DevSecOps Adventures

A Game-Changing Approach with Chocolate, LEGO, and Coaching Games

Second Edition

Dana Pylayeva

Apress®

DevSecOps Adventures: A Game-Changing Approach with Chocolate, LEGO, and Coaching Games

Dana Pylayeva
Brooklyn, NY, USA

ISBN-13 (pbk): 979-8-8688-0396-3   ISBN-13 (electronic): 979-8-8688-0397-0
https://doi.org/10.1007/979-8-8688-0397-0

Copyright © 2024 by The Editor(s) (if applicable) and The Author(s), under exclusive license to APress Media, LLC, part of Springer Nature

This work is subject to copyright. All rights are reserved by the publisher, whether the whole or part of the material is concerned, specifically the rights of translation, reprinting, reuse of illustrations, recitation, broadcasting, reproduction on microfilms or in any other physical way, and transmission or information storage and retrieval, electronic adaptation, computer software, or by similar or dissimilar methodology now known or hereafter developed.

Trademarked names, logos, and images may appear in this book. Rather than use a trademark symbol with every occurrence of a trademarked name, logo, or image we use the names, logos, and images only in an editorial fashion and to the benefit of the trademark owner, with no intention of infringement of the trademark.

The use in this publication of trade names, trademarks, service marks, and similar terms, even if they are not identified as such, is not to be taken as an expression of opinion as to whether or not they are subject to proprietary rights.

While the advice and information in this book are believed to be true and accurate at the date of publication, neither the authors nor the editors nor the publisher can accept any legal responsibility for any errors or omissions that may be made. The publisher makes no warranty, express or implied, with respect to the material contained herein.

   Managing Director, Apress Media LLC: Welmoed Spahr
   Acquisitions Editor: Melissa Duffy
   Development Editor: Laura Berendson
   Coordinating Editor: Gryffin Winkler
   Copy Editor: April Rondeau

Cover designed by eStudioCalamar

Distributed to the book trade worldwide by Apress Media, LLC, 1 New York Plaza, New York, NY 10004, U.S.A. Phone 1-800-SPRINGER, fax (201) 348-4505, email orders-ny@springer-sbm.com, or visit www.springeronline.com. Apress Media, LLC is a California LLC and the sole member (owner) is Springer Science + Business Media Finance Inc (SSBM Finance Inc). SSBM Finance Inc is a **Delaware** corporation.

For information on translations, please e-mail booktranslations@springernature.com; for reprint, paperback, or audio rights, please e-mail bookpermissions@springernature.com.

Apress titles may be purchased in bulk for academic, corporate, or promotional use. eBook versions and licenses are also available for most titles. For more information, reference our Print and eBook Bulk Sales web page at http://www.apress.com/bulk-sales.

Any source code or other supplementary material referenced by the author in this book is available to readers on GitHub (https://github.com/Apress). For more detailed information, please visit https://www.apress.com/gp/services/source-code.

If disposing of this product, please recycle the paper

To my daughter, Erica, who inspires me, challenges me, and supports me all the way. Thank you for being a sounding board for my game design ideas and for making this book better by editing my writing.

Table of Contents

About the Author xiii
About the Technical Reviewer xv
Acknowledgments xvii

Chapter 1: Introduction 1
  Who This Book Is For 2
    Audience 3
    Facilitators 4
    Organizations 5
  Facilitating Culture Change with Games 6
  How I Got Started with Designing Coaching Games 9
  How About You Now? 11

Chapter 2: About This Book 13
  What's New in the Second Edition? 13
  How to Use This Book 14
  What's Included in the Appendices 16
    Role Cards 17
    Mod Cards: Special Instructions That Modify the Game ... 17
    Team Handouts 17
    In-room Posters 18
    Debriefing and Ideas Crowdsourcing Resources 18
    Coaching Games for Psychological Safety 19
  Electronic Version of the Appendices 19

TABLE OF CONTENTS

Chapter 3: Brief History of DevOps and DevSecOps............................21

DevOps..22

Functional Silos and a Low-Trust Culture......................................22

The Movement of People Who Cared..25

No Longer "for Unicorns Only"..27

Refocusing on Culture..28

Psychological Safety..32

DevSecOps...34

Summary...36

Chapter 4: What You Will Teach with *LEGO and Chocolate* Simulation 39

Ideas from "The Phoenix Project"..40

The First Way of DevOps..42

Bottlenecks..43

Technical Practices Supporting The First Way.............................44

The Second Way of DevOps...49

"Shift Left" and "Shift Right" of DevSecOps..51

Scrum and Agile..54

Summary...55

Chapter 5: *LEGO and Chocolate*: Rules of the Game 57

Summary and Aim of the Game..57

Player Roles and Avatars..58

Scrum Team..59

IT Operations Team..65

Security Team: Sara Security..70

Business Team (Benjamin Business)..73

Surprise Character: Harry Hacker..74

vi

TABLE OF CONTENTS

Basic Game Flow and Modifications 75
    Sprint 1: Feel the Pain 76
    Sprint 2: First Steps to DevSecOps 78
    Sprint 3: Continuous Delivery of Value 82
Summary 83

Chapter 6: Game Components 85

Role Cards 85
Mod Card 86
Supplies for One Scrum Team 87
Supplies for Operations Team 89
Supplies for Sara Security 90
Supplies for Business Team 91
Supplies for Harry Hacker 92
Supplies for the Facilitator 92
Complete List of Component Links 94
Summary 94

Chapter 7: Setting the Space 97

Setting Up the Room Posters 98
    Visible Posters 98
    Hidden Posters 101
Room Configuration Options 104
    Optimal Configuration (4 Tables x 21 People) 105
    Small Group Setup (3 Tables x 9–14 People) 106
    Medium Group Setup (4 Tables x 15–25 People) 106
    Medium Group Setup (5 Tables x 18–28 People) 108
    Large Group Setup (6 Tables x 28–42 People) 109
    Large Group Setup (7 Tables x 38–56 People) 110

TABLE OF CONTENTS

    Extra Large Group Setup (11 Tables x 57–84 People) 111

    Scaling Beyond Extra Large (22 Tables x 124+ People) 112

Summary 114

Chapter 8: Know Your Timebox 115

Visible Interval Timer 116

Session Plan for an Experiential DevSecOps Training (3 hours) 117

Session Plan for a Standalone LEGO and Chocolate
Simulation (90 minutes) 125

Room Setup and Teardown Timebox 130

Chapter 9: Be the Gamemaster 131

Facilitation Script for DevSecOps Training with LEGO and
Chocolate Game (3 hours) 132

    Turn and Talk (5 min) 132

    Introduce Yourself (3 minutes) 133

    Introduce the First Topic: Misalignment of Goals (10 minutes) 133

    Introduce the Flow of Sprint 1 (6 minutes) 139

    Sprint 1: Feel the Pain (18 min) 143

    First Debriefing (12 minutes) 145

    Introduce the Next Topic: First Way of DevOps (7 minutes) 146

    Introduce Process Modifications of the Second Sprint (2 minutes) 149

    Sprint 2: First Steps to DevSecOps (18 minutes) 150

    Spring 2 Debriefing (15 minutes) 153

    Optional Break (10 minutes) 155

    Introduce the Final Topic (8 minutes) 155

    Introduce Process Modifications for the Final Sprint (4 minutes) 158

    Sprint 3: Continuous Value Delivery (18 minutes) 160

    Introduce the Final Debriefing Activity (3 minutes) 161

    Final Debriefing: User Experience Fishbowl (27 minutes) 163

TABLE OF CONTENTS

Facilitation Script for a Standalone Version of the LEGO and Chocolate Game (90 minutes) 163
    Introduce the Game (8 minutes) 164
    Sprint 1: Feel the Pain (15 minutes) 166
    First Debriefing (10 minutes) 167
    Introduce Process Improvements and Modifications for the Second Round (2 minutes) 168
    Sprint 2: First Steps to DevSecOps (15 minutes) 169
    Spring 2 Debriefing (10 minutes) 172
    Introduce Process Improvements and Modifications for the Final Round (2 minutes) 174
    Sprint 3: Continuous Value Delivery (15 minutes) 175
    Final Debriefing (13 minutes) 176
Summary 177

Chapter 10: *Fear in the Workplace* Coaching Game 179
When DevSecOps and Organizational Culture Collide 181
Symptoms and Impact of Fear in Organizations 183
Fear-Inducing Organizational Changes 186
    DevSecOps Transformations 186
    Mergers and Acquisitions 188
Reorgs and Layoffs, Is There a Better Way? 189
Team-level Fears 193
Facilitating the Fear in the Workplace Game 194
    Option One: A Competitive Game 194
    Option Two: A Collaborative Game 195
    Option Three: A Short Activity for an Extra-large Group 196
Teaching the Third Way of DevOps with the Fear in the Workplace Game 197
Summary 202

ix

TABLE OF CONTENTS

Chapter 11: Safety in the Workplace Coaching Game 205

How to Use This Game 206

Safety Enhancers Collection 208

    SCARF® model 208

    Status 209

    Certainty 215

    Autonomy 222

    Relatedness 227

    Fairness 232

Summary 238

Chapter 12: Master Your Debriefing 239

Why Is Debriefing Important? 240

Debriefing Models 242

Debriefing Tips for DevSecOps Games 244

    Debriefing Sprint 1 246

    Debriefing Sprint 2 247

    Debriefing Sprint 3 248

    Debriefing Sprint 4 251

    Summary 252

Chapter 13: Key Takeaways 255

Visualizing Bottlenecks and Silos 255

Benefits of Cross-training 256

Concerns about the Cross-training 257

"Shift-left" on Security 258

DevSecOps' Impact on Business 259

Fearless Culture 261

Summary 262

TABLE OF CONTENTS

Chapter 14: Frequently Asked Questions 265
    LEGO and Chocolate Simulation 265
    Fear in the Workplace and Safety in the Workplace Games 269
    Facilitation with Remote Teams 269
    Summary 275

Chapter 15: Play History and Modifications: It's All about the Feedback! 277
    2013: Minimum Playable Version 277
    2014–2015: First Public Workshops (v 1.0) 279
        Global Scrum Gathering New Orleans, May 2014 280
        Global Scrum Gathering Berlin, September 2014 282
        Toronto Agile and Software, November 2014 283
        Play4Agile in Rückersbach, February 2015 284
    2016–2018: More Public Workshops (v2.0) 286
        Agile Days 2015, March 2015 286
        XP2015, May 2015 288
        Agile2015, August 2015 291
        Global Scrum Gathering Prague, November 2015 293
        Rakuten Technology Conference, November 2015 294
        US, Brazil, and Portugal Conferences in 2016 295
        Content Delivery Redesign with TBR in 2017 296
    2018: The *Fear in the Workplace* Is Born! 297
        Fear-Focused Retrospective at HBC Digital 299
        AgileCamp2018 Conference, New York, September 2018 300
        Agile + DevOps East Conference, Orlando, Florida, November 2018 301
    Train-the-Trainer Workshops 303
    2019–2020: More Workshops, Design Iterations, and Global Pandemic 304

TABLE OF CONTENTS

AgileCamp2019, New York, October 2019 305
OOP2020, Munich, Germany, February 2020 306
Agile India 2020 and the Failed Attempt at Online Conversion 306
2021: *Fear in the Workplace* and *Safety in the Workplace*,
Online Edition 307
2022: DevOps Coaching Games Are Back! 308

Chapter 16: Kickstarting Transformations with Games: Field Stories 311

Karl Métivier, Canada 312
1. Ensure Buy-in and Continuity 313
2. Watch Out for Habitual Behaviors 314
3. Draw Attention to Business Needs 315
4. Ask: "How Can We improve?" 315
5. First Master the Games, Then Modify Them 316
Dr. Peter Fassbinder, Germany 317
    Virtual Adaptation with a Focus on Flow 318
    Key Observations 319
Wayne Hetherington, Canada 322
Norma Hernandez Garcia, José Luis Ortiz González, and Jorge Gándara,
Grupo Salinas, Mexico 325
    Virtual Adaptation 327
    Dealing with Skeptics 327
    Trainer's Attitude Plays an Important Role 328
It's a Wrap! 328

Appendix: Design Assets, Posters, and More 331

Index 369

About the Author

Dana Pylayeva is a business games designer, trainer, and DevOps culture coach who is known for infusing playfulness into the most serious workplaces. She offers a unique blend of expert-level knowledge, exceptional facilitation skills, professional coaching mindset, and a diverse technical background (as a former Java developer, DBA manager, and application architect).

Dana is equally effective in coaching teams, coaching leaders, and navigating the complexity of enterprise transformations. She enjoys working with clients across a diverse span of industries (legal publishing, automotive, digital marketing, retail, fintech, music streaming, non-profits, etc.). In her 25+ years of experience, she has been fortunate to work with clients from the United States, Canada, the United Kingdom, Ireland, France, India, Japan, Malaysia, and Australia. She speaks at conferences internationally and has delivered her workshops at 80 conferences in 18 countries.

Dana holds a Certified Enterprise Coach (CEC) designation from Scrum Alliance, Professional Certified Coach (PCC) credentials from the International Coaching Federation (ICF), and a Certified Professional Co-Active Coach (CPCC) certification from Co-Active Training Institute.

Dana is passionate about helping others grow and giving back to the Agile/Scrum community. Through the years, she has been involved in various community roles as a volunteer, reviewer, track chair, program chair, and conference chair at Agile Alliance and Scrum Alliance organizations. She is the founder of the Big Apple Scrum Day conference in NYC and a co-organizer of several local user groups.

About the Technical Reviewer

Bernie Maloney's career started with a flash and a bang. Literally. His first position was designing devices that protect telephone networks from lightning strikes. A few career pivots later, he had a flash of insight: it was possible to tap into latent potential in every person, every team, and every organization.

The teams he's worked with have grown businesses to beyond $1B/qtr, delivering products from consumer electronics to network infrastructure to services and payments at firms including TiVo, Cisco, Wells Fargo, and more. He teaches private and public workshops, including several on Agile Product Development and Agile Leadership at Stanford Continuing Studies.

As a trainer, speaker, and coach, Bernie helps clients achieve performance breakthroughs with their teams, their organizations, and themselves. More, he believes that Accelerating Genius[SM] is possible in every person and business, and leads both to outrageous effectiveness and a whole lot more fun.

Acknowledgments

My very first appreciation goes to Gene Kim, Kevin Behr, and George Spafford for writing *The Phoenix Project*. If it wasn't for their inspiring and eye-opening book that resonated so strongly with my own experience, I wouldn't have started thinking about creating a game to share these insights with my "reluctant to read" colleagues.

Thank you, Bryan Beecham, for recognizing the potential in that MVP version of the game, collaborating with me on the very first public version of it, inspiring me to start speaking at conferences, and co-presenting with me at Global Scrum Gathering in New Orleans (SGNOLA) in May 2014.

When I later brought this version to the Global Scrum Gathering in Berlin, the feedback I got from Mark Van Bezel, Andy Mutton, Jaya Shrivastava, and Charlles Pinon was immensely helpful. Thank you, folks, for taking the time to debrief with me on the players' experiences! It gave me several ideas to experiment with in the next iteration.

I am grateful to every conference participant who played these very first versions of the *Chocolate, LEGO, and Scrum* game at SGNOLA, SGBER, Toronto Agile and Software, Agile Days 2015, XP2015, and Agile2015. Your active engagement, excitement, questions, and feedback inspired me to continue refining this game further. Your inquiries and interest in bringing this simulation to your organizations convinced me to start working on the very first facilitator's guide for it on Leanpub.

I want to thank *myself* for jumping into the unknown and signing up for Play4Agile 2015 unconference—a three-day event on the top of a mountain in the middle of German woods. (What was I thinking?)

ACKNOWLEDGMENTS

Ari-Pekka Lappi, Antti Kirjavainen, Omar Bermudez, Ellen Grove, Udo Wiegärtner, Falk Kühnel, Roland Schöler—the opportunity to playtest this game with all of you, the Agile Games pros from around the world, was invaluable. Your very candid feedback and game improvement ideas propelled this game to an entirely new level!

Alexander Kylburg and Bernie Maloney, I am glad our paths crossed at the Global Scrum Gathering Prague. Your feedback on the 2.0 version of the game was helpful in further improving the game. Who would've thought that this encounter would lead to our collaboration on both editions of this book, Bernie? I consider myself very lucky!

I am grateful to my first Leanpub readers, who helped me validate the interest in this book. I loved answering your questions, reading your success stories, and learning about the game modifications that worked best for you!

Thank you, Steve Anglin, Mark Powers, and the editorial team at Apress for later discovering this book on Leanpub and for all your help and guidance during the first edition publishing process. Thank you to Melissa Duffy for inviting me to start working on the second edition, and to Laura Berendson, Gryffin Winkler, and Nirmal Selvaraj for being extremely supportive and patient as I was discovering that I had so much more content to share (or completely rewrite) in the second edition.

Laura M. Powers and Bernie Maloney, you both are truly amazing people. I can't thank you enough for your readiness to step in and help at a moment's notice. Your ability to re-shuffle priorities and lend your support with the technical review of the first edition of this book unblocked me (and the book) from being published.

Bernie, after being blown away by the quality of your technical review of the first edition, I knew there was no other expert in my network who would be more suited for reviewing the second one. I appreciate you for agreeing to support me once again! Your detailed and methodical reviews of each chapter, ability to spot any inconsistencies, and all the ideas you've shared improved the quality of the final product.

ACKNOWLEDGMENTS

I am grateful to all the trainers and coaches around the world who have been running my DevSecOps coaching games, translating materials to their languages, modifying them to their contexts, and even taking these games online during COVID. Thank you Karl Métivier, Dr. Peter Fassbinder, Wayne Hetherington, Norma Hernandez Garcia, Jorge Gándara, and José Luis Ortiz for taking the time to speak with me about your experiences, and for your permission to include the highlights of our conversations as the field stories in the final chapter of this book.

Finally, to my dearest family (my husband, Alex Indman, and my daughter, Erica Indman) I appreciate you for playing along with my crazy aspirations and ideas, being the first readers, first players, tireless LEGO-sorting assistants, and so much more. Thank you for giving me the freedom to experiment and for supporting me all the way!

CHAPTER 1

Introduction

It's been ten years since my very first attempt to share my own excitement about DevOps ideas with a small group of reluctant co-workers at an internal Agile community of practice. Little did I know back then that a small experiment in making ideas from *The Phoenix Project*[1] more digestible through a gamified experience would turn into an internationally acclaimed collection of DevOps culture games, open doors to conference-speaking experiences in 15 different countries, and even give me enough courage to quit my full-time job and start my own Agile Play Consulting business.

The book you are holding in your hands today (or reading on your screens) is a second edition. A lot has changed since 2013 in the DevOps space. As the DevOps community has been learning more about safety culture and embracing ideas from Ron Westrum and Amy Edmondson in the past 10 years, I've also recognized that the original version of my game (published by Apress in 2017) was lacking in-depth coverage of this important topic. The version of the workshop I run today includes extensive coverage of the third way of DevOps (culture of experimentation and learning) with two supplemental games: *Fear in the Workplace*[2] and *Safety in the Workplace*.[3]

---

[1] https://www.amazon.com/Phoenix-Project-DevOps-Helping-Business-ebook/dp/B078Y98RG8
[2] https://www.thegamecrafter.com/games/fear-in-the-workplace
[3] https://www.thegamecrafter.com/games/safety-in-the-workplace

CHAPTER 1   INTRODUCTION

As a reader of this second edition, you will benefit from my continued facilitation experience and the experience of the many trainers who've incorporated these coaching games into their DevOps trainings and coaching worldwide. Together we've been able to bring this workshop to public conferences and private workshops, influencing the mindsets of organizations and helping kick-start their DevSecOps transformation initiatives in automotive, FinTech, insurance, academia, and even government. In this book, you will get a glimpse into these experiences, read about key takeaways from participants, and appreciate the modifications of the game that they inspired.

You will be pleased to find improved facilitation instructions, an expanded list of debriefing techniques, as well as a list of frequently asked questions I've encountered from various participants.

By now, this is a solid, tried-and-true workshop that you can rely on in your stand-alone training sessions or as a part of a larger DevSecOps transformation initiative. Equally accessible to techies and non-techies, it will reliably generate excitement, introduce participants to fundamental ideas of DevSecOps, and create shared understanding of the cultural changes required for its successful implementation in your organization.

Who This Book Is For

Congratulations on picking up this book! It makes you a curious person who is at least open to the idea of experimenting with non-conventional ways of teaching and training. Using simulations and coaching games in one's training is not for the faint of heart, yet it is a rewarding experience for the facilitator (NPS scores anyone?) as well as for their workshop participants.

Executed well, this workshop will make the experience more engaging, help with long-term knowledge retention, and trigger a change in participants' mindsets. Sounds hard? Fear not! This is exactly the reason I am writing this book—to set you up for success in delivering impactful training, facilitating tough conversations, and prepping the way for DevSecOps transformation success.

Audience

This workshop is designed to resonate equally well with technical and non-technical participants. If you are running it internally at your organization or for a private client where you can influence the workshop roster, consider inviting people from different parts of the organization. Development teams, business personnel, information security professionals, architects, IT operations staff—every role currently involved in product development, software delivery, security, and operations in your organization—will benefit from it and will be able to grasp the concepts from this training. Encourage them to take on a role in the game that is different from their current "real life" role for added benefit.

If you are a functional manager, a director, or a chapter lead involved in DevSecOps transformation or team design, performance management, and skills development planning, you can benefit from running this workshop as well. The *LEGO and Chocolate* game will give you a good understanding of foundational DevOps concepts as well as lead you through an experience of shifting bottleneck dynamics. The bottlenecks in the game will feel strikingly familiar! The learnings from this workshop will help you to avoid inadvertently creating the same bottlenecks. You will be able to make better team design choices and to establish more impactful goals and policies to enable knowledge silo reduction.

It is even more crucial for you and your peers to experience a "safe" introduction to conversations about fear, learn about the detrimental effect it can have on innovation capacity, as well as showcase the importance of destigmatizing failure. The *Fear in the Workplace* and *Safety in the Workplace* games are perfect for experimenting with these initial conversations.

Another type of audience that can benefit from these games is a team with an unhealthy dynamic, fear symptoms, and/or interpersonal conflict. If you are a Scrum Master, an Agile Coach, or a team lead working with a team in conflict, make sure to check out Chapters 9 and 10 for more info.

Facilitators

This book is written with you in mind. If you are an internal DevOps/DevSecOps trainer, an Agile Coach, or a Scrum Master, this collection of games and this book will be a welcomed addition in your toolbox. Consider bringing these in when you notice any one of the following dynamics:

- Your organization is experiencing a typical misalignment of goals between business/customers, development team, operations team, and security (see Figure 1-1).

- Agile practices and principles are used in the development organizations only, while Operations continues to use a plan-driven waterfall approach.

- Your developers have no idea about the post-deployment performance of their software.

- Delayed, infrequent deployments of product increments cause service disruption in production.

- Every new security vulnerability causes a major panic, requiring a lengthy manual patching of all the environments. Security is an afterthought.

If you are an external trainer offering public workshops, these games can be facilitated as part of a stand-alone multi-day DevSecOps training, or as a DevOps extension to a standard Scrum training. Alternatively, they can be brought in as individual coaching games for improving Agile team dynamics, enabling psychological safety, and facilitating difficult conversations with teams.

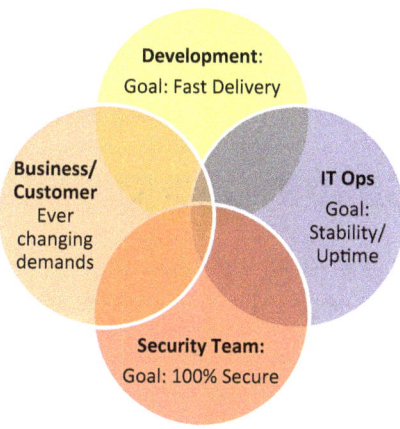

Figure 1-1. Misalignment of goals in a typical product development organization

Organizations

LEGO® and Chocolate simulation resonates the most in medium- to large-size organizations, the ones that are either just starting their DevSecOps initiatives, or the ones disappointed with not seeing the benefits expected from their "tools first" DevSecOps transformation approach.

The *Fear in the Workplace* and *Safety in the Workplace* coaching games can be effective in organizations of any size and any DevSecOps maturity level. My latest successful experience was applying them both in facilitating a team conflict resolution for my client, a well-regarded music company known in the Agile/DevOps communities as an innovator and culture trendsetter.

CHAPTER 1   INTRODUCTION

Keep your eyes open for symptoms of fear in your workplace, as they may show up in unexpected places! Bring out the deck of fear monster cards in coaching sessions or introduce them at your community of practice (CoP). You will be surprised at how many places the little fear monsters will come in handy.

Debriefing tips from Chapter 11 as well as a selection of special facilitation techniques (*Liberating Structures*)[4] described in this book can be applied independently from the rest of the book and can enhance group collaboration in organizations of any size.

Facilitating Culture Change with Games

This book is making a case for being very intentional about facilitating a cultural change as part of your DevSecOps transformation initiative. Too many initiatives start with automation, building CI/CD pipelines, and implementing monitoring dashboards as the most tangible parts of DevOps, while leaving the other parts of CAMS[5] acronym to chance.

Cultural change, however, is the most difficult one as it involves changing people's perception of their reality. Luc de Brabandere, a professor at École Centrale in Paris, calls it a "forgotten half of change"[6] and argues that for a change to stick we must change both our reality (tools, practices, skills, policies) and our perception of this reality (culture change, or "this is how we work around here") for ourselves, our management, and our clients.

---

[4] https://www.liberatingstructures.com/
[5] CAMS (Culture, Automation, Measurement, and Sharing) is a term describing DevOps pillars coined by John Willis, one of the luminaries of the DevOps movement.
[6] Luc de Brabandere, *The Forgotten Half of Change: Achieving Greater Creativity Through Changes in Perception*, Dearborn Trade Publishing, 2005.

CHAPTER 1 INTRODUCTION

In my experience, people respond well to skillful and meaningful introduction of playful elements, games, and role-playing simulations in training, coaching, and change management. In addition to the games described in this book, I've had success with using games for facilitating organizational restructure after layoffs at a large Canadian retailer, for reorganizing development teams at the time of their rapid growth at a healthcare company in Chicago, and many others.

Games allow people to disconnect from their challenges and roles in "the real world" and transition into a "magic world" of a simulation—a safe space for experimenting, failing, and learning together, the world where their current titles don't matter and winning/losing is not a big deal. The fascinating part of this transition is that they typically bring their behavioral patterns and their mindsets with them!

People act in the game as they would in the real world; however, the playful setting of the "game world" makes it easier to learn as a group. The game flow and rounds of debriefing make it possible to step back, debrief these dysfunctions, discuss the impact, and continue experimenting with a new set of behaviors in the next round of the game. This shared playful experience gives the group a common vocabulary, powerful metaphors to invoke from their "real world" when similar situations emerge. Still not convinced?

Check out the work of Nick Wignall, who has a PhD in clinical psychology and speaks about seven benefits of playfulness for adults, which include unlocking our creative thinking and enacting smarter decision making, as well as helping us shift from worry and anxiety to curiosity and passion.[7]

There is one more reason for using games and simulations to facilitate change. They increase the "stickiness" of your training message as well as participants' "Aha!" moments. Sharon Bowman in her "Training from the Back of the Room" work emphasized positive emotional experiences,

---

[7] https://nickwignall.com/benefits-of-playfulness/

multi-sensory stimulation, and novelty among the elements used in brain-friendly training.

Studies at Martinos Center for Biomedical Imaging, Department of Radiology, Massachusetts General Hospital, and Harvard Medical School found that our brain assembles the data received from sensory inputs into a complete picture that becomes a memory of an event. Engaging multiple senses while learning helps amplify its effectiveness. Additionally, when we experience an emotional reaction, it becomes a part of the memory, strengthening it dramatically.

The *LEGO and Chocolate game* is designed to engage all five senses and tap into the emotional side of the brain. Working with LEGO bricks, stickers, colorful labels, and chocolate candies, participants experience the downside of local optimization and learn to expand their view to include the entire system. Using avatars, personas, and role cards, participants gain an understanding of Dev, Ops, and Security roles as well as their interdependencies. They try out a mindset of each role for the duration of the game.

Throughout the game, they experience a range of emotions and learn to expand the boundaries of individual roles, acquire T-shaped skills, and incorporate security practices through the entire life cycle. They build new environments, protect them from hackers' attacks, and work with demanding customers, trying to satisfy their ever-changing demands. The game takes players through a gamified DevSecOps transformation journey, facilitating their first baby steps toward embracing the DevOps culture.

What you will notice when facilitating the *Fear in the Workplace* game is that its playful "monster" cards allow players to really go deep into discussions. Visually engaging and silly, these cards help players externalize their emotions and feelings; make fears less personal, less scary; and enable serious conversations about conflicts or culture challenges in teams or their workplaces.

The culture of an organization will not change overnight. As a change agent, you know the multitude of change management models (Kotter,

ADKAR, Kanban, and others) designed to increase the likelihood of successful organizational change. Thoughtful and skillful use of coaching games (followed by in-depth debriefing) can help you lessen resistance to change and create more awareness and more desire for the participants to embrace a new way of working, and a new culture. While not a magic wand, playfulness is your gentle wind that over time can make a dune by moving tiny grains of sand in a new direction.

How I Got Started with Designing Coaching Games

My interest in the DevOps movement originated when I stepped into a DBA manager role. I had years of experience under my belt as a PowerBuilder developer and Java developer, an application architect, and as a typical developer in 2013, with a very limited understanding of what happens in the Operations world. It was an opportunity for me to try something new. I remember thinking:

> *"How hard can it be? I know how to write a CREATE TABLE statement or implement a stored procedure, among other things. I am sure I can figure out how to manage DBAs!"*

Little did I know what I was getting myself into—a "second level of escalation" meant carrying a pager 24x7x365 and responding to a page if a DBA on call did not acknowledge it within five minutes. Thanksgiving weekend, which I've always enjoyed, turned into a nightmare after accepting this new role. The round-the-clock support, war room, and hourly conference calls with senior management—all to ensure that Black Friday traffic would not be impacted by database performance. If it wasn't for the help of my amazing team members, I doubt I would've survived!

A few years later, I came across *The Phoenix Project* by Gene Kim, Kevin Behr, and George Spafford, and I couldn't put the book down! It was describing my experience and my pain, yet it was also showing the way out. I wanted everyone to read this book!

At that time, I was one of the organizers of a company-wide internal learning forum designed to cross-pollinate knowledge among various technology groups. I tried facilitating a book club, running a book raffle, but people didn't want to read. I was at my wits' end, until one day I came across a Gamification course on Coursera. Bingo! Creating a game was one idea I hadn't yet tried. Luckily, our October agenda was wide open and gave me a perfect opportunity to play-test the minimum playable version of the game. The rest is history, which you can read about in Chapter 16.

The *Fear in the Workplace* game was born out of necessity much later as I was already working as an Agile Coach at another company. My own team was experiencing a lot of pain and dysfunction caused by a lack of alignment with a new manager, post-merger culture clashes, and many other issues. My observations, experiments, and desire to help the team (myself included) became a breeding ground for this new game. Around the same time, I was invited to keynote the Agile Games 2018 conference and settled on a "Team up to Eradicate Fear" title, committing to the very first public appearance of the *Fear in the Workplace* game. This was my first card game designed and published on The Gamecrafter.

While doing research for my keynote, I discovered the fascinating work of William A. Kahn[8] and Amy C. Edmondson on psychological safety.

When Amy C. Edmondson's book *The Fearless Organizations*[9] came out later that year, it inspired me to start working on the Safety in the Workspace extension. This new addition to my games collection helped me amplify the impact of coaching conversations about fears and toxic cultures in workplaces and teams.

---

[8] Kahn, W.A. (1990). Psychological conditions of personal engagement and disengagement at work. *Academy of Management Journal*, 33, 692–724.
[9] https://www.amazon.com/Fearless-Organization-Psychological-Workplace-Innovation/dp/1119477247

CHAPTER 1   INTRODUCTION

How About You Now?

As you flip through this book and try out these coaching games, I hope you will start noticing the impact they make for your team. Perhaps you may even consider designing a coaching game of your own!

If you'd like to deep dive into it, pick up a copy of Jesse Schell's *The Art of Game Design: A Book of Lenses!*[10] This book is a treasure, a "must read" for anyone interested in creating games. Consider exploring a community games collection on TastyCupcakes.org. Connect with me and other geeks from Agile Games communities[11] for brainstorming, play testing, and collaboration. Let's bring more playfulness into workplaces near and far!

---

[10] https://www.amazon.com/Art-Game-Design-Lenses-Third-ebook/dp/B07X59RN6N

[11] A few of my favorite community events: Play4Agile (Germany), Play4AgileNA (Canada), Agile Games (Boston).

CHAPTER 2

About This Book

This book is a facilitation guide. It provides a set of detailed instructions on how to prepare for, facilitate, and debrief three coaching games. It also shares stories, questions, and reflections from previous workshop participants, allowing you to be well prepared with the answers when it is your turn to run these games with your audience.

The book is focused on a few essential key concepts of DevOps/DevSecOps culture and is not trying to be an all-encompassing primary source of learning in these fields. It does, however, describe a unique approach to introducing these concepts in a way that resonates with techies and non-techies alike (including those non-techies who are in charge of managing budgets, and the ones who can either support or limit your ability to fully implement tooling, infrastructure, and upskilling necessary for the success of DevSecOps).

What's New in the Second Edition?

If you have the original book handy, the first thing you'll notice is that the second edition has twice as many chapters. My intention is to not only double the size, but also double the impact for trainers, coaches, and organizations who are using these games to kick-start their DevOps/DevSecOps initiatives.

This edition includes the latest version of the *LEGO and Chocolate* game with a description of modified flow in Sprint 3, redesigned game components (updated role cards and handouts, new in-room facilitator's signage), and new in-depth coverage of my two other games: *Fear in the Workplace* and *Safety in the Workplace*. Together, these three coaching games provide comprehensive gamified coverage across the three ways of DevOps.

There is expanded coverage of practices and ideas from DevSecOps and added emphasis on the importance of debriefing (Chapter 12). I am especially excited about integrating several Liberating Structures[1] into the latest workshop design. In the second edition, I will describe how you can use them to amplify the effectiveness of debriefing, bring out all voices in a large group discussion, and equally engage both the introverts and the extroverts in the room.

I hope you will also find the second edition easier to read. I've streamlined facilitation instructions based on feedback from my train-the-trainer workshop participants (including those who were non-native English speakers).

How to Use This Book

You will find a brief history of DevOps/DevSecOps in Chapter 3 and an overview of the key learning concepts in Chapter 4. Use these chapters as a quick refresher in preparation for facilitating this workshop, or skip them if you are already familiar with the concepts described there.

A good portion of this book (Chapters 5-9) provides a detailed description of the *LEGO and Chocolate* simulation, including room setup for various group sizes (allowing you to scale the game from 12 to 100+ participants), facilitation scripts, a list of game supplies/components,

---

[1] McCandless, K., Lipmanowicz, H. "The Surprising Power of Liberating Structures: Simple Rules to Unleash A Culture of Innovation." https://www.amazon.com/Surprising-Power-Liberating-Structures-Innovation

and in-room posters. You will be coming back to these chapters often: when packing for your next workshop and when preparing for an effective session facilitation.

Chapters 10 and 11 cover the *Fear in the Workplace* and *Safety in the Workplace* coaching games, respectively. This is the first time you will get to read about every fear monster (and corresponding organizational dysfunctions) included in this game, as well as 32 safety practices (for individuals, teams, and leadership) that can positively influence organizational culture and start shifting it from pathological or bureaucratic cultures to a generative culture of experimentation and learning.[2]

Chapter 12 offers you several debriefing practices that will help you connect learning from the game with the "real life" application of this learning for the workshop participants. You will find some of the most salient insights from previous workshops' participants in Chapter 13, and their most frequently asked questions in Chapter 14.

This edition mentions several of the Liberating Structures in Chapters 8, 9, 10, and 12 as part of the main facilitation script and debriefing instructions. Additionally, Chapter 14 mentions a few additional structures (TRIZ and Tiny Monsters) that can be used to facilitate culture-focused DevSecOps conversations with teams. Facilitation instructions for all six of the above referenced structures are included in Appendix 2 for easy access.

If you are exploring the option of applying these coaching games for remote participants, check out Chapter 14 for tips and ideas. Chapter 15 of this book includes play history and modifications. I have also collected several stories from other DevOps coaches and trainers about their experience facilitating change with these coaching games. You will find the highlights of their experience in the final chapter of this book.

---

[2] Westrum, R. "A Typology of Organizational Cultures." https://www.ncbi.nlm.nih.gov/pmc/articles/PMC1765804/pdf/v013p0ii22.pdf.

CHAPTER 2   ABOUT THIS BOOK

What's Included in the Appendices

This book contains two versions of the appendix. The printed version includes photos of all the flipcharts to be created by a facilitator, images of optional workshop handouts, role cards (see Figure 2-1), and the packing checklist. In addition, it includes facilitation instructions for the six Liberating Structures referenced in this book.

Figure 2-1. *Sample role cards included in the appendix*

The electronic version of the book's appendix provides facilitator slides, workshop handouts, packing checklist, and print-ready versions of the *LEGO and Chocolate* role cards, and the *Fear in Workplace* and the *Safety in the Workplace* cards. You can access it by clicking on "Download Source Code" on the book's information page on Apress.

Role Cards

- Scrum Team (Danny Developer, Tim Tester, Patricia Product, and Samuel Scrum)
- Operations Team (Adam Admin, Robert Release)
- Security Team (Sara Security)
- Business Team (Benjamin Business)
- Hacker (Harry Hacker)

Mod Cards: Special Instructions That Modify the Game

- Mod cards for Sprint 1 (Sara Security, Adam Admin)
- Mod cards for Sprint 2 (Benjamin Business, Sara Security)
- Mod card for Sprint 3 (Patricia Product)

Team Handouts

- "Definition of Done" page with a photo of a small "developed" package and a large "deployable" package
- *LEGO and Chocolate* game flow for Sprint 1

In-room Posters

There are several posters that will allow you to facilitate the simulation more effectively. You can prepare them ahead of time, have them laminated, or hand draw them in preparation for each session.

Visible Posters

- LEGO Animal Exchange poster
- Delivery Board poster
- Key Takeaways poster

Hidden Posters

- Cross-training (FEEL) poster
- Known Good Environment Configuration poster

Debriefing and Ideas Crowdsourcing Resources

- 1-2-4-All
- User Experience Fishbowl
- What? So What? Now What?
- 25-10 Crowdsourcing
- TRIZ
- Tiny Monsters

Coaching Games for Psychological Safety

- *Fear in the Workplace*
- *Safety in the Workplace*

Electronic Version of the Appendices

An electronic version of the appendices is available for download at this book's information page on Apress: `https://github.com/Apress/DevSecOps-Adventures-2nd-ed`.

CHAPTER 3

Brief History of DevOps and DevSecOps

In the first two chapters, we went over the new and updated material included in the second edition, including the following:

- Expanded coverage of DevOps/DevSecOps history

- Latest version of the *DevOps with LEGO and Chocolate* simulation

- Addition of the two new coaching games designed for enabling a culture of innovation and learning

- A robust collection of debriefing practices that will support you in facilitating group conversations with more impact

- Books and experiences that inspired me to start designing Agile/DevOps coaching games, embracing playfulness in my training and coaching

The following two chapters will offer you a few notable highlights of the DevOps/DevSecOps history and walk you through a variety of concepts these games are designed to teach. My goal is to offer you a DevOps primer, including some key theories, as well as important highlights from notable industry reports. Think of these chapters as "minimum viable basics"—just enough to grasp the ideas built into this gamified DevOps/DevSecOps introduction, and to be able to connect them with real-life practices during debriefing. This will be sufficient to get you started, and by no means do I expect you to stop here. Continue your own DevOps upskilling with a new edition of *The DevOps Handbook*,[1] and other great resources published by IT Revolution Press.

If you are already familiar with these ideas, feel free to skip directly to Chapter 5 and start diving into the dynamics and mechanics of the simulation game.

DevOps

What is DevOps? What kind of fundamental challenges created a fertile ground for it to emerge in the first place? What are the key principles underpinning DevOps? Where is it now, 14 years since the term "DevOps" was coined by Patrick Debois? What kind of technical DevOps practices are modeled in the *LEGO and Chocolate* simulation, and what do you need to know about them to successfully run this simulation?

Functional Silos and a Low-Trust Culture

It is hard to imagine now that less than fifteen years ago we didn't even have the term "DevOps" in our vocabulary. In fact, organizations around the world were mostly still at the beginning of their Agile journeys. According to the 2009 State of Agile Report by VersionOne, only 31% of

---

[1] Kim, G., Humble, J., Debois, P., Willis, J., Forsgren, N. (2021). *The DevOps Handbook: How to Create World-Class Agility, Reliability, & Security in Technology Organizations*. IT Revolution Press.

respondents worked in organizations with "two teams or less" practicing Agile, while others were still applying the traditional Waterfall approach to managing and delivering projects.

While a change in the speed of delivery and collaboration patterns at least started to happen on the development side at that time, the processes, tools, and behaviors on the operations side were still largely unchanged. It was the time of large data centers, expensive relational databases, and physical servers that had to be ordered from hardware vendors three to nine months in advance. Building a new QA environment, loading production-like data, or deploying new code into production required long, error-prone manual efforts on the part of IT operations.

It was the time of monthly (or even quarterly) deployments. Handling post-production deployment emergencies, carrying pagers, and invoking escalation procedures were all parts of "business as usual" for IT operations. While many of these emergencies were caused by the release of new versions of applications (implemented earlier by the development teams), it was the on-call database administrator (DBA) or the on-call system administrator (SA) who was paged to handle the issues in the middle of the night.

In a typical organization, development teams had very few insights into the world of IT operations, and vice versa. Collaboration between the two departments was minimal, they operated as functional silos. Andrew Clay Shafer would later call this disconnect a "wall of confusion,"[2] referring to the lack of visibility between the two groups as well as the opposing, even conflicting, goals of the two departments. With development teams focused on the speed of building and delivering new features, while operations teams were focused on stability, reliability, and "keeping the lights on" for the revenue-generating systems already running in production, the disconnect was inevitable.

---

[2] Shafer, A.C. AgileRoots 2009 - Agile Infrastructure. https://www.youtube.com/watch?v=Y_u84PNrX9g

CHAPTER 3   BRIEF HISTORY OF DEVOPS AND DEVSECOPS

> **NOW, PUT ON AN "OPS HAT" FROM 2008 AND TAKE A STAB AT ANSWERING THIS QUESTION**
>
> What is the most reliable way to ensure that the production environment is stable and no new defects can be introduced into production by a new code deployment?
>
> That's right! Limit the number of production deployments, of course!

This misalignment of goals between the two departments in traditional organizations created a breeding ground for a low-trust culture. Why would that be a problem, you ask? Lee Reid explained it best in his "Simple math of DevOps[3]" blog post (see also Figure 3-1):

> *"Tasks we do in a delivery cycle are impacted by the degree of trust we have in the hand-offs from one to another. If we have zero trust, then our $T_{DELIVERY}$ will be infinite (divide by zero). 100% trust and our $T_{DELIVERY}$ will be only limited by how fast each task can be performed."*
>
> Lee Reid, "Simple math of DevOps"

When we operate in an environment of low trust, we add extra steps and extra sign-offs, in part to protect ourselves from potential blame later. We pad our project estimates because we don't trust the other party to be "on time" with their deliverables. We introduce "code freeze" around the days that are important to our business from reliability, stability, and performance perspectives because we don't trust the quality of the code being deployed. As a result, we limit our ability to delight our customers with the timely delivery of new features and new applications.

---

[3] http://devops.com/the-simple-math-of-devops/

CHAPTER 3   BRIEF HISTORY OF DEVOPS AND DEVSECOPS

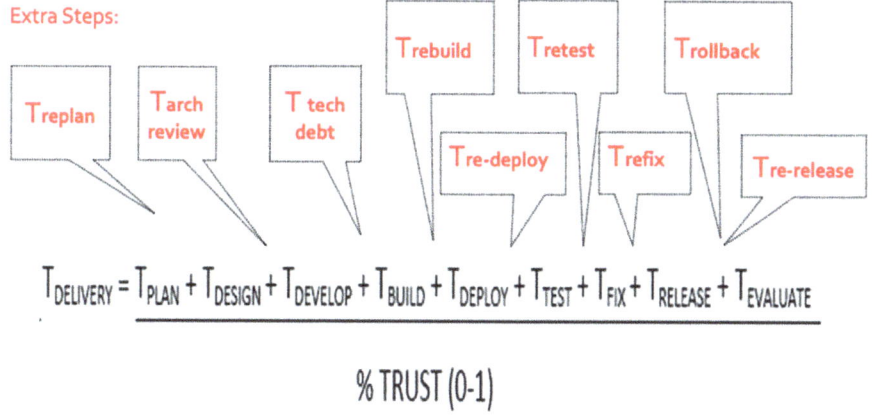

Figure 3-1. Extra steps we add to the delivery timeline to compensate for a low-trust culture. Inspired by Lee Reid, "Simple math of DevOps"

The Movement of People Who Cared

Back in 2008, Patrick Debois, a Belgian IT consultant, was among the very few people aware of this striking difference in goals, incentives, processes, and tools between development and operations. His awareness came from the experiment he had embarked on, aiming to expand his knowledge by working at every part of an IT organization.

Armed with these shocking discoveries, and desperately trying to find like-minded people interested in closing the gap between Dev and Ops, Patrick stumbled upon a bird-of-a-feather session on "Agile Infrastructure" proposed by Andrew Clay Shafer at the Agile 2008 conference in Toronto. The two of them later formed the "Agile System Administration" Google group. However, at that time, there were so few people interested in the topic that the group didn't get much traction.

CHAPTER 3   BRIEF HISTORY OF DEVOPS AND DEVSECOPS

This all changed after the Velocity 2009 conference when John Allspaw and Paul Hammond shared the groundbreaking results of Dev and Ops collaboration at Flickr in their pivotal talk "10+ Deploys Per Day." This talk pushed the limits of what was possible at that time and inspired many followers.

Encouraged by this talk and disappointed that he couldn't attend it in person, Patrick decided to organize his own conference in Belgium. He put together a two-day event, creating a space for developers and operations to collaborate and exchange ideas. This inaugural DevOpsDays conference brought to Belgium several leading practitioners from around the world, who continued the conversations on Twitter long after the event. Due to its massive use in the post-conference conversations, the original #DevOpsDays Twitter hashtag became too long. The "Days" was dropped. The #DevOps hashtag and the DevOps movement were born.

The early unicorns of the DevOps movement continued to push the boundaries of what was possible, inspiring others with their experiments:

- Amazon reported 11.6 seconds as their deployment frequency in 2011 (or about seven thousand deploys per day); that number increased to 130,000 deploys per day by 2015!

- Spotify, Facebook, and LinkedIn all went through a complete re-architecture, implementing CI/CD pipelines and embracing DevOps culture.

- Netflix and Etsy became known for their experiments with Chaos Engineering, blameless postmortems, and many other safety culture–enhancing practices.

CHAPTER 3   BRIEF HISTORY OF DEVOPS AND DEVSECOPS

No Longer "for Unicorns Only"

The next big influencer in the DevOps space showed up in 2014—DevOps Enterprise Summit. Created by Gene Kim, this conference put DevOps in the spotlight for leaders of large, established organizations and created space for them to inspire each other with their experiments, introducing the idea that large organizations were precisely the ones that could benefit the most from bringing in DevOps practices and tools, as well as instigating DevOps cultural change.

By 2015, DevOps practices, tools, and philosophy became widely adopted by large enterprises and small startups alike. The DevOps Enterprise Summit 2016 highlighted success stories from Macy's, Nordstrom, GE Capital, Disney, Capital One, 1-800-Flowers, Target, the US Department of Homeland Security, and many others.

Even this *LEGO and Chocolate* simulation game expanded its reach from public conferences only to being invited to kick-start DevOps transformations in several organizations worldwide. From 2017 to early 2020, this simulation taught DevOps culture in a large US-based insurance company, a global bank with 14 technology hubs around the world, an electric service company, a government organization, and many others. Check out Chapter 18 for additional stories from trainers and DevOps coaches who have been successfully running this simulation in their DevOps transformations in the United States, Canada, Germany, Mexico, and the rest of the world.

How about now? According to the 2023 "State of DevOps" report by Puppet Labs, DevOps became so widely adopted in many organizations and so deeply ingrained in their current way of working that they no longer even use the term "DevOps." By the same token, the researchers also noted a distortion of the meaning that "DevOps" has taken in large organizations:

CHAPTER 3 BRIEF HISTORY OF DEVOPS AND DEVSECOPS

> *"[...] vast spectrum between teams that are so 'DevOps' that they don't use the term at all, and teams that use the term 'DevOps' but work in a way that runs counter to the spirit of the movement [...]"*
>
> Puppet | State of DevOps Report 2023

Whether you picked up this book today to help your organization catch up with the DevOps movement or to help your teams reconnect with the spirit of DevOps, start your quest by clarifying what "DevOps" means in your context. My personal favorite definition of "DevOps" is this one:

> *"A mix of patterns intended to improve collaboration between development and operations. DevOps addresses shared goals and incentives as well as shared processes and tools."*
>
> —Michael Hüttermann, *DevOps for Developers*

Refocusing on Culture

Flipping back through the older "State of DevOps" reports (2013-2019), one can observe the gradual increase in emphasis on the cultural changes in DevOps transformations.

2013

This year's report provided recommendations on developing some rudimentary collaboration skills for people from the different functional groups:

> *"If you're in operations, find a developer who writes the code you deploy. If you're a developer, find one of the ops people who deploys your code. Have coffee. Hang out."*

Another recommendation was directed toward managers, suggesting they "foster a culture of direct communication" instead of using a top-down approach.

2014

A major contribution of this year's report was the introduction of Ron Westrum's work on the typology of organizational cultures. Westrum, a professor of sociology who spent decades studying complex organizations, identified three major organizational cultures—Pathological, Bureaucratic, and Generative—and highlighted the difference in the flow of information, especially in the case of "bad news." (See Figure 3-2 for my interpretation of Westrum's typology of organizational cultures.)

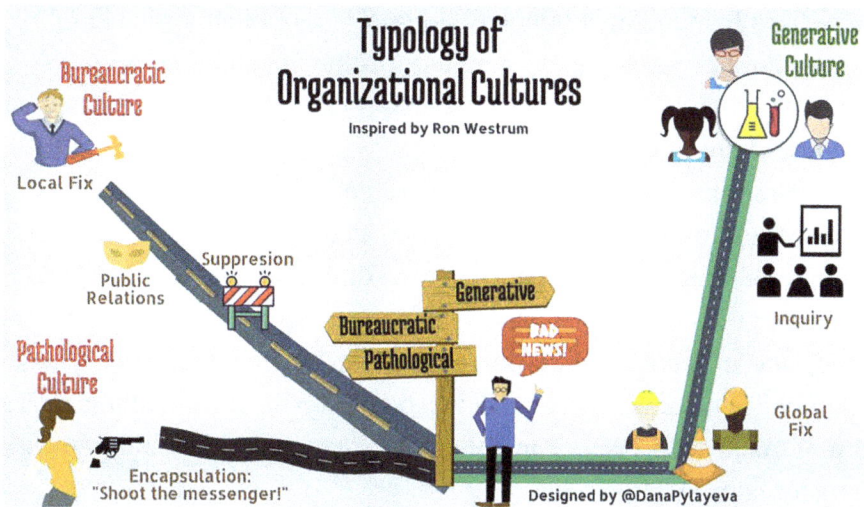

Figure 3-2. Typology of organizational cultures (inspired by Ron Westrum)

What he noticed about organizations with *Pathological/fear-ridden cultures* was that they typically exhibit low levels of cooperation and absolutely no tolerance for any kind of failure. "Shoot the messenger" and encapsulations are the most typical responses to bad news in this culture. Not surprisingly, this type of culture has the lowest level of innovation, experimentation, and organizational learning.

When a bad event happens in *Bureaucratic cultures*, the most common response is to downplay the severity of the failure, "save the face" of the department, and only implement the fix locally. While there exists some limited cooperation and collaboration, innovation isn't encouraged.

The highest level of collaboration and organizational learning that he observed was in organizations with *Generative cultures.* In these cultures, the flow of information is unobstructed by fear. Even if a failure happens, it typically leads to an inquiry, a blameless postmortem, and sharing of the lessons learned with the others in the organization, enabling global learning. One of the well-known examples of this type of shared learning comes from Etsy and their famous "Morgue"[4]—a publicly available collection of blameless postmortem reports that documented various systems failures, as well as results of the root-cause analysis performed by countless teams in Etsy.

Typology of organizational cultures helped me clarify what I was missing: the early unicorns of DevOps had all been the organizations with Generative cultures! As larger and more traditional organizations began to enter the DevOps space, the need for an increased focus on the cultural shift in DevOps transformations became clear. DevOps and Agile thrive in Generative cultures. When introduced in Bureaucratic or Pathological cultures, Agile and DevOps can potentially trigger new fears and even face strong resistance!

As I started running my DevOps simulation with more traditional organizations around that time, I observed several new concerns showing up in the reflections shared by the participants. You will have an opportunity to examine some of the most representative ones in Chapter 13 of this book.

---

[4] https://github.com/etsy/morgue

2018

From 2018 onward, researchers behind the original "State of DevOps" report split and began to produce two separate reports, which offered even more insights into the cultural changes and the obstacles on the road to DevOps adoption. One of this year's reports (by Puppet and Splunk) included the results of several interviews they'd conducted with C-level executives, management, and team members assessing their views on the level of DevOps practices penetration in their respective organizations. This is where the infamous "illusion of success" emerged!

On average, C-level executives reported 58% better DevOps penetration levels than those observed by teams in the trenches, with the astounding 97% variance in response to the "Incident responses are automated" statement (see Figure 3-3).

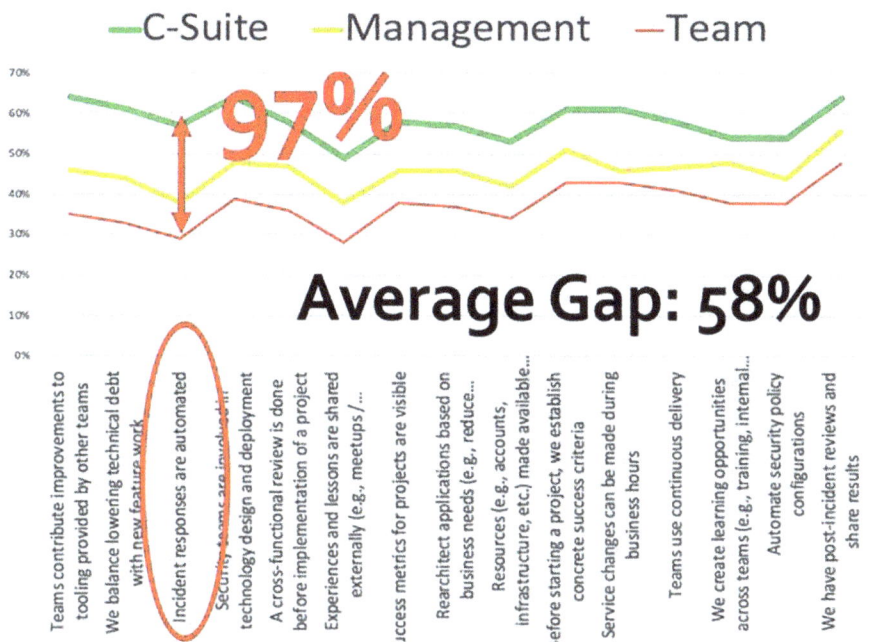

Figure 3-3. *Gap in the DevOps adoption progress perception, based on the 2018 "State of DevOps" report by Puppet*

2019

This was the year when psychological safety entered the DevOps space for the first time and was called out by the researchers of this year's report as the key contributing factor for software delivery and operations performance:

> "A culture of psychological safety contributes to SDO performance, organizational performance, and productivity, showing that growing and fostering a healthy culture reaps benefits for organizations and individuals."
>
> Accelerate | 2019 State of DevOps Report

I was excited while flipping through that year's report! It was confirming the hunch I had about the connection between DevOps and the other topic I am passionate about—psychological safety.

Psychological Safety

In parallel to my work in the DevOps space, I also have been focusing on coaching Scrum teams and learning about ways to help them reach their peak performance. Around 2016, I came across the newly published Google's "Project Aristotle."[5] While the term "psychological safety" already existed (thanks to the work of Willian A. Kahn and Amy C. Edmondson), it was Google's research that really put it into the spotlight for me, and for many other Agile practitioners. Psychological safety immediately became a hot topic at Agile conferences, and the more I learned about it, the more I was beginning to feel that it must be related to the third way of DevOps. I wanted to confirm this assumption.

---

[5] https://www.nytimes.com/2016/02/28/magazine/what-google-learned-from-its-quest-to-build-the-perfect-team.html

CHAPTER 3   BRIEF HISTORY OF DEVOPS AND DEVSECOPS

> **IS THERE A CHANCE THAT THE "THIRD WAY OF DEVOPS" AND "PSYCHOLOGICAL SAFETY" MIGHT BE RELATED?**
>
> What do you think?
>
> I asked the same questions for the first time at the Agile + DevOps East 2018 conference during my lightning keynote session. To my surprise, only a few hands went up in response to my question. Since then, I've been running this "informal survey" with every new audience in my DevOps workshops, and the results have been consistent.
>
> Very few people recognized the connection between these two ideas at that time!

The link between these two topics remained relatively weak for another few years, until the 2019 "State of DevOps" report pulled them together! Right around the same time, Gene Kim in his new book doubled down on the significance of psychological safety:

> *"The Fourth Ideal is Psychological Safety, where we make it safe to talk about problems, because solving problems requires prevention, which requires honesty, and honesty requires the absence of fear."*
>
> Gene Kim, "The Unicorn Project"

Reflecting on my own gap helped me understand why so many organizations would discount the Third Way of DevOps in their DevOps transformations. The Third Way of DevOps sounds like "common sense." Why wouldn't it happen organically? As these organizations kick off an "automation only" DevOps transformation, hire DevOps engineers, create new DevOps teams, or simply rebrand their Sys Admins into DevOps, they miss the opportunity to truly break down silos between development and operations.

CHAPTER 3   BRIEF HISTORY OF DEVOPS AND DEVSECOPS

Without deliberate and intentional cultural changes, people in these organizations are likely to continue to operate in a culture of fear and risk aversion, unable to realize the full benefits of DevOps.

DevSecOps

How about the term "DevSecOps"? What is the significance of inserting "Sec" in the middle of "DevOps"? Wasn't security already included in the original DevOps concept? Yes, the core idea of "shifting left" on security has always been a part of DevOps! Nevertheless, sometime around 2013 the term "DevSecOps" emerged, explicitly bringing additional attention to security as a critical part of any DevOps initiative.

One of the key factors that necessitated this move at the time was the exponential increase in the use of open-source software components, resulting in an increased frequency of data security breaches and vulnerability exploits.[6] No longer could information security professionals stay isolated from the rest of the process. No longer was it acceptable to delay security validation until the code was about to go to production. Security had to become integrated into every step of the development and deployment process, effectively shifting away from being "bolted on" to becoming everyone's responsibility (Figure 3-4).

Injecting "Sec" right in the middle of "DevOps" became, to some extent, an effective branding strategy. It brought DevOps into the spotlight for InfoSec professionals, clarifying their critical role in DevSecOps initiatives. In addition, it made DevSecOps more appealing to a broader range of C-level executives, helping further drive their interest in sponsoring DevSecOps initiatives.

---

[6] https://www.rsaconference.com/library/webcast/31-a-brief-history-of-devsecops-and-where-we-go-from-here

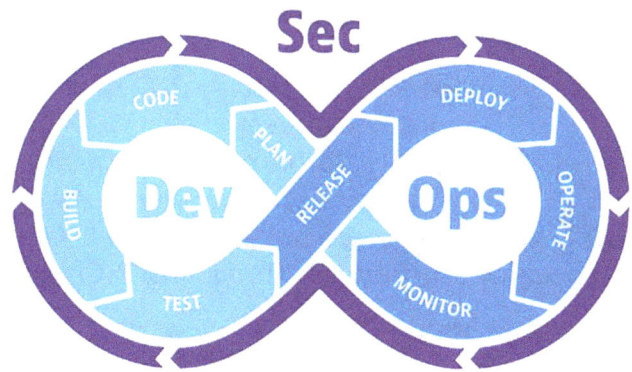

Figure 3-4. *Security integrated during development and after the deployment Image source:* `https://www.dynatrace.com/news/blog/what-is-devsecops/`

And yet, it has been so much more than a simple rebranding. DevSecOps called out a need for a partnership with security as well as a need for security professionals to become nimbler and more adaptable in the face of constant changes. The DevSecOps Manifesto, created under the leadership of Shannon Lietz, one of the thought leaders of DevSecOps, accentuated this partnership and the alignment on the key values as follows:

> *"Through Security as Code, we have and will learn that there is simply a better way for security practitioners, like us, to operate and contribute value with less friction. […] We will strive to be a better partner by valuing what you value:*
>
> ***Leaning in*** *over Always Saying 'No'*
> ***Data & Security Science*** *over Fear, Uncertainty and Doubt*
> ***Open Contribution & Collaboration*** *over Security-Only Requirements*
> ***Consumable Security Services with APIs*** *over Mandated Security Controls & Paperwork*

> ***Business Driven Security Scores*** *over Rubber Stamp Security*
> ***Red & Blue Team Exploit Testing*** *over Relying on Scans & Theoretical Vulnerabilities*
> ***24x7 Proactive Security Monitoring*** *over Reacting after Being Informed of an Incident*
> ***Shared Threat Intelligence*** *over Keeping Info to Ourselves*
> ***Compliance Operations*** *over Clipboards & Checklists"*
>
> DevSecOps Manifesto: `https://www.devsecops.org/`

This partnership is the only way forward for modern organizations, where the software delivery cadence is shortened to days or even hours. By integrating security in all aspects of software development and operation, teams are now able to remove or significantly reduce the pre-deployment security scans, reducing the need for last-minute security issue remediation and delivering "software, safer, sooner."

I want to point out another significant contribution to safety culture and destigmatizing failure that originated from the DevSecOps community—the "Epic Failures in DevSecOps[7]" report. This collection of failure stories continues to inspire others with its transparency, supporting the notion of celebrating failure as a way to promote community learning and making it safe to talk about mistakes.

Summary

The DevOps movement emerged in response to the low-trust culture that was impeding organizations' ability to deliver software to their customers. From the very beginning, the DevOps movement was driven by practitioners, who have seen the "wall of confusion" from both sides

---

[7] Miller, M., Stearn, A., Schleen, DJ., Wong, C., Lim, F., Roberts, C., Conikee, C., Kwan, E., Streichsbier, S. (2018) Epic Failures in DevSecOps, DevSecOps Days.

and desperately wanted to bring it down! Over the last 14 years, DevOps expanded its reach from small start-ups and unicorn companies to large enterprises and government organizations. Nowadays, as more development teams leverage open-source software components, and the number of security vulnerabilities rises, DevSecOps is emerging to help bring security into the spotlight.

As DevOps/DevSecOps continues to move further through the innovation adoption life cycle, more focus is needed on cultural change, especially in organizations with pathological and bureaucratic cultures. Psychological safety becomes an essential ingredient in fostering a generative culture of learning and in enabling successful DevOps/DevSecOps initiatives.

CHAPTER 4

What You Will Teach with *LEGO* and *Chocolate* Simulation

Let's take you through the key principles and practices that can be taught with the main simulation described in this book. Some of the more evident ones are systems thinking, flow, and feedback loop. This chapter will offer you a high-level overview of these concepts as well as their associated technical practices: Continuous Delivery, containerization, microservices, automated environments provisioning, and Infrastructure as Code. You will find "How to introduce this…" panels with an outline of specific models and metaphors used in the simulation that will help you bring these practices to life in your training, without writing a single line of code or building a CI/CD pipeline for real. The essential ideas of "shift left" and "shift right" of DevSecOps will also be described in this chapter.

CHAPTER 4   WHAT YOU WILL TEACH WITH LEGO AND CHOCOLATE SIMULATION

Ideas from "The Phoenix Project"

As you already know, the *LEGO and Chocolate* simulation game was inspired by one of the most famous books in DevOps—*The Phoenix Project*. This business novel brilliantly distills the essence of ideas and principles from Lean, Agile, Theory of Constraints, and the Safety Culture into a short and memorable image: flow, feedback loop, and series of small repeatable loops of learning. (See Figure 4-1)

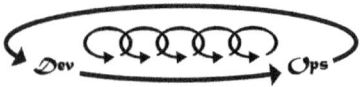

Figure 4-1. *The Three Ways: The principles underpinning DevOps Source: Gene Kim* `https://itrevolution.com/articles/the-three-ways-principles-underpinning-devops/`

This creative image represents the key principles that serve as pillars for all the behaviors, practices, and tools that enable the breakthrough of DevOps: "The Three Ways of DevOps."

To facilitate the learning of these core ideas, the *LEGO and Chocolate* simulation helps you create an immersive experience for your participants, connecting them with the three principles in a very visual and very tangible way:

- *First Way of DevOps* and, very specifically, the idea of flow of value from Dev to Ops, bottleneck optimization, and *systems thinking*. The game will start by bringing to life the day-to-day operation and the culture of a heavily sub-optimized organization. As you start experimenting with bottleneck optimization after Sprint 1, you will lead the participants through an experience of developing "T-shaped" skills. This is one of the most powerful activities in the game! Even skeptics will be able to recognize the positive impact of cross-training and upskilling. Technical practices for accelerating flow (containerization, microservices, Infrastructure as Code, CI/CD, etc.) will also be introduced here.

- *Second Way*, and the various practices that enable *amplifying feedback loop*. As you continue with further improvements to the way of working in the following rounds, the players will begin to experience the benefits of a shorter feedback loop from the business. They will have an opportunity to discuss telemetry, on-call rotation, and the "you build it, you run it"[1] mantra introduced by Amazon's CTO Werner Vogels in 2006, as examples of embracing the essence of the Second Way of DevOps.

- While the *Third Way of DevOps* is taught using supplemental material (*Fear in the Workplace* and *Safety in the Workplace* coaching tools), the topic of safety, as well as job security, resistance to change, and other barriers to DevOps adoption, often come up during debriefing rounds of the *LEGO and Chocolate* simulation (see Chapter 12 for tips on effective debriefing).

- Another concept this simulation will help you explore is the *role of security*. With a dedicated Sara Security role and a built-in "Shift-Left" dynamic, it will be easy

---

[1] "A Conversation with Werner Vogels: Learning from the Amazon technology platform." https://queue.acm.org/detail.cfm?id=1142065

to articulate how DevOps (and later DevSecOps) turns security into the whole team's concern. "Shift-left," static code analysis, vulnerability scans, and intruder attacks are discussed in the DevSecOps section of this chapter.

The First Way of DevOps

This principle specifically addresses the culture of functional silos and its negative impact on an organization's ability to accelerate delivery of value to the customers. *Systems thinking* (as opposed to focusing on local sub-optimizations of each silo) is the way to optimizing flow and achieving better organizational performance.

Building on the ideas from the Theory of Constraints and Lean, this principle highlights the importance of gaining visibility into the entire end-to-end value stream and understanding the different types of work existing in the system. It brings attention to the following practices:

- Visualize the entire end-to-end technology value stream: from business, to development, to IT operations ("planned work").

- Understand the "unplanned" or emergency work that causes the biggest disruption to the flow of value.

- Uncover the "non-value-adding" activities and "waits" in your current processes that can be reduced or eliminated to shorten the overall time to delivery.

- In the best tradition of Lean manufacturing, limit the work in progress and reduce the batch sizes of the work items.

- Double down on identifying bottlenecks in the flow of value and select the biggest one, which will need to be addressed first. In fact, the authors of the *Phoenix Project* emphasize that "any improvements made anywhere besides the bottleneck are an illusion."

Bottlenecks

Once we start paying closer attention to the performance of the entire end-to-end flow, many bottlenecks will become apparent. Take a closer look at the list of most typical bottlenecks uncovered in DevOps transformations. Does anything look familiar? Do you currently experience any of these in your organization?

- Environment creation delays
- Large batch size code merges (feature branches)
- Code deployment executed by a centralized group in a large organization
- Test setup and manual execution
- Two weeks of regression testing
- Monolithic legacy architecture
- Lack of skills or silos of knowledge
- People unwilling to change

You will be able to lead the group through experiencing some of these bottlenecks in the *LEGO and Chocolate* simulation. Sprint 1 of the game was intentionally designed to showcase the negative impact of the traditional organizational structures on the firm's ability to deliver value with speed and at scale.

Technical Practices Supporting The First Way

When it comes to technical practices that enable the First Way of DevOps, there are several that are modeled in the *LEGO and Chocolate* simulation. What follows is a summary of each practice as well as some information on how each of them comes to life in the simulation. You will find detailed facilitation instructions for introducing each round of the simulation and facilitating the debriefing in Chapters 8, 9, and 12.

Continuous Delivery

One of the technical practices modeled in Sprint 3 is Continuous Delivery (CD). This is an approach to developing/deploying software that relies on a set of automated processes for moving a change (new feature, configuration change, bug fix, etc.) through each stage of the software development lifecycle in a safe, fast, predictable, and repeatable way. "Continuous Delivery" is defined as follows:

> *"[...] software development strategy that optimizes your delivery process to get high-quality, valuable software delivered as quickly as possible [...]"*
>
> Jez Humble, David Farley, *Continuous Delivery*

As a natural evolution of Continuous Integration (CI) practices from Extreme Programming (XP), Continuous Delivery relies heavily on version control, automated testing, and configuration management. It aims to take the emergency and all-nighters out of the deployments, turning them into a non-event. CI/CD makes this possible by ensuring that the code is always in the deployable state, no matter how large or how complex the codebase and environments are.

CHAPTER 4 WHAT YOU WILL TEACH WITH LEGO AND CHOCOLATE SIMULATION

A key enabler for this lofty goal is configurational management, as well as automated, repeatable environment provisioning that makes it possible for a developer, a tester, and anyone else on the team to re-create a production-like environment on demand.

CI/CD fundamentally shifts the way development teams collaborate on developing software! Instead of the traditional approach of working in feature branches, infrequently committing the code to trunk, and incurring high costs of merge conflicts when finally merging the code, in CI/CD shops developers use a trunk-based development approach.

Trunk-based development requires that every developer checks in the code directly into the main trunk of the codebase, the same one used for production deployment, at least once a day. While this practice sounds scary at first, it eliminates the need for large batch size code merges, removes the stabilization phase of the project, and significantly shortens the cycle time of application delivery. Trunk-based development relies heavily on the following practices:

- Breaking the work into smaller chunks so that each can be completed in less than a day.

- Implementing fast and reliable automated builds so that they don't slow down the developers on the code check-in.

- Maintaining efficient, reliable, and automated test suites that can provide immediate feedback on the quality of the newly checked-in code.

- Embracing the "everyone is responsible" principle, swarming on fixing the broken build, maintaining the code in an "always deployable" state.

Containerization and Microservices

These two powerful technologies often go together in modern application development and deployment. While containerization can be applied to the deployment of traditional monolithic applications as well, when applied to the deployment of microservices and used with a CI/CD pipeline, it can become a true illustration of optimizing flow with "small batches"—the First Way of DevOps.

What is *containerization*? It is a process of packaging software code with all associated libraries, dependencies, and configurations so that it can be isolated in its own lightweight and portable container. Development, testing, production—these containers can be easily deployed to and run in any of these environments!

Docker was the first company to introduce robust containerization technology, in 2013. Today, using containers, teams can create and deploy applications faster and more securely, completely avoiding the infamous "Worked on my machine, Ops' problem now!" scenario.

You can think about *microservices* as a modern version of service-oriented architecture (SOA). Microservice architecture is an approach to application development where every service is isolated and only communicates with other services through lightweight APIs. This approach breaks up an application into smaller, more specialized core functions, allowing developers to work on a specific area of an application, simplifying development, testing, and deployment, as well as minimizing the impact on the app's overall performance.

CHAPTER 4   WHAT YOU WILL TEACH WITH LEGO AND CHOCOLATE SIMULATION

> **HOW TO INTRODUCE THESE PRACTICES IN LEGO AND CHOCOLATE SIMULATION**

There are three rounds (or Sprints) in this game (see Chapters 8 and 9):

- Sprint 1: pre-DevSecOps
- Sprint 2: first steps to DevSecOps (with cross-training)
- Sprint 3: DevSecOps with CI/CD and containerization

All three concepts (CI/CD, microservices, and containerization) come together in Sprint 3 when you instruct the team to experiment with the following modifications in their way of working:

- Split large batches into smaller ones—one LEGO animal per batch (a metaphor for user story splitting, minimizing the use of feature branches, trunk-based development, and microservices).
- Start using the "green" secure packages that can be deployed directly into production—no additional release packaging required (a metaphor for Docker containers).
- Deploy green packages to production (one by one) as soon as each one is ready. (This is a metaphor for Continuous Delivery of the increments of the product that meet Definition of Done.[2])

Infrastructure as Code

Infrastructure as Code (IaC) is one more practice that is modeled in this simulation. IaC is a technology and process for automating environments configuration, provisioning, and management of infrastructure resources

---

[2] https://scrumguides.org/scrum-guide.html#increment

(servers, network, databases) with code. Unlike the manual provisioning and configuration of physical servers of the past, IaC automates and simplifies environment creation by templating all manual configurations into machine-readable files.

These configuration files can be version controlled, peer reviewed, approved, and audited. The approach avoids manual, undocumented configuration changes, minimizes configuration drift, and promotes compliant infrastructure management processes. Reproducible and scalable, the IaC process makes self-service provisioning of the environments available to others outside IT operations.

First introduced by Puppet in 2009, IaC removes the time-consuming bottleneck of manual environment configuration, significantly reducing the cycle time of the value delivery. Other notable choices for IaC implementation are Chef, Red Hat Ansible, AWS CloudFormation, and others.

HOW TO INTRODUCE THIS CONCEPT IN LEGO AND CHOCOLATE SIMULATION

After the cross-training has been completed in Sprint 2, participants with System Administrator roles (Adam Admin) typically discover that they have a little more availability. This is the time when you can ask them to join you in the "innovation center" by a room poster with "known good environment configuration" (See Figure 4-2).

CHAPTER 4 WHAT YOU WILL TEACH WITH LEGO AND CHOCOLATE SIMULATION

Figure 4-2. *"Chef recipes" created in the Innovation Center by Adam Admins, Sprint 3*

They will now start learning Infrastructure as Code tools and build their first "Chef recipes" (simulated by a green painter tape). They will be working ahead of the development team to enable automated environment provisioning in Sprint 3.

The Second Way of DevOps

The Second Way of DevOps is about *amplifying feedback loops* and putting information into the hands of developers, testers, security engineers, and operations involved in the end-to-end value stream. Here are just a few examples of the Second Way of DevOps in action:

- Immediate feedback about potential security issues and suboptimal code quality from static code analysis tools in developers' IDE

- Early feedback on quality of the newly checked-in code from continuous integration (CI) server: are the test suites passing or failing in response to the new code?

49

CHAPTER 4   WHAT YOU WILL TEACH WITH LEGO AND CHOCOLATE SIMULATION

- Implementing telemetry and collecting feedback on the server load, stability, and performance of the application under production load, making it visible to all.

- Collecting feedback on the new feature adoption and performance from A/B testing

- Inviting development team into user experience interviews, involving them in the early discovery phase where the feedback from reviewing paper-prototyping and wireframes with the users can influence the course of the product development

- Shared on-call rotation for the entire team (including developers and architects) to amplify upstream feedback loop on the architecture, design, and coding decisions they've made

HOW TO INTRODUCE THIS CONCEPT IN LEGO AND CHOCOLATE SIMULATION

You will discuss the Second Way of DevOps concept with the group prior to the third round of the simulation, when introducing Continuous Delivery, containerization, and microservices. Using one LEGO animal per batch and deploying directly into production with "secure" green Docker containers allows the teams to shorten the cycle time, as well as to amplify feedback loops, bringing business closer to the development team and enabling our fictional organization to become more profitable in this simulation.

"Delivery board" and "Animal Exchange" posters will help you model monitoring dashboards that track (and make visible to teams) the value being delivered and the business demand fluctuation in each round.

During the debriefing, you can help the group explore the impact of process improvements and transparency, call out changes in the dynamic of the group, and point out the shifts in collaboration patterns. By this time players in the business role are typically drawn into collaborating closely with the developers, who can now respond to the market demand's fluctuation of the "Animal Exchange board" more effectively.

"Shift Left" and "Shift Right" of DevSecOps

One of the earlier innovations in the application security space was the idea of "shifting left" on security. This approach emphasized a shift away from the traditional security scans performed by security professionals immediately prior to production deployments. The new approach extended an invitation into the security world to the developers, educating them on secure coding practices and providing the tools to identify and remediate vulnerabilities as early in the development process as possible.

Static code analysis tools (Sonar Lint/SonarQube, Checkmarx, Veracode, Snyk, and others) emerged at that time to enable building the security in from the very first lines of code. These tools have the ability to integrate with existing developers' IDEs, help to identify security issues, and flag expired compliance standards as well as offer fast, reliable, just-in-time feedback on critical defects, often providing guidance on their resolution. With this approach, the teams can proactively reduce their potential security tech debt.

CHAPTER 4   WHAT YOU WILL TEACH WITH LEGO AND CHOCOLATE SIMULATION

While the "shift-left" approach expands the circle of security-conscious roles to include developers, the "shift-right" approach expands it to include operations, bringing security testing to post-deployment and into production environments. Also known as "shield right," this approach ensures that the application can perform under production load with an appropriate level of runtime security controls. The tools enabling the "shield right" approach provide consistent monitoring and real-time threat detection, and offer a security feedback loop, allowing development teams to correlate issues from production with the underlying code, enabling them to effectively prioritize fixing the most exploitable production vulnerabilities.

HOW TO INTRODUCE THESE DEVSECOPS CONCEPTS WITH LEGO AND CHOCOLATE SIMULATION

The role of Sara Security is the one that allows this game to bring basic DevSecOps ideas to life. The game uses a security catalog artifact (see Figure 4-3) as Sara's reference for "known vulnerabilities and threats." At the beginning of each Sprint, Sara is asked to write down three random numbers in her catalog. These become known security issues for that Sprint.

CHAPTER 4   WHAT YOU WILL TEACH WITH LEGO AND CHOCOLATE SIMULATION

SARA SECURITY

MOD CARD

1. At the start of each Sprint, write down 3 random numbers between _____ and _____. These numbers will be your **known security issues** for this Sprint for team_____.
2. Check the **deployment packages**. If any of them contain an animal with a label that's matching your number, send the **entire package back** to the Dev team for a fix.
Sprint 1 ____   ____   ____
Sprint 2 ____   ____   ____
Sprint 3 ____   ____   ____

THREATS AND SECURITY BUGS CATALOG

Figure 4-3. *Sara Security's known vulnerabilities and security threats catalog*

As the team delivers large deployment packages in Sprint 1, Sara scans them prior to production deployments, trying to find a LEGO animal with one of the three identified numbers from the catalog. If she finds a matching number, the entire large package containing an animal with that number will be sent back to the development team for security issues remediation.

Potential debriefing topics: large, painful deployments. Silos of knowledge and lack of transparency causing a lot of rework if/when a security issue is found.

As a part of Sprint 2 modifications, you will ask Sara to join her Scrum team and share the knowledge about three new security issues with them. Now they will avoid using these numbers on the new animals from the start, effectively "shifting left" on security.

Another game modification you'll introduce will be the role of Harry Hacker—an intruder who will be instructed to hack all the physical environments by drawing hearts and holes on the "environment tape." Soon after, you will instruct Sara to monitor environments for new vulnerabilities and lead the remediation effort in partnership with the entire team.

Lastly, the focus on security will come up again in Sprint 3 of the simulation. There the group will be introduced to secure Docker containers (green packages), and Total Security Suite will be made available through implementation of Chef Recipes and on-demand environment provisioning (green tape).

Scrum and Agile

Occasionally you may still find yourself facilitating this simulation for a group that's looking to bring the DevOps/DevSecOps practices to an organization with a heavy Waterfall environment. This simulation assumes some level of familiarity with the 2020 version of The Scrum Guide[3] as well as the Agile Manifesto.[4] If you find yourself in front of a group with limited knowledge in these areas, you may need to take a few minutes to explain the basics of the Scrum framework (accountabilities, events, and artifacts) and the Agile values to this group. Introducing either of these bodies of knowledge is beyond the scope of this book.

---

[3] https://scrumguides.org/docs/scrumguide/v2020/2020-Scrum-Guide-US.pdf
[4] https://agilemanifesto.org/

CHAPTER 4   WHAT YOU WILL TEACH WITH LEGO AND CHOCOLATE SIMULATION

Summary

Incorporating the *LEGO and Chocolate* simulation in your training will allow you to teach the fundamental ideas from DevSecOps. Optimizing end-to-end flow, amplifying feedback loop principles, and the associated technical practices are modeled well in this simulation. Continuous Delivery, containerization, microservices, Infrastructure as Code, and "shift left" on security have been intentionally designed into the dynamic of this game. Just like with any other simulations or business games, remember that the main learning will always emerge for the participants through the discussions and reflections that they will share during the debriefing. This is also where the game may surprise you with opportunities to extend the learning beyond what was originally intended by me. Keep your eyes and ears open for these opportunities!

CHAPTER 5

LEGO and Chocolate: Rules of the Game

Now that you are aware of the key learning concepts that the *LEGO and Chocolate* simulation is designed to teach, let's dive into the game dynamic and learn about the various roles and their interaction patterns. In this chapter, I will share with you the basic game flow and several hidden modifications that you, as a facilitator, will be introducing during the game. Some of these modifications are there to create new process bottlenecks; others are to alleviate them and highlight the benefits of collaboration. This chapter will also shed light on the emotional side of each round so that you know exactly what may emerge and how to set the right expectations with the participants.

Summary and Aim of the Game

The *LEGO and Chocolate* simulation is a collaborative role-playing game set in the current time in a fictional company—a large player on the LEGO animals' market. This is an asymmetric game in which players take on one of the nine roles and play differently according to their role description. All players share a common purpose: to maximize the total value delivered and help their fictional organization remain profitable in the increasingly complex and competitive market. Unlike other simulations that engage players at a single table, this one unfolds in the entire room as it attempts to showcase elements of organizational dynamics before and after transitioning to DevSecOps culture.

The game is played in three identically time-boxed rounds (see Chapter 8 for timebox recommendations). The first round models the organizational structure, role boundaries, and interaction patterns of a large traditional organization. I call this round "Feel the Pain." In the second round ("First Steps to DevSecOps") participants begin to experiment with culture changes by building T-shaped skills through cross-training, "shifting left" on security, blurring the boundaries of their roles, and adopting new interaction patterns. The third round ("Continuous Value Delivery") brings in a few additional DevOps-inspired process improvements (on-demand environments provisioning, containerization, and CI/CD pipeline), dialing up collaboration, fun, and performance of the group to the max! At the end of each round, teams spend a few minutes debriefing and adapting their process before the next round starts. With additional game modifications introduced by the facilitator (you!) the players learn to respond to change and adjust their strategy accordingly.

Player Roles and Avatars

Based on the individual roles selected at the beginning of the game, all participants arrange themselves into several *Scrum* teams, an *IT Operations* team, a *Security* team, and a *Business* team (refer to Chapter 7 for ideas on setting up the space for optimal balance of the game). Players carry out the first round according to their predefined roles, engaging in interactions with other roles at their tables as well as across the entire room.

CHAPTER 5 LEGO AND CHOCOLATE: RULES OF THE GAME

The Business team provides direction to the Scrum teams on the types of LEGO animals that need building. Players use the LEGO Animal Exchange board (see Figure 5-1) as an information radiator of the current market demand as well as an impromptu Product Backlog.

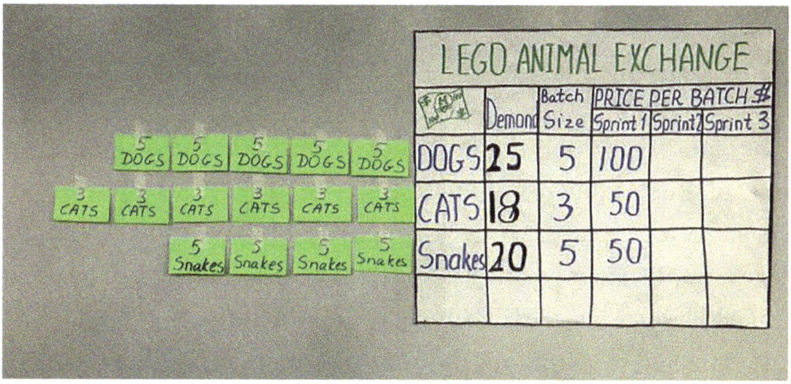

Figure 5-1. *LEGO Animal Exchange board and Product Backlog items*

Scrum teams work to build and test these LEGO animals as well as deliver them to IT Operations for packaging and production deployment. The Security team ensures that all environments and the final products are free from security issues and that opportunities for vulnerability exploits are minimized.

Scrum Team

There are four different roles intentionally included in each of the Scrum teams of this simulation: Product Owner, Scrum Master, Developer, and Tester. Since the game starts in the context of a "traditional" organization, this separation of functional roles of Developer and Tester represents one of the typical anti-patterns found in these organizations. As the game progresses, the intra-team dynamic will naturally shift to the dynamic of a

Scrum team, as defined in the Scrum Guide. With increased cross-training and focus on optimizing for the flow of values, the role boundaries begin to fade and both roles will integrate into one that is "committed to creating any aspect of a usable Increment each Sprint," irrespective of the specialized skills required to build and deliver the high-quality product.

Patricia Product

Patricia (Figure 5-2) is a Product Owner. She is accountable for maximizing the value of the product resulting from the work of the Scrum team. Patricia starts the game in Sprint 1 by approaching the Business team, selecting a few Product Backlog item (PBI) work cards from the Animal Exchange Marketplace, and clarifying the characteristics of the LEGO animals expected by *Benjamin Business*. She then brings these work cards to her team (*Danny Developer* and *Tim Tester*) and guides them through the implementation of these items.

Figure 5-2. *Patricia Product*

Note that PBIs are defined as small batches of three to ten animals per PBI and must be delivered in the quantity indicated on each work card. *Patricia* works with *Benjamin Business* to collect feedback and receive money for the products accepted by business stakeholders.

Patricia will receive a special Mod Card in the last Sprint with instructions to start splitting the PBIs, reducing the size of the unit of work to *one* per batch, and enabling a "one-piece flow" mode of operations for her team. See "Mod Cards" section in the appendix.

Danny Developer

Danny (Figure 5-3) is a member of the Scrum team. His goal is to create any aspect of usable product increment each Sprint—i.e., build quality LEGO animal products fast.

When *Patricia Product* shows him the first PBI, he is ready to roll up his sleeves and start building. Unfortunately, he doesn't have an environment to work in and doesn't know how to provision one. *Danny* needs to find a system administrator (a.k.a. infrastructure engineer) from IT Operations (*Adam Admin*) who can provision the development environment for *Danny*.

Once the environment is created, *Danny* can start working on the first PBI and build the LEGO animals that *Benjamin Business* needs. Another surprise—there are no standard assembly instructions! *Danny* needs to work with *Patricia Product* and/or *Benjamin Business* to understand what is currently needed on the market.

CHAPTER 5   LEGO AND CHOCOLATE: RULES OF THE GAME

Figure 5-3. Danny Developer

According to the team's Definition of Done, *Danny* must not forget to attach a small number label to each LEGO animal, place every animal into a small clear package, add a chocolate candy, and close the package. Now it is ready to be tested by *Tim Tester*.

Danny may have to redo his work if defects are found during testing, including security testing. Just like any other member of the Development team in the first Sprint, *Danny* can't independently deploy into production and has a dependency on another member of IT Operations (*Robert Release*).

As the game unfolds, and we start embracing DevSecOps ideas, *Danny* will learn to modify his interaction patterns when working with his IT Operations and Security counterparts. Through cross-training, role shadowing, automation, and involving Security/Operations early in the process, *Danny* will be able to expand the boundaries of his role. Not only that! This new way of working will enable *Danny*, and his entire team, to respond faster to the changing demands of *Benjamin Business*, earn more money for the team, and bring joy into everyday work.

CHAPTER 5 LEGO AND CHOCOLATE: RULES OF THE GAME

Tim Tester

Tim (Figure 5-4) is a new member of the Scrum team. His goal is to ensure product quality. He has recently transitioned from a functional QA/QE department. *Tim's* interaction model in the first Sprint highlights a very common dysfunction. He hasn't embraced a new mindset and still operates within narrow boundaries of his traditional role. Through the game, he will acquire new skills and become a fully integrated member of the Scrum team.

Figure 5-4. *Tim Tester*

During the first Sprint, *Tim* must validate that each small development package created by *Danny Developer* meets the Definition of Done as defined by the team (see Figure 5-5). If a development package fails validation, *Tim* sends the package back to *Danny* for rework. *Tim Tester* also works with another member of IT Operations, a release engineer (*Robert Release*), and runs integration tests on the deployment package assembled and packaged for deployment by *Robert*. *Tim Tester* verifies the Definition of Done for the deployment package as well.

CHAPTER 5   LEGO AND CHOCOLATE: RULES OF THE GAME

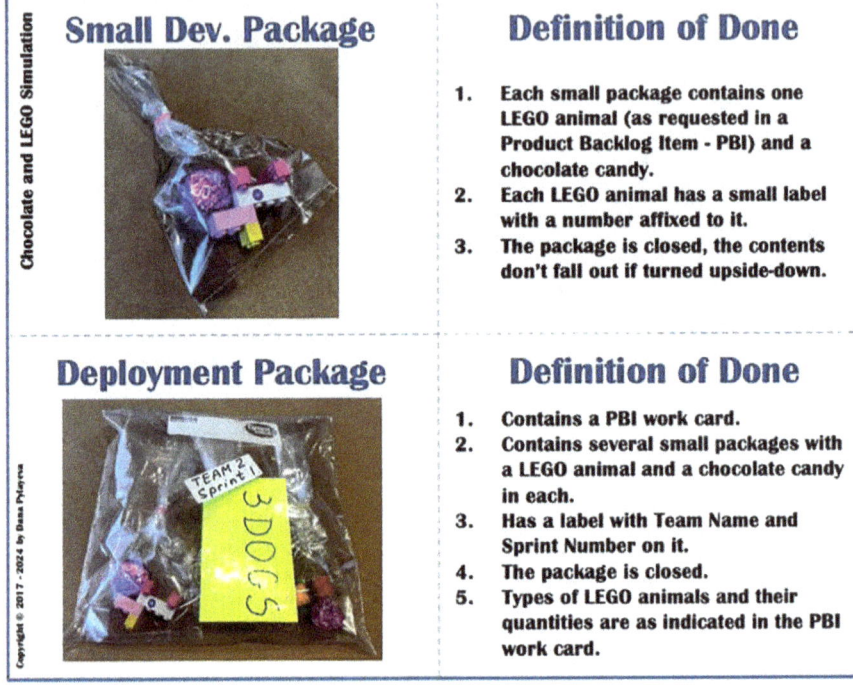

Figure 5-5. Definition of Done: small development package and a deployment package

The game is configured with a 1:2 ratio of players in the *Tim Tester* role versus the ones in the *Danny Developer* role. This intentionally created bottleneck feels very real and highlights the need for cross-training, expanding the boundaries of roles, and making quality the "entire team's concern."

Samuel Scrum

Samuel (Figure 5-6) is a Scrum Master. His goal is to enable the Scrum team's effectiveness. *Samuel Scrum* is always busy! He coaches team members in self-management and cross-functionality.

Figure 5-6. *Samuel Scrum*

He can support *Patricia Product* and assist in her communication with *Benjamin Business* and the team. He can request additional supplies from the facilitator, removing impediments. He can work with the IT Operations group to find people with the right skills.

As all rounds of the game are timeboxed, they are modeled after events in the Scrum framework. *Samuel Scrum* is the one who ensures that all Scrum events take place and are positive, productive, and kept within the timebox. He helps the team and organization to continuously improve through empirical process development with practices like retrospectives. *Samuel* is a true leader who serves the team and the organization at large.

IT Operations Team

There are two key roles from a traditional IT Operations team that are featured in the *LEGO and Chocolate* simulation: a system administrator (a.k.a. an infrastructure engineer) and a release engineer (a.k.a. release/build manager). While there are more roles and broader responsibilities that exist in a traditional IT Operations team, for the purpose of this game's learning objectives we will zoom in on these two.

CHAPTER 5   LEGO AND CHOCOLATE: RULES OF THE GAME

At the start of the game, the IT Operations team exists as a functional silo. The Scrum teams think about them only in the case of a crisis—an environment needs to be provisioned or patched ASAP, or a new deployment package needs to be built at the last minute, just before the deadline. The limited communication and non-existent collaboration between the groups causes numerous bottlenecks in the delivery of value. The dynamic begins to change in Sprints 2 and 3, as the players adopt a DevSecOps mindset, facilitate cross-training (T-shape building activity with sticker exchange), invest in upskilling, and enable self-service environment provisioning.

Adam Admin

Adam (Figure 5-7) is a system administrator in the IT Operations team. His goal is to keep the production environment stable. *Adam* is the only one in the organization who knows how to build environments for *Danny Developer* or *Tim Tester*, and how to perform environment upgrades, install security patches after *Harry Hacker's* attacks, or completely rebuild the environments. *Sara Security* calls for *Adam Admin's* help any time she discovers security issues with the environments.

Figure 5-7. *Adam Admin*

Adam uses household masking tape as a model for provisioning the environments (see Figure 5-8) or patching them. (This is a special supply item available to players in *Adam Admin*'s role only. See Chapter 6 for more info.)

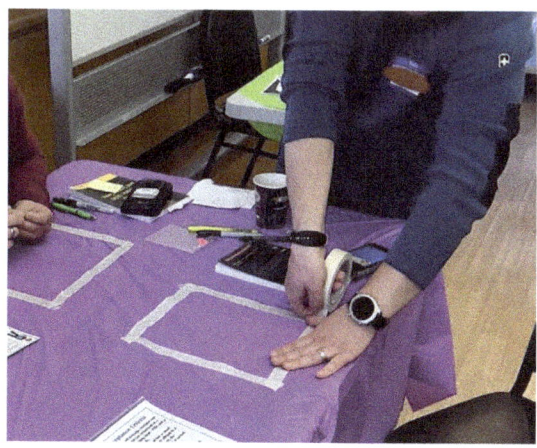

Figure 5-8. *Adam Admin in the process of provisioning development environments: square-shaped spaces created by applying a layer of household masking tape*

In addition to environment creation, *Adam* monitors the production environment to prevent unauthorized deployments. *Adam* controls the production deployment schedule and is the only person who can give a "go ahead" to *Robert Release* for production deployment. *Adam* is also the first one who gets notified about the production deployment moratorium (a.k.a. "code freeze") via a special "secret" Mod Card in Sprint 1. (See "Mod Cards" section in the appendix.)

There is a limited number of players in *Adam Admin*'s role. Often, he must support more than one Scrum team in the first round of the game. This bottleneck is intentionally built into the simulation; however, it reflects the reality and the pain point of many large traditional organizations today.

Adam Admin's role will become less painful in the second round, as it will shift from firefighting to fire-prevention mode. *Adam* will have an opportunity to research, learn, and implement on-demand self-service environment provisioning technology for the Scrum teams.

Robert Release

Robert (Figure 5-9) is a release engineer in the IT Operations team.

Figure 5-9. *Robert Release*

His goal is to keep the production environment stable. *Robert Release* is the only one who has release management knowledge and experience. He is authorized by the organization to build deployment packages and deploy them into production.

Every deployment package (Figure 5-10) contains a PBI work card and a corresponding number of individual development packages.

CHAPTER 5 LEGO AND CHOCOLATE: RULES OF THE GAME

Figure 5-10. *Deployment package built by Robert Release*

Robert labels each deployment package with the development team name and the Sprint number in which this package has been created. Once a deployment package is ready, it is verified by *Tim Tester* and sent for a pre-production security scan to *Sara Security*. If no security issues are found, the package is ready for deployment.

Robert now works with *Adam Admin* to identify the timing of the next deployment window. If the deployment window is on, *Robert* delivers the deployment package to *Benjamin Business*. If deployment is not allowed, the package remains on the Operations table, waiting for future deployment opportunities. Similar to *Adam Admin*'s role, the number of players in the role of *Robert Release* is limited to one release engineer per one or two Scrum teams (see Chapter 7 for guidance on the optimal balance of roles for various groups).

CHAPTER 5   LEGO AND CHOCOLATE: RULES OF THE GAME

Security Team: Sara Security

Sara (Figure 5-11) is an information security engineer in the Security team. Her goal is to keep the production environment secure. *Sara* is well-versed in the latest vulnerabilities and security bugs. *Robert Release* works with her to perform final pre-deployment security scans.

Figure 5-11. *Sara Security*

Sara works with her designated Scrum team. At the start of each Sprint, *Sara* randomly selects three numbers (within a designated range, provided by the facilitator), and writes them into her "known security issues catalog" (see Figure 5-12). These random numbers become the "security bugs" for her designated Scrum team during the Sprint. When *Sara* performs a pre-production security scan, she cross-checks the small number labels on each LEGO animal against her catalog of known security issues.

SARA SECURITY

MOD CARD

1. At the start of each Sprint, write down 3 random numbers between _____ and _____. These numbers will be your **known security issues** for this Sprint for team_____.
2. Check the **deployment packages**. If any of them contain an animal with a label that's matching your number, send the **entire package back** to the Dev team for a fix.
Sprint 1 ____ ____ ____
Sprint 2 ____ ____ ____
Sprint 3 ____ ____ ____

THREATS AND SECURITY BUGS CATALOG

Figure 5-12. *Known security issues catalog, used by Sara Security to record the latest vulnerabilities in each Sprint*

She fails a test of a development package if a LEGO animal has one of these numbers on the small label. When this happens, an entire deployment package is sent back to the Scrum team for rework. *Sara* will receive a special instruction Mod Card in Sprint 2 that will expand her role to monitoring environments against *Harry Hacker* attacks and leading vulnerability remediation efforts if/when the attacks occur (See the "Mod Cards" section in the appendix).

CHAPTER 5   LEGO AND CHOCOLATE: RULES OF THE GAME

In terms of role ratio, ideally you'll have one *Sara Security* per Scrum team. This ratio enables an effective visualization of the popular "shift left on security" concept. In the second round of the simulation, *Sara Security* will be asked to sit with her Scrum team and share the new vulnerability numbers with them from the start! This way the team can start building more-secure products from the very beginning, embracing the "build security in" mindset as a team.

FACILITATOR TIP

As a facilitator, you will instruct each *Sara Security* to work with a specific Scrum team. Ensure that the range of the small number labels you distribute to her designated Scrum team is the same as the range of numbers in the "known issues catalog" used by *Sara Security* (see Figure 5-13).

Figure 5-13. *Sara Security's threats catalog for Scrum Team Two, and the corresponding set of number labels from Scrum Team Two*

CHAPTER 5 LEGO AND CHOCOLATE: RULES OF THE GAME

Business Team (Benjamin Business)

Benjamin (Figure 5-14) is a business stakeholder who represents various markets and has insights into current LEGO animals market demands. In the first Sprint, *Benjamin* works primarily with *Patricia Product* to communicate the demand for specific LEGO animals, provide feedback on the products delivered, and pay the current market price for these products. If asked by *Patricia Product* or other members of Scrum teams, he can provide early feedback on the LEGO animals "in progress" or even join a Scrum team for just-in-time continuous feedback.

Figure 5-14. *Benjamin Business*

Benjamin may also reject the entire deployment package if LEGO animals don't meet his expectation. (Entirely possible with Scrum teams that have made unvalidated assumptions about the LEGO animals' characteristics expected by the *Business Team*!)

When *Benjamin* accepts the products, he pays the current market price for LEGO animals and updates the Delivery Board (see Figure 5-15) to reflect the amount he paid to each of the Scrum teams for the packages they delivered.

The full power and the impact of *Benjamin Business*'s role will become apparent with changes introduced in Sprint 2. He will be able to ask for new products and drop prices on the old LEGO animals that haven't been delivered into production by teams yet. As the group transitions into the Continuous Delivery model, the dynamic of *Benjamin Business*'s interaction with the Scrum teams significantly improves, leading to amplified organizational effectiveness.

Figure 5-15. *Benjamin Business in the process of updating the Delivery Board*

Surprise Character: Harry Hacker

This is an optional role that you may choose to skip (or play it yourself) if the group is small, or if players are already struggling with the game's complexity.

CHAPTER 5   LEGO AND CHOCOLATE: RULES OF THE GAME

Harry (Figure 5-16) is a cybercriminal. His goal is to exploit the security vulnerability of various websites, penetrate environments, and hack the LEGO animal packages. *Harry Hacker* exploits security holes (simulated by cutting gaps in the masking tape of the "environments"). He takes advantage of the "Heartbleed" bug and exploits the "Ghost" vulnerability (simulated by drawing hearts and ghosts on the masking tape of the "environments").

Figure 5-16. *Harry Hacker*

Harry Hacker attacks when players expect him the least—during the cross-training simulation. At the time of cross-training, when everyone is engaged in teaching others about the role that they do in this game and learning from other players about their role, the tables (and environments) are left unattended. This is exactly when *Harry Hacker* strikes!

Basic Game Flow and Modifications

Let's bring the roles together with the end-to-end basic game flow and modifications. The dynamic of the first round reflects the interdependency and the divide between Development, Operations, Security, and Business. It is typical for players in the first round to experience some confusion and disconnect due to an obscure organizational landscape and a strong presence of functional silos. As the game progresses, the mood of the room shifts. The cross-training simulation in Sprint 2 creates a sense of connection and empowerment. At the same time, it is known to bring out questions about job security and career prospects in certain environments. Sprint 3 elevates these concerns and brings the mood of the group to a peak with excitement and a sense of accomplishment.

Sprint 1: Feel the Pain

In the first part of the simulation, everything starts with *Benjamin Business* (see Figure 5-17). He knows exactly what sells on the LEGO animal market. During the setup time of the first Sprint, *Patricia Product* interacts with the business team to learn more about the current demand and to select a few Product Backlog items (PBIs) for her team. In the meantime, the *Danny Developers* and *Tim Testers* realize that they don't have their environments built out, and approach *Adam Admin* for help.

Once the environments have been provisioned, and *Patricia* has made the selection of the PBI cards, *Danny Developer* can start building products and will require additional guidance from *Patricia Product*. All packages built by the developers must meet the Definition of Done. This is what *Tim Tester* will be testing for, only sending the packages forward to *Robert Release* if they pass the test.

CHAPTER 5   LEGO AND CHOCOLATE: RULES OF THE GAME

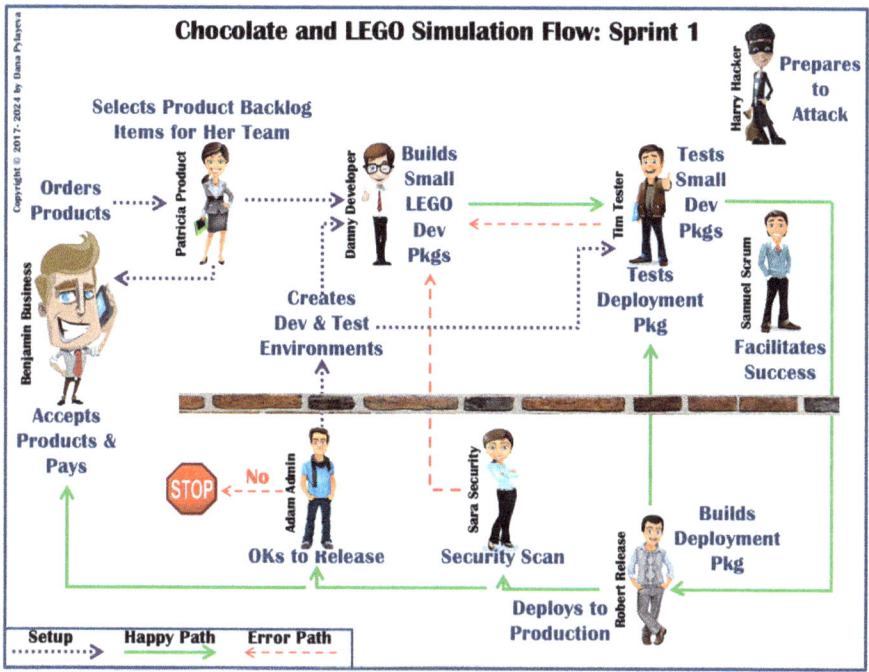

***Figure 5-17.** Basic game flow – Sprint 1*

When *Robert* receives a batch of development packages from a Scrum team, he validates the PBI card, cross-checks with the development packages, and builds a deployment package, labeling it appropriately. *Tim Tester* performs the final integration test and returns the deployment package to *Robert Release* for further processing. The deployment package is now sent to *Sara Security* for the final pre-production security scan. If the package fails her security scan (a number label on the LEGO animal matches the security issues catalog), it is sent back to the developers in its entirety. If the security scan was successful and *Adam Admin* gives his "OK to release," a product finally makes it into the hands of *Benjamin Business*. If *Benjamin* likes the product, he pays for it based on the current market price.

CHAPTER 5   LEGO AND CHOCOLATE: RULES OF THE GAME

> **SPECIAL INSTRUCTIONS IN SPRINT 1**
>
> During the second part of Sprint 1 you will deliver a special instructions mod card to *Adam Admin*. The card will announce that as of this moment, we are in a Code Freeze. No production deployments are allowed for the remainder of this Sprint. *Adam* will keep this information to himself and only share it with *Robert Release* if/when he asks for *Adam's* permission to deploy into production. This creates a major bottleneck in the process.

By the end of the first Sprint, it becomes apparent that the current way of working is dysfunctional. The group is primed for experimenting with process changes and taking the first steps toward DevSecOps.

Sprint 2: First Steps to DevSecOps

There are a few changes that occur in the second round of the game to bring in the basic ideas from DevSecOps culture.

First, the group is invited into a round of T-shape building. You will distribute sets of small stickers to each of the technical roles (Developers, Security, and Operations) and invite them to share with each other the details of their roles (as performed in the simulation). At the end of this cross-training, players will exchange their different color stickers as a token of "certification"—the other person has been trained in a new skill (as visualized in Figure 5-18).

CHAPTER 5   LEGO AND CHOCOLATE: RULES OF THE GAME

Figure 5-18. *T-shape building steps "FEEL" instructional poster*

SPECIAL INSTRUCTIONS IN SPRINT 2

Benjamin Business will receive a special mod card with the secret instructions to update the LEGO Animal Exchange board, reflecting the current demand and the current market price of various LEGO animals. Any products that haven't been delivered by the end of the Sprint will be discounted by 50% or more (see Figure 5-19). In addition, *Sara Security* will receive a mod card alerting her about *Harry Hacker* attacks and the need to start monitoring environments.

79

Figure 5-19. *Benjamin Business updates prices at the LEGO Animal Exchange board*

Something else will happen in Sprint 2. *Harry Hacker* attacks! Right when everyone is distracted with T-shaped skills building, the environments are left unattended, creating a golden opportunity for *Harry*. *Harry*'s actions create a lot of impediments for the Scrum teams, as they must stop building LEGO animals and wait until all security patches are applied. Luckily, *Adam Admin* has crossed-trained a lot of players, and now they all can help with installing security patches in their own environments. A bottleneck has been effectively managed with cross-training!

More improvements emerge from another modification: Scrum teams are encouraged to invite *Operations* to their tables and "shift left" on *Security*. From this round onward, *Sara Security* will sit with her Scrum team and share the new vulnerability numbers with them from the start!

CHAPTER 5   LEGO AND CHOCOLATE: RULES OF THE GAME

This way, the team can start building more-secure products from the very beginning, embracing the "build security in" mindset as a team. *Sara Security* will also start monitoring the environments now, proactively anticipating and mitigating hackers' attack attempts.

A Scrum team's ability to carry out simple environment patching (in response to *Harry Hacker* attacks) has another important implication. This frees up some capacity for *Adam Admin* and allows him to take the time for some serious upskilling. *Adam* will learn how to enable automated on-demand self-service environment provisioning. This activity is simulated by preparing small strips of green household masking tape ("known good environment configuration") at the Innovation Center (see Figure 5-20).

Figure 5-20. *Adam Admin at the Innovation Center learning how to enable self-service environment provisioning for Scrum team members*

CHAPTER 5   LEGO AND CHOCOLATE: RULES OF THE GAME

Sprint 3: Continuous Delivery of Value

The rules of the game, and the dynamic of the third round, are designed to improve flow and amplify the feedback loop—two of the pillars of DevOps culture. As such, the teams will be asked to re-think the sizes of their PBIs (with the help of *Patricia Product*) and the sizes of their deployment packages, moving away from large batch sizes toward a "one-piece flow."

To support this process change, *Benjamin Business* will update the "batch size" column on the LEGO Animal Exchange board, dropping it to a "one." You will also distribute a new set of supplies—green packages (a model for containerization, built-in security libraries, etc.). Now each LEGO animal with the chocolate can be built, packaged, and deployed in its own individual secure green package, reducing wait time and allowing the teams to respond faster to the demands of *Benjamin Business*.

> **SPECIAL INSTRUCTIONS IN SPRINT 3**
>
> *Patricia Product* will receive a special Mod Card with instructions to start splitting the large PBIs into several single–LEGO animal PBI cards. She will be provided with small-sized index cards to help with splitting.

As Dev, Ops, and Security collaboration flourishes, and the speed of deployment accelerates, the business team can request more innovative LEGO animal designs, experiment with new models, and finally outperform the competitors. By the end of Sprint 3, the business table overflows with the newly delivered LEGO animals (see Figure 5-21), Scrum teams and their Operations partners celebrate their accomplishments, and our fictional organization becomes a market leader in the LEGO animal market and leads the way in DevSecOps culture adoption.

CHAPTER 5   LEGO AND CHOCOLATE: RULES OF THE GAME

Figure 5-21. *Benjamin Business is in the process of paying for the LEGO animals delivered by the team. The business table is full of green packages—continuous delivery of value in action!*

Summary

In this chapter you got to know more about the setting of the *LEGO and Chocolate* simulation, learned how the nine different roles collaborate, and saw how their interaction patterns change throughout the three rounds of the game. In the next chapter, I will walk you through all the game components required to enable this experience. I will also offer you several links for online stores where you can purchase them, and share my packing cheat-sheet that saves me every single time!

CHAPTER 6

Game Components

There are a lot of different components that you will need to assemble in preparation for facilitating this game. You will be distributing them to players at specific times throughout the three rounds. This chapter will help you make packing for your next workshop simple and repeatable. It will also provide you with suggestions on where to shop for these supplies in case you can't find them in your local craft or discount stores. Most of these components are reusable and can be repurposed for running this simulation more than once. Chocolate is certainly the exception—you will need to buy some for every new group.

Role Cards

Every workshop participant will use a Role Card as a reference for their role and its dependencies in this simulation. There are nine distinct roles in this simulation; however, the distribution of players across these roles is not even.

There is a 2:1 ratio of Danny Developers to Tim Tester. For each Scrum team in the room, you will need to have one player in each of the Sara Security, Robert Release, and Adam Admin roles. Don't create more than two Benjamin Business players per each Scrum team. Please reference Table 6-1 for group configuration ideas. Order the high-quality sets of Role Cards and Mod Cards (21 players per set) from The Gamecrafter store (`https://tinyurl.com/LCRoleCard`). Alternatively, you may access the electronic version of this book's appendix to print the required quantity of the Role Cards. Consider printing them on cardstock paper at your local printer.

Table 6-1. Number of Role Cards for Each Role That Need to Be Packed Based on the Size of the Group

Group Size	15–22	22–28	31–42	42–56	69–84
Number of Scrum Teams	2	2	3	4	6
Benjamin Business	2	2–4	3–6	4–8	12
Sara Security	1–2	2	3	4	6
Robert Release	1–2	2	3	4	6
Adam Admin	1–2	2	3	4	6
Harry Hacker	0	2	1–3	2–4	3–6
Patricia Product	2	2	3	4	6
Samuel Scrum	2	2	3	4	6
Tim Tester	2–4	2–4	3–6	4–8	6–12
Danny Developer	4–6	6–8	9–12	12–16	18–24

Mod Card

In addition to the main Role Cards, you need to pack these additional Mod Cards (see Table 6-2). You will distribute them to their recipients at the designated time during the workshop. Use the electronic version of this book's appendix to print the required quantity of the Mod Cards. Consider printing them on cardstock paper at your local printer. If you choose to order the high-quality Role Card sets from The Gamecrafter store (`https://tinyurl.com/LCRoleCard`), corresponding Mod Cards will already be included in your package.

Table 6-2. *Number of Special Instructions Mod Cards for Each Role That Need to Be Packed Based on the Size of the Group*

Group Size	15–22	22–28	31–42	42–56	69–84
Benjamin Business (Sprint 2)	2	2–4	3–6	4–8	12
Sara Security (Security Issues Catalog, Sprint 2)	1–2	2	3	4	6
Robert Release	-	-	-	-	-
Adam Admin (Sprint 1)	1–2	2	3	4	6
Harry Hacker	-	-	-	-	-
Patricia Product (Sprint 3)	2	2	3	4	6
Samuel Scrum	-	-	-	-	-
Tim Tester	-	-	-	-	-
Danny Developer	-	-	-	-	-

Supplies for One Scrum Team

This is what you need to pack for **one** Scrum team in this simulation (see Figure 6-1). Remember to pack for the number of Scrum teams you anticipate in your workshop.

1. A mix of basic building blocks (650–700 pieces)

    a. Option 1: LEGO Classic Large Creative Brick Box (https://tinyurl.com/LCBricksOptMain)

    b. Option 2: Building Bricks Regular Colors (https://tinyurl.com/LCBricksOpt2)

CHAPTER 6   GAME COMPONENTS

2. Small chocolate candies, individually wrapped (up to 1 lb.)

    a. Option 1: Dove (https://tinyurl.com/LCChocoOpt1)

    b. Option 2: Hershey's (https://tinyurl.com/LCChocoOpt2)

3. Clear Small 9 1/2" x 4" bags (1 pkg x 25) (https://tinyurl.com/LCBagClear)

4. Small rubber bands (~100 bands). One of these packages will be enough for the entire group (https://tinyurl.com/LCRBands).

5. Small number labels (1 page). One of these packages will be enough for the entire group (https://tinyurl.com/LCLabelNumber).

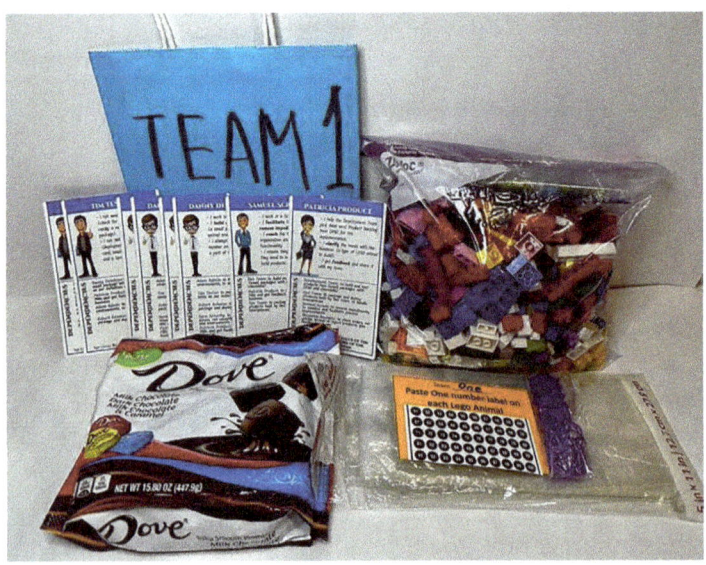

Figure 6-1. *Supplies for one Scrum team*

There will be a point in the game when members of the Operations team will need to start working closely with Scrum teams. To help Operations locate the right team, give each Scrum team a number. Write a team number on a medium-size paper bag and use it to pack Scrum team supplies.

Supplies for Operations Team

Here is what you need to pack for the Operations team (see Figure 6-2):

1. Roll of 1" household masking tape (1 per Adam Admin) (https://tinyurl.com/LCTapePlain)

2. Gallon-sized resealable bags (14 per Robert Release) (https://tinyurl.com/LCBagGallon)

3. All-purpose 1" x 3" rectangular white labels (14 per Robert Release) (https://tinyurl.com/LCLabelWhite)

CHAPTER 6   GAME COMPONENTS

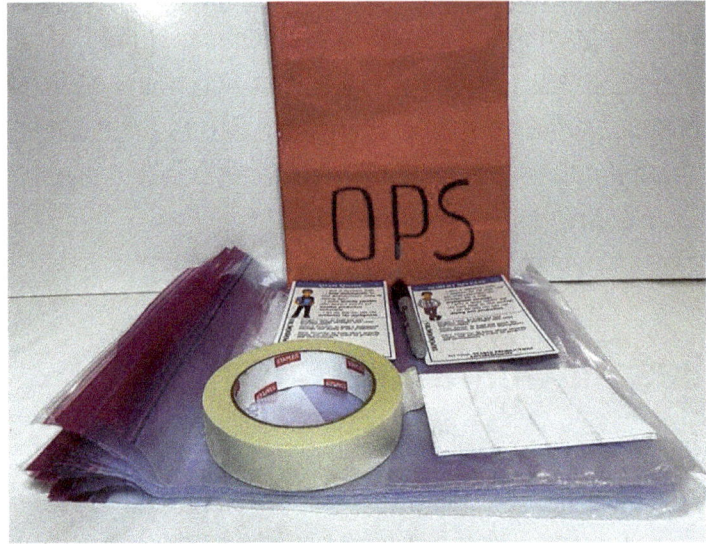

Figure 6-2. *Supplies for the Operations team*

Supplies for Sara Security

Here is what you need to pack for this role (in addition to the Role Card):

1. "Known Security Issues Catalog" Mod Card (see Figure 6-3)

CHAPTER 6 GAME COMPONENTS

Figure 6-3. *Supplies for the Security team*

Supplies for Business Team

Here is what you need to pack for this role (in addition to the Role Card):

1. Play Money — use Monopoly money or purchase (https://tinyurl.com/LCMoneyPlay)

2. 3" x 5" index cards in any color (about 20 per team). One pack (https://tinyurl.com/LCIndexReg) will be sufficient for up to five Scrum teams.

3. *LEGO Animal Exchange* board and the *Delivery Board posters*. These will be described in Chapter 7.

CHAPTER 6　GAME COMPONENTS

Supplies for Harry Hacker

1. Red marker (https://tinyurl.com/LCMarkerRed)
2. Blunt scissors (https://tinyurl.com/LCScissors)

Supplies for the Facilitator

1. Online interval timer (https://tinyurl.com/LCIntTimer)
2. Camera, phone, or tablet to take pictures
3. 3" x 3" sticky notes, any color (2 pads per workshop table) (https://tinyurl.com/LCStickies)
4. Black fine-point marker (1 per person) (https://tinyurl.com/LCMarkerBlack)
5. Disposable table cover (1 per table) (https://tinyurl.com/LCTableCover) to denote different functional teams, and to simplify the room cleanup after the workshop (see Figure 6-4)

CHAPTER 6 GAME COMPONENTS

Figure 6-4. Disposable table covers

6. Team handout (Game flow + Definition of Done) (2 per table); see appendix

7. Special Instruction Mod Cards (see Table 6-2) to distribute to specific roles (Sprint 1 – Adam Admin; Sprint 2 – Benjamin Business, Sara Security; Sprint 3 – Patricia Product)

8. Small round stickers of at least 3 distinct colors for cross-training simulation activity in Sprint 2 (https://tinyurl.com/LCLabelRound)

9. Two rolls of 1" painter's green masking tape to simulate the on-demand self-service environment provisioning in Sprint 2 (https://tinyurl.com/LCTapeGreen)

10. Transparent green party bags for Sprint 3 (1 pkg x 25 per Scrum team) (https://tinyurl.com/LCBagGreen)

CHAPTER 6   GAME COMPONENTS

Complete List of Component Links

https://tinyurl.com/LCBagClear
https://tinyurl.com/LCBagGallon
https://tinyurl.com/LCBagGreen
https://tinyurl.com/LCBricksOptMain
https://tinyurl.com/LCChocoOpt1
https://tinyurl.com/LCBricksOpt2
https://tinyurl.com/LCChocoOpt2
https://tinyurl.com/LCIndexReg
https://tinyurl.com/LCIntTimer
https://tinyurl.com/LCLabelNumber
https://tinyurl.com/LCLabelRound
https://tinyurl.com/LCLabelWhite
https://tinyurl.com/LCMarkerBlack
https://tinyurl.com/LCMarkerRed
https://tinyurl.com/LCMoneyPlay
https://tinyurl.com/LCRBands
https://tinyurl.com/LCRoleCard
https://tinyurl.com/LCScissors
https://tinyurl.com/LCStickies
https://tinyurl.com/LCTableCover
https://tinyurl.com/LCTapeGreen
https://tinyurl.com/LCTapePlain

Summary

In this chapter, I have provided you with a comprehensive list of supplies and game components you will need to pack for creating the *LEGO and Chocolate* experience. After the initial purchase of all the supplies, you will mostly be returning to this chapter to adjust your packing to your specific group size. If your workshop size remains mostly the same, you may find my packing cheat sheet handy (see the appendix). Feel free to adjust it to the most common group size in your workshops.

In the next chapter, we will look at the room setup and adjustments for various group sizes. I will also demonstrate several in-room posters that you will need to prepare ahead of the workshop.

CHAPTER 7

Setting the Space

As you already know from the previous chapters, the *LEGO and Chocolate* simulation is an asynchronous role-playing game in which every player acts in accordance with one of the nine predefined roles. The power of this game is in its ability to make visible the interaction patterns and showcase process bottlenecks. This chapter will help you understand how to split the participants into these nine roles based on the size of your group and the physical constraints of the workshop space so that the process bottlenecks will become visible. I will share my optimal setup with you and offer seven additional options for various group/room sizes. Each option has been play-tested and optimized for the best player experience.

In addition to table setup, there are several information radiators you will need to prepare. These can be prepared ahead of time as flipchart posters (and hung in the room before the workshop), or they can be executed as simple handwritten instructions on a whiteboard. I will share the Bikablo®-style[1] posters I create for my workshops. Feel free to copy them as is, simplify them, or create your own.

---

[1] See Bikablo® icons Icon Card Set: https://bikablo.com/en/tools/

CHAPTER 7   SETTING THE SPACE

Setting Up the Room Posters

When you facilitate the *LEGO and Chocolate* simulation, you are creating the end-to-end player experience. From the moment they walk into the room, they know that this is going to be different from any other technical workshops they've experienced before. From the tables' arrangement to the colorful (and delicious) supplies on these tables, to the engaging posters on the walls, this workshop draws the participants in, tapping into their curiosity and preparing them for a rich learning experience. Here are the posters that will help you create that.

Visible Posters

There are several posters that are visible from the beginning of the workshop and act as information radiators during the game.

LEGO Animal Exchange Board

This is the main poster (Figure 7-1) in the simulation that serves as a dashboard for the current market demand (the type of LEGO animals, demand, batch size, and the current price per batch). I always start the game with simple animals—dogs, cats, and snakes—to reduce the complexity.

There is a correlation between the number of Scrum teams in your workshop and the initial demand for each item.
Demand = "number of teams" x ("batch size" + 1)

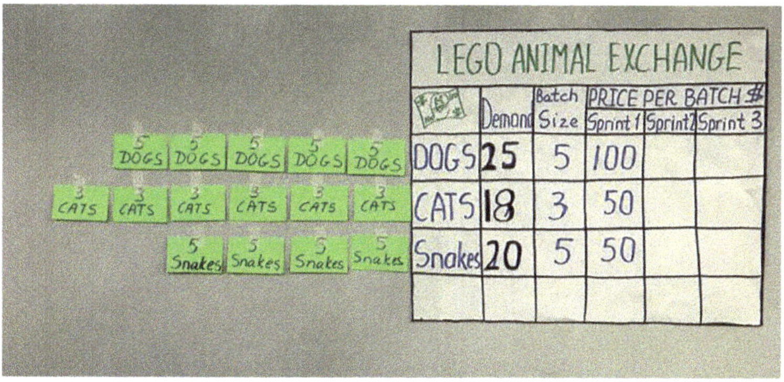

CHAPTER 7 SETTING THE SPACE

Figure 7-1. Setting up the LEGO Animal Exchange board

In Sprints 2 and 3, as the game progresses, *Benjamin Business* will start adding new animal requests to this board. (Have an empty flipchart sheet to further extend this grid as needed.) Don't be surprised to see requests for elephants, giraffes, dragons, and even unicorns on this board—as business team gains confidence in Scrum teams' abilities to deliver, they become more innovative with their needs.

The small green index cards that you see to the left of the grid are the product backlog items (PBIs). You will need to set them up at the start and instruct *Benjamin Business* to create new ones if and when they ask for new LEGO animals (starting in Sprint 2).

Delivery Board

What is the impact of introducing the DevSecOps culture and Continuous Delivery in this simulation? This Delivery Board poster (Figure 7-2) will help you track the value delivered by teams in each of the Sprints of the simulation and make visible the striking difference in the volume of product delivery. You will instruct *Benjamin Business* to record the price he paid for each of the products delivered in the appropriate team column.

CHAPTER 7　SETTING THE SPACE

Figure 7-2. Delivery board poster

Learning/Debriefing Poster

One of the important steps in training with games is debriefing (Figure 7-3). During debriefing, workshop participants have time to integrate the "Aha!" moments from their experience, reflect on the interaction patterns, and connect the lessons from the game to the "real life" challenges of the participants. I will cover various debriefing facilitation techniques in Chapter 12.

This poster will clearly designate a space for consolidating the "Aha!" moments and key takeaways from the workshop participants. It will also serve as your own feedback loop mechanism when you are ready to reflect on the effectiveness of the simulation and your own facilitation style. You will find a sample collection of key takeaways from previous workshop participants in Chapter 13 of this book.

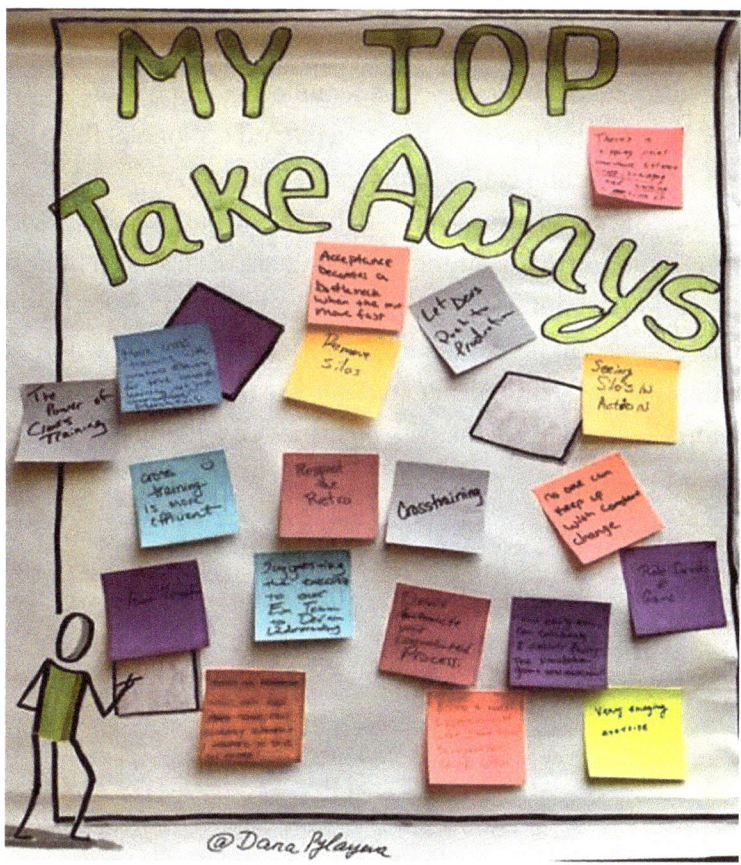

Figure 7-3. *Takeaways poster for collecting players' reflections and learning*

Hidden Posters

There are several posters that will be hidden at the beginning and will be revealed throughout the game as it unfolds. You can hang them on the walls during the setup time and cover them up with another flipchart sheet, then introduce them at the right moment of the simulation.

CHAPTER 7   SETTING THE SPACE

Cross-training "FEEL" Poster

One of the hidden posters is the T-shape building "FEEL" poster (Figure 7-4). While this poster can be considered optional, I find that it offers reinforcement and clarity to players as they carry out the dynamic of the cross-training simulation (aka T-shaped skills building). As it visualizes the four steps of the cross-training process, it also delivers an important message: learning about each other's roles and sharing the details of one's own responsibilities cultivates empathy development within the organization. Note that the poster contains the instructions as well as the actual sample color stickers that will be used by each role participating in the simulation.

CHAPTER 7 SETTING THE SPACE

Figure 7-4. *Cross-training "FEEL" poster for facilitating cross-training*

Innovation Center: "Known Good Configuration"

This last poster (Figure 7-5) will be revealed in the second Sprint and serve as a repeatable pattern for the self-service on-demand environment configuration activity.

CHAPTER 7   SETTING THE SPACE

Figure 7-5. Known good environment configuration

You will bring *Adam Admin* to this poster and ask him to prepare strips of green masking tape next to it. These will be used later in the game to rebuild the environments according to the pattern on this poster.

Room Configuration Options

Let's take a look now at the suggested placement of these posters in a workshop room, various options for effective arrangement of tables, as well as the distribution of game roles. In the remaining part of this chapter, I will share the room configurations, starting with the one I use most often in full-length workshops with private clients

CHAPTER 7   SETTING THE SPACE

Optimal Configuration (4 Tables x 21 People)

This particular configuration (Figure 7-6) creates very strong bottlenecks on the *Adam Admin*, *Tim Tester*, and *Robert Relea*se roles, magnifying the need for change. Use it as an opportunity to drive parallels with organizations that practice allocating team members to more than one project, or more than one squad.

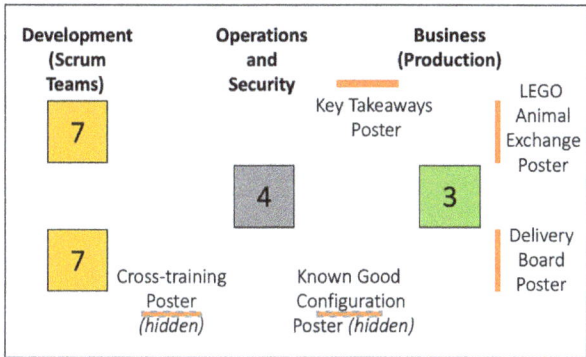

Figure 7-6. *Optimal room setup and group size – 21 players*

Note that tables in the room are placed to roughly mimic stages in the product development life cycle. Ideally, all Dev tables (Scrum teams) will be located equidistant from the Operations table. The Operations table must be placed between Dev and Business so that it can potentially "block the flow of value" between them.

In this configuration, the room is set up with two *Scrum* teams (*Patricia Product, Samuel Scrum, Danny Developer* (4), and *Tim Tester* (1)). There is a combined *Operations/Security* team with *Sara Security* (2), *Adam Admin* (1), and *Robert Release* (1). There are also (3) *Benjamin Business* players. The role of *Harry Hacker* is either played by you or by one of the players in the *Benjamin Business* role.

105

CHAPTER 7   SETTING THE SPACE

Small Group Setup (3 Tables x 9–14 People)

Since the game is focused on organizational dynamics before and after the DevSecOps transformation, you will need a minimum of 9 players to run it (see Figure 7-7). This group size is one of the least effective; however, it may still be valuable as a pilot with a small group of innovators or early adopters.

This configuration has only one *Scrum* team (*Danny Developer* (2-4), *Tim Tester* (1-2), *Patricia Product*, and *Samuel Scrum*), a small *Operations/Security* team (*Adam Admin, Robert Release,* and *Sara Security*), *Benjamin Business* (1-2), and may or may not have *Harry Hacker*.

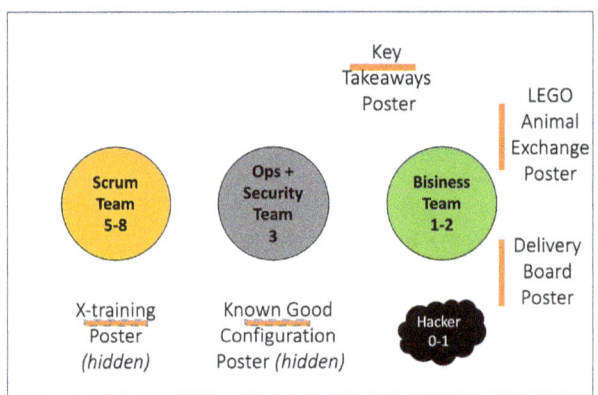

Figure 7-7. *Room setup for 9-14 players*

Medium Group Setup (4 Tables x 15–25 People)

If you are planning a workshop for a group of 15-25 people and your room is set up with four tables, you can experiment with the following layout (Figure 7-8). In this configuration you will set up two *Scrum* teams with the following roles:

CHAPTER 7 SETTING THE SPACE

- Option for a five-person *Scrum* team: *Patricia Product, Samuel Scrum, Danny Developer* (2), and *Tim Tester*

- Option for an eight-person *Scrum* team: *Patricia Product, Samuel Scrum, Danny Developer* (4), and *Tim Testers* (2)

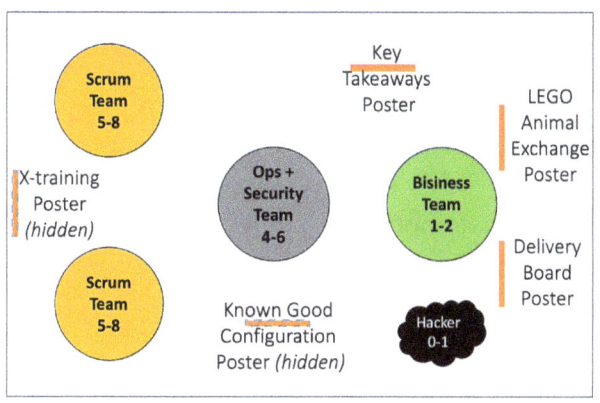

Figure 7-8. *Room setup for 15–25 players*

Ideally you will have one of each Operations role (*Adam Admin, Robert Release,* and *Sara Security*) per *Scrum* team table. In this configuration, you can have six people play the Operations/Security roles, and up to two *Benjamin Business* players.

CHAPTER 7   SETTING THE SPACE

Medium Group Setup (5 Tables x 18–28 People)

If you have an option to have five tables in the room, here is another possible configuration for a medium-sized group (see Figure 7-9). The main difference between this version and the previous one is a separate *Security* team. Again, you will have the option to set up two *Scrum* teams:

- Option for a five-person *Scrum* team: *Patricia Product, Samuel Scrum, Danny Developer* (2), and *Tim Tester*

- Option for an eight-person *Scrum* team: *Patricia Product, Samuel Scrum, Danny Developer* (4), and *Tim Tester* (2)

In this room configuration, the *Operations* table will have *Adam Admins* (2) and *Robert Releases* (2), one per *Scrum* team table. A separate *Security* table will have *Sara Securities (2)* and *Harry Hackers (2)*.

There will be 2–4 *Benjamin Business* players.

If you have a group of 18–25 people, your choice of room setup will depend on the number of tables in the room and your personal preference between this setup (Figure 7-9) and the previous one (Figure 7-8).

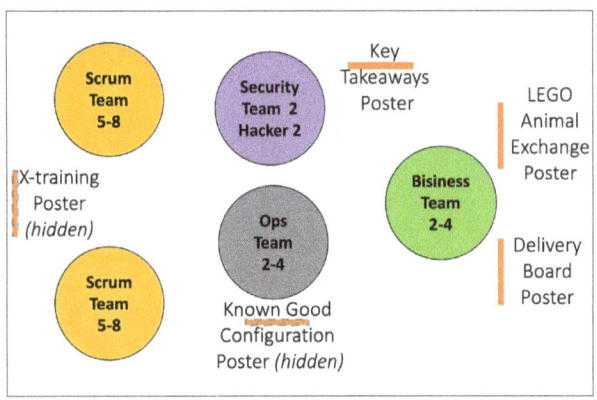

Figure 7-9. *Room setup for 18-28 players*

CHAPTER 7 SETTING THE SPACE

Large Group Setup (6 Tables x 28–42 People)

This setup and the group size work really well for a hands-on workshop at a conference. In fact, this is exactly how I set up the room when I ran this simulation as half-day tutorials at *Agile + DevOps* conferences by TechWell.

This configuration has an additional *Scrum* team table and a proportionally scaled number of Operations, Security, and Business roles (see Figure 7-10).

In this room configuration, there are three *Scrum* teams:

- Option for a five-person *Scrum* team: *Patricia Product, Samuel Scrum, Danny Developer* (2), and *Tim Tester*

- Option for an eight-person *Scrum* team: *Patricia Product, Samuel Scrum, Danny Developer* (4), and *Tim Tester* (2)

The *Operations* table has *Adam Admins* (3) and *Robert Releases* (3), one per *Scrum* team table. A separate security table has *Sara Securities* (3) and *Harry Hackers* (3). There are 3–6 *Benjamin Business* players.

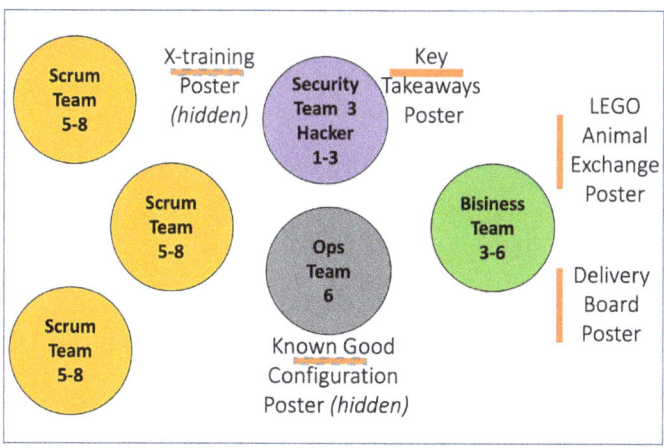

Figure 7-10. Room setup for 28–42 players

109

CHAPTER 7   SETTING THE SPACE

If you have a group of exactly 28 people, your choice of room setup will depend on the number of tables in the room and your personal preference between this setup (Figure 7-10) and the previous one (Figure 7-9).

Large Group Setup (7 Tables x 38–56 People)

This room setup is appropriate for a large room with seven tables and a group size of 38 to 56 people (see Figure 7-11).

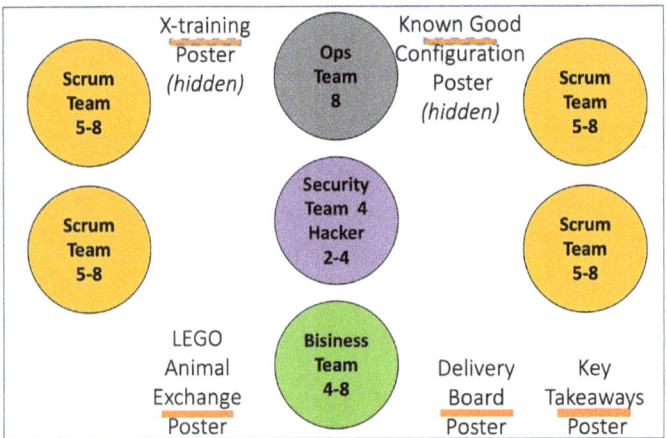

Figure 7-11.   Room setup for 38–56 players

In this room configuration, you will set up four *Scrum* teams:

- Option for a five-person *Scrum* team: *Patricia Product, Samuel Scrum, Danny Developer* (2), and *Tim Tester*
- Option for an eight-person *Scrum* team: *Patricia Product, Samuel Scrum, Danny Developer* (4), and *Tim Tester* (2)

CHAPTER 7   SETTING THE SPACE

The *Operations* table will have *Adam Admins* (4) and *Robert Releases* (4), one per *Scrum* team table. A separate *Security* table will have *Sara Securities* (4) and *Harry Hackers* (2-4). There will be 4-8 *Benjamin Business* players.

If you have a group of 38–42 people, your choice of room setup will depend on the number of tables in the room and your personal preference between this setup (Figure 7-11) and the previous one (Figure 7-10).

Extra Large Group Setup (11 Tables x 57–84 People)

This configuration is the one I used for a 1.5-hour version of this simulation at *Global Scrum Gathering Prague*. For this type of group size, you will need to enlist help from an additional facilitator and set up two independent *Animal Exchange Boards* and two *Delivery Boards*.

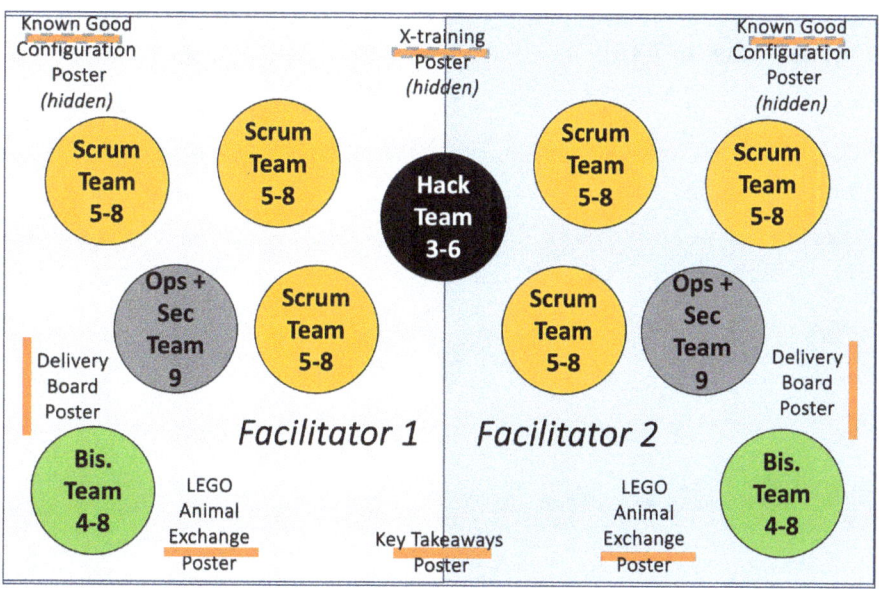

Figure 7-12.   Room setup for 57–84 players

111

In this room configuration, you will set up six *Scrum* teams:

- Option for a five-person *Scrum* team: *Patricia Product, Samuel Scrum, Danny Developer* (2), and *Tim Tester*
- Option for an eight-person *Scrum* team: *Patricia Product, Samuel Scrum, Danny Developer* (4), and *Tim Tester* (2)

There will be two *Operations/Security* tables (one per facilitation area) with *Adam Admins* (3), *Robert Releases* (3), and *Sara Securities* (3). In this option only, there will be a separate *Hackers* team with *Harry Hackers* (3-6) sitting at their own table! There will be two business tables (one for each facilitation area) with *Benjamin Business* (3-6) players.

Scaling Beyond Extra Large (22 Tables x 124+ People)

Scaling this simulation beyond 84 people will mean running multiple instances of the Large (28-42) configuration with the help of multiple facilitators (Figure 7-13).

Figure 7-13. *Room setup for a parallel run of the game with four facilitators (124–168 participants)*

This will require independent *LEGO Animal Exchange Boards*, independent *Delivery Boards,* and multiple *Key Takeaways* posters available around the room. Due to the added complexity of this setup, more time will be required for clarification and debriefing. Running the game in parallel will also benefit from establishing clear physical boundaries between every simulation instance. This could be achieved by setting up a row of flipchart stands or stretching a long ribbon alongside the "border," etc. Feel free to experiment with what works best in your specific room.

You will need to enlist multiple facilitators (one per simulation instance). As the main facilitator, you will be delivering the presentation part, providing game onboarding instructions to the entire group, establishing the overall timeboxes (as per the facilitation script in Chapter 9), and running large group debriefings. This room setup will require multiple hand-held microphones to be available throughout the room.

CHAPTER 7 SETTING THE SPACE

CO-FACILITATION

Please plan on preparing your additional facilitators ahead of time on game dynamics and their role in the workshop. While the workshop will be facilitated by the main facilitator (you), the additional facilitators' involvement will simplify the distribution of supplies throughout the game, greatly enhancing participants' comprehension and their overall satisfaction with the game.

The additional facilitators' goal is to help spot-check every team in their area for any confusion among the participants as well as address any "red flags"— lack of engagement or lack of understanding of the roles.

Summary

There are several options for setting up the room in this simulation, and it is important to be mindful of the right balance of players and roles in each group. While it might be tempting to add more people to the *Operations* team, remember that the purpose of this game is to highlight the bottlenecks, making them painful in the first round and amplifying the need for change. This chapter offered you a few ideas. Experiment and discover what works best for you.

CHAPTER 8

Know Your Timebox

Here is the chapter you've been waiting for—a structured session plan for the *LEGO and Chocolate* simulation with a timeline, instructions, and timeboxes for each individual activity! Unlike the first edition of this book, which offered 75-minute, 90-minute, and 180-minute versions of DevOps training based on this simulation, the second edition will take a different approach.

As I continued modifying the simulation and running it in various settings after the first edition was published, anything shorter than 90 minutes proved to be a subpar learning experience for the participants. This chapter will offer you the most effective version of the simulation in the following two formats:

1. The 3-hour version of a DevSecOps training in which each round of the *LEGO and Chocolate* simulation is used as one of the "Concrete Practice" activities within the 4C framework[1] (an approach to designing experiential learning workshops coined by Sharon L. Bowman) and is interwoven with the bite-size "Concept" lecture segments and "Conclusion" debriefing activities.

2. The standalone *LEGO and Chocolate* simulation.

---

[1] Bowman, S.L. (2008). *Training from the BACK of the Room! 65 Ways to Step Aside and Let Them Learn*. Pfeiffer.

CHAPTER 8 KNOW YOUR TIMEBOX

Visible Interval Timer

As you already know, each round of the simulation is based on a simplified and abbreviated version of the Scrum events. You will need to configure an interval timer (Figure 8-1) to timebox the overall duration of the round (Sprint) as well as to display the timing and the progress of the simulation (blue highlight) through the individual intervals (Sprint Planning, Sprint Execution, Sprint Review, and Sprint Retrospective).

Figure 8-1. Interval timer configured for the 18-minute round

Once the timer starts, it will be *Samuel Scrum*'s responsibility to keep an eye on the intervals and ensure that Scrum events are happening as designed.

Session Plan for an Experiential DevSecOps Training (3 hours)

You will find this session plan (see Table 1-1) useful if you are getting ready for an internal training for a wide range of participants (technology, operations, management, information security, business, HR/people operations, etc.).

This session plan is structured according to the 4C framework, introduced by Sharon L. Bowman in her *Training from the BACK of the Room!* book. Inspired by various research from the cognitive neuroscience field, Bowman's work suggests that a traditional lecture-based approach to adult learning is not the most effective when it comes to long-term content retention. The framework proposes that learners' engagement and content retention can be significantly improved if instead of a long lecture, the training is delivered in the format of 4Cs: Connection, Concept, Concrete Practice, and Conclusion.

The workshop follows this model, starting with a Connection activity that facilitates the initial interaction of the participants and connects them with the topic of this workshop—DevSecOps. As the workshop unfolds, it progresses through the three short cycles. Each cycle includes a bite-size lecture (Content), an 18-minute round of the *LEGO and Chocolate* simulation (Concrete Practice), and a debriefing (Conclusions). Debriefing is where the magic happens!

If you are new to using simulations or Agile games in your training, the time allocated to debriefing in this session plan may surprise you. Don't shorten the debriefing time! The simulations you facilitate are only a means to an end. Debriefing is important as it helps players integrate their learning and connect the gamified experience to their real-life challenges.

Table 8-1. *Session Plan for a 3-hour DevSecOps Training with the LEGO and Chocolate Simulation*

Starting Time (Duration)	Description	Goal of This Activity
0:00 (5 min)	**Turn and Talk** Invite participants to work at their tables on answering the following three questions: • What is your name? • What is your current role? • What's your experience with DevOps or DevSecOps?	C1: Connection: Connect participants with each other and the topic.
0:05 (3 min)	**Introduce Yourself** Your own introduction. Keep it short.	C1: Connection Instructor introduction
0:08 (10 min)	**Introduce the Topic** Briefly introduce the fundamental goals misalignment between functional silos in traditional organizations, share highlights from the history of the DevOps movement, and agree on definitions of DevOps and DevSecOps (Chapters 3 and 4).	C2: Concept: Present concepts introduced in the first round (Sprint 1).

(continued)

Table 8-1. (continued)

Starting Time (Duration)	Description	Goal of This Activity
0:18 (4 min)	**Setup** Introduce the role-playing simulation. Invite participants to: • select one of the available roles and take a minute to read their role card, • raise their hands when you call out their role characters during the game overview, and • for the duration of the simulation, fully embrace their selected character—name, gender, mindset, and behaviors.	Simulation onboarding
0:22 (6 min)	**Introduce the Simulation Flow of Sprint 1** Use the facilitation script from Chapter 9 to introduce the simulation flow of the first round (Sprint 1).	Simulation Setup—Sprint 1
0:28 (18 min)	**Sprint 1—Feel the Pain** Instruct the participants to start the first round of the simulation with these timeboxes: • Setup – 3 min • Sprint Planning – 2 min • Sprint Execution – 8 min • Sprint Review – 2 min • Sprint Retrospective – 3 min Remember to always keep the interval timer visible.	C3: Concrete practice: Expose a negative impact from the culture of silos, and goals misalignment on the overall performance of an organization.

(continued)

Table 8-1. (*continued*)

Starting Time (Duration)	Description	Goal of This Activity
0:46 (12 min)	**First Debriefing** Follow this specific order for maximum impact. Start with the Scrum teams, then switch to Business team, and finish with Operations and Security. Highlight the differences in the goals of each group and recognize the groups' most painful process bottlenecks. You may also choose to use the 1-2-4-All or W3 Liberating Structures (see Chapter 12).	C4: Conclusion: Rebuild a system-level view based on the individual reflections, highlighting https://tinyurl.com/LCMoneyPlay bottlenecks.
00:58 (7 min)	**Introduce the Topic** Use the facilitation script from Chapter 9 to introduce the following topics: First Way of DevOps, Optimize Flow, Systems Thinking, and typical bottlenecks in DevSecOps transformation.	C2: Concept: Present the concepts introduced in the second round of the simulation (Sprint 2).

(*continued*)

Table 8-1. (*continued*)

Starting Time (Duration)	Description	Goal of This Activity
01:05 (2 min)	**Introduce process improvements and modifications of the second round:** • T-shaped skills-building activity • "Shift left on Security": Sara Security will work with the Scrum team from the beginning. She will also start monitoring development/QA environments for Hacker's attacks and request security patching when "Heartbleed bugs" are discovered. • Benjamin Business will start adjusting prices and will ask for new animals.	Simulation setup—Sprint 2
01:07 (18 min)	**Sprint 2—First Steps to DevSecOps** Distribute additional supplies and Mod Cards for Sprint 2 (See Chapter 6). Instruct the surprise character (Harry Hacker) to start hacking during the T-shape building activity. Instruct the participants to start the second round of the simulation with these timeboxes: • T-shape Building Activity – 3 min • Sprint Planning – 2 min • Sprint Execution – 8 min • Sprint Review – 2 min • Sprint Retrospective – 3 min Remember to always keep the interval timer visible. A few minutes into this round, invite Adam Admin to join you at the Innovation Center for upskilling.	C3: Concrete practice: Improved ability to handle planned and unplanned work after the T-shaped skills cross-training activity, collaboration across functional silos, and "Shift Security to the Left." Upskilling opportunity with DevSecOps.

(*continued*)

Table 8-1. (*continued*)

Starting Time (Duration)	Description	Goal of This Activity
1:25 (15 min)	**Sprint 2 Debriefing** Bring attention to the Delivery Board. What was different about the Sprint 2 experience? What have participants observed in each group? Use the 1-2-4-All[2] activity to facilitate this debriefing. (See debriefing tips in Chapter 12.)	C4: Conclusion: Debrief Sprint 2 experience with different teams. Gain a system-wide perspective.
1:40 (10 min)	**Break** You may choose to offer a 10-minute break (or skip it) based on the needs/energy of the group.	
1:50 8 min	**Introduce the Topic** Use the facilitation script from Chapter 9 to introduce the following topics: "Amplify Feedback Loop." Discuss technical practices that support the Second Way of DevOps. Bring the group's attention to the escalating rate of security vulnerability exploits.	C2: Concept: Present concepts introduced in the final round of the simulation (Sprint 3).

(*continued*)

---

[2] https://www.liberatingstructures.com/1-1-2-4-all/

Table 8-1. (*continued*)

Starting Time (Duration)	Description	Goal of This Activity
1:58 (4 min)	**Introduce process improvements and modifications of the final round:** • Request a full environment rebuild for all development and QA environments. • Introduce changes to support the "one-piece flow": • Benjamin Business needs to drop the batch size to a "one" on all new LEGO animal requests. • Patricia Product needs to help the team with splitting large PBRs. • The teams need to start building into secure green packages that can be deployed directly into production.	Simulation Setup—Sprint 3
2:02 18 min	**Sprint 3—Continuous Value Delivery** Distribute special instructions Mod Card to Patricia Product, and additional supplies for Sprint 3 (see Chapter 6) to the Scrum team. Instruct the participants to start the final round of the simulation with these timeboxes: • Rebuild all environments – 3 min • Sprint Planning – 2 min • Sprint Execution/Review/ Deployment – 10 min • Sprint Retrospective – 3 min Remember to always keep the interval timer visible.	C3: Concrete practice: One-piece flow, secure, automated, and continuous deployment.

(*continued*)

Table 8-1. (*continued*)

Starting Time (Duration)	Description	Goal of This Activity
2:20 3 min	**Introduce the final debriefing activity** (Create a space with five chairs arranged as a semi-circle in preparation for this step). Introduce the dynamic and self-organizing nature of User Experience Fishbowl[3] activity. (See Chapter 12 for debriefing instructions.) Give participants a minute to reflect on their learning from the final round of the *LEGO and Chocolate* simulation, and to write them down on the sticky notes.	Simulation setup—debrief
2:22 27 min	**Final Debriefing—User Experience Fishbowl** Open the Fishbowl and invite the first volunteers in. If you want to add your own observation, remember to jump into a fishbowl as one of the fishbowl participants.	C4: Conclusion - final debrief. Allow for the final reflection in a self-organized group discussion format. Collect written reflections and "Aha!" moment for the Key Takeaways poster.

(*continued*)

---

[3] https://www.liberatingstructures.com/18-users-experience-fishbowl/

Table 8-1. (*continued*)

Starting Time (Duration)	Description	Goal of This Activity
2:50 10 min	**Buffer Time** Things happen! Use this built-in buffer time to help you get back on track with the timeboxes or to slightly expand a timebox of a particularly insightful conversation in debriefing.	Simulation Buffer

Session Plan for a Standalone LEGO and Chocolate Simulation (90 minutes)

This session plan (see Table 8-2) will come in handy if you want to include this simulation as one of the activities in your own full-length DevSecOps training or offer it as an extension to a Scrum training.

The standalone version can also be facilitated as a team-building activity at an off-site event to promote collaboration across the functional departments and to create a safe space for conversations about the biggest bottlenecks (or dysfunctions) in their current ways of working.

Table 8-2. *Session Plan for a 90-minute Standalone LEGO and Chocolate Simulation*

Starting Time (Duration)	Description
0:00 (8 min)	**Introducing the Game** Introduce the role-playing simulation and explain the flow of the first Sprint. Invite participants to • select one of the available roles and take a minute to read their Role Card, and • use the handout to follow along as you walk them through the game and raise their hands when you call out their role.
0:08 (15 min)	**Sprint 1—Feel the Pain** Instruct the participants to start the first round with these timeboxes: • Setup – 2 min • Sprint Planning – 2 min • Sprint Execution – 7 min • Sprint Review – 2 min • Sprint Retrospective – 2 min Remember to always synchronize your countdown timer with the ones used by each Samuel Scrum.
0:23 (10 min)	**First Debriefing** Follow this specific order for maximum impact. Start with the Scrum teams, then switch to Business, and finish with Operations and Security. Highlight the differences in the goals of each group and recognize the process bottlenecks.

(continued)

Table 8-2. (*continued*)

Starting Time (Duration)	Description
00:33 (2 min)	**Introduce process improvements and modifications for the second round of the simulation** • T-shaped skills building activity • "Shift left on Security": Sara Security will work with the Scrum team from the beginning. She will also start monitoring development/QA environments for Hacker's attacks and request security patching when "Heartbleed bugs" are discovered. • Benjamin Business will start adjusting prices and will ask for new animals (market change).
00:35 (15 min)	**Sprint 2—First Steps to DevSecOps** Distribute additional supplies and Mod Cards for Sprint 2. Instruct the surprise character (Harry Hacker) to start hacking during the T-shape building activity. Instruct the participants to start the second round with these timeboxes: • T-shape building activity – 2 min • Sprint Planning – 2 min • Sprint Execution – 7 min • Sprint Review – 2 min • Sprint Retrospective – 2 min Remember to always synchronize your countdown timer with the ones used by each Samuel Scrum. A few minutes into this round, invite Adam Admin to join you at the Innovation Center for upskilling.

(*continued*)

Table 8-2. (*continued*)

Starting Time (Duration)	Description
0:50 (10 min)	**Sprint 2 Debriefing** Bring attention to the Delivery Board. What was different about the Sprint 2 experience? What have participants observed in each group? Use the 1-2-4-All activity to facilitate this debriefing. (See debriefing tips in Chapter 12.)
1:00 (2 min)	**Introduce process improvements and modifications for the final round of the simulation** • Request a full environment rebuild for all development and QA environments. • Introduce changes to support the "one-piece flow": • Benjamin will need to drop the batch size to a "one" on all new LEGO animal requests. • Patricia will need to help the team by splitting PBIs. • The teams will need to start building into secure green packages that can be deployed directly into production.

(*continued*)

Table 8-2. (*continued*)

Starting Time (Duration)	Description
1:02 15 min	**Sprint 3** Distribute special instructions Mod Card to Patricia Product, and additional supplies for Sprint 3 (see Chapter 6) to Scrum team. Instruct the participants to start the final round with these timeboxes: • Rebuild all environments – 2 min • Sprint Planning – 2 min • Sprint Execution/Review/Deployment – 9 min • Sprint Retrospective – 2 min Remember to always synchronize your countdown timer with the ones used by each Samuel Scrum.
1:17 13 min	**Final Debriefing** Give participants a few minutes to reflect on their learning from the final round and facilitate 1-2-4-All to close the game.
1:30	**The end of the standalone simulation.**

CHAPTER 8   KNOW YOUR TIMEBOX

| **A WARNING ABOUT SHORTENING THE GAME** |

Sometimes you may have a need to shorten the game even further; for example, when offering it as a teaser to a pilot group, running it at a local meetup, or facilitating a team-building activity. If this is your case, then skip the third round of the simulation from this session plan to bring it down to 60 minutes. Beware of the significant reduction in the game's learning outcomes.

Room Setup and Teardown Timebox

Please allow 30–45 min for the room setup and 60–75 min for the teardown after the workshop (see Chapter 7 for instructions on setting up the space). If possible, enlist the participants, a training host, or your friends to help you with the post-workshop teardown and supplies packing. There will be a lot of LEGO animals! Don't underestimate the time you'll need to break down everything that teams have created during the three rounds of the simulation.

CHAPTER 9

Be the Gamemaster

Now that you have an idea about the game flow, the nine characters, and the interaction patterns in the *LEGO and Chocolate* simulation, let's review two sample facilitation scripts that can help you run it like a pro!

Expanding upon the two options outlined in Chapter 8, I will share with you two scripts. The first one is a script for a 3-hour version of DevSecOps training that relies on this simulation for experiential component ("Concrete Practice"). The second script is a standalone version of this simulation that you can integrate with your own training or run as a team-building activity at an off-site.

As a facilitator/trainer, you will play the role of the Gamemaster. You will be creating an environment for players to engage with the game and each other. You will also be introducing surprise elements of the game, advancing the storyline, as well as helping the players debrief on their experience and reconstruct the full picture. Be sure to understand well what each character may or may not do and how they contribute to the overall simulation experience (see Chapter 5). In addition, familiarize yourself with the key takeaways (see Chapter 13) and typical questions that arise during the simulation (see Chapter 14).

If you choose to use either of the scripts from this chapter, feel free to also leverage the supporting slides provided in the electronic version of the appendix. These scripts are your starting point, and they are neither final nor set in stone. Experiment with them, enhance them with your stories, update them with the latest industry reports, or simplify them as you see fit.

You will be timeboxing a lot of activities in this workshop. Use the timer of your choice and make it visible to the workshop participants. This workshop will be very noisy. Make sure to adjust the sound volume of the timer so that it can be heard by the players. You may find this interval timer handy: `bit.ly/CLS_timer_interval`.

Facilitation Script for DevSecOps Training with LEGO and Chocolate Game (3 hours)

As people gather in the workshop room, welcome them to their tables:

> *"Hello, welcome to the workshop! We will be learning about DevSecOps through a gamified simulation experience. You will become a part of a large enterprise. Every table in the room is set up to be a separate functional group: development tables, operations, security, and business. I suggest you select a role that's different from the one you have in the real world. Go ahead and pick your table now."*

Turn and Talk (5 min)

Introduce the activity and display this slide (Figure 9-1) so that the latecomers can immediately join in when they arrive:

> *"Once I finish explaining, you will turn around to your neighbors and for the **next 4 minutes** connect with each other using the questions from this slide. Make sure everyone gets a chance to speak. If new people join during this time, integrate them into your conversation. Go!"*

CHAPTER 9   BE THE GAMEMASTER

Figure 9-1. Turn and Talk slide

Introduce Yourself (3 minutes)

Your own introduction. Keep it short and, ideally, connected with your own experience in DevOps/DevSecOps. Why are you teaching this workshop?

Introduce the First Topic: Misalignment of Goals (10 minutes)

Refer to the slides in Figures 9-2 and 9-3 as you introduce the group to the fundamental misalignment of goals in traditional organizations, using this script:

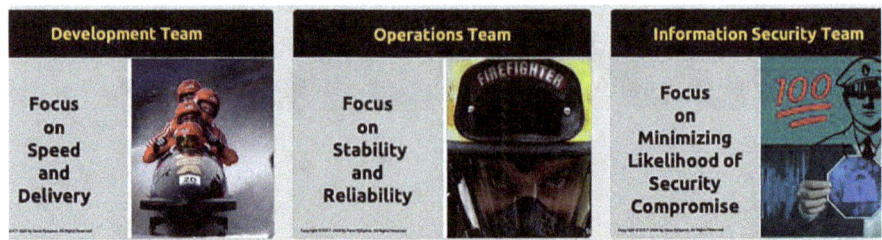

Figure 9-2. *Misalignment of goals between Development, Operations, and Security*

> *"Let's look closely at some of the issues in a traditional organization, where Development teams practice Scrum while Operations teams operate in a traditional sequential manner. Scrum teams are focused on delivering features and maintaining good flow. By the end of each Sprint, they are expected to deliver one or more usable, valuable increments as stepping stones toward the Product Goal. Often, they end up throwing these increments 'over the wall' and moving onto the next Sprint. What happens to it afterward is not their concern—their Sprint is DONE!*
>
> *What do we have on the other side of the wall? Life isn't pretty—escalation procedures, on-call rotation, monitoring—everything to ensure that current systems that generate revenue are stable and have adequate throughput. The Operations team is focused on Stability and Reliability.*
>
> *Operations resist change. They know that when all these increments accumulate in IT operations, they can cause deployment issues and lead to post-deployment firefighting in production.*
>
> *How does Information Security fit into this picture? This team is focused on Security. They run security scans on the new increments, seeking to identify and document issues with the code that could lead to data security breaches and vulnerability exploits if deployed to production.*

CHAPTER 9   BE THE GAMEMASTER

Add to that a continuously increasing pressure from the customers with ever-changing demands and you get a complete picture. In traditional organizations, these groups have completely opposite goals.

Display the slide shown in Figure 9-3 and introduce it with the following script:

Why is this a problem? As Lee Reid, senior IT specialist at IBM, highlighted in his guest article[1] on DevOps.com: 'key factor that will determine the speed to value is TRUST.'

The misalignment of goals between Development, Operations, and Security often becomes a breeding ground for a low-trust culture. Each of the extra steps that the groups introduce to compensate for the lack of trust extends the overall delivery timeline. When deployments are manual, and security is an afterthought, the delivery timeline can stretch into years."

---

[1] https://devops.com/the-simple-math-of-devops/

CHAPTER 9   BE THE GAMEMASTER

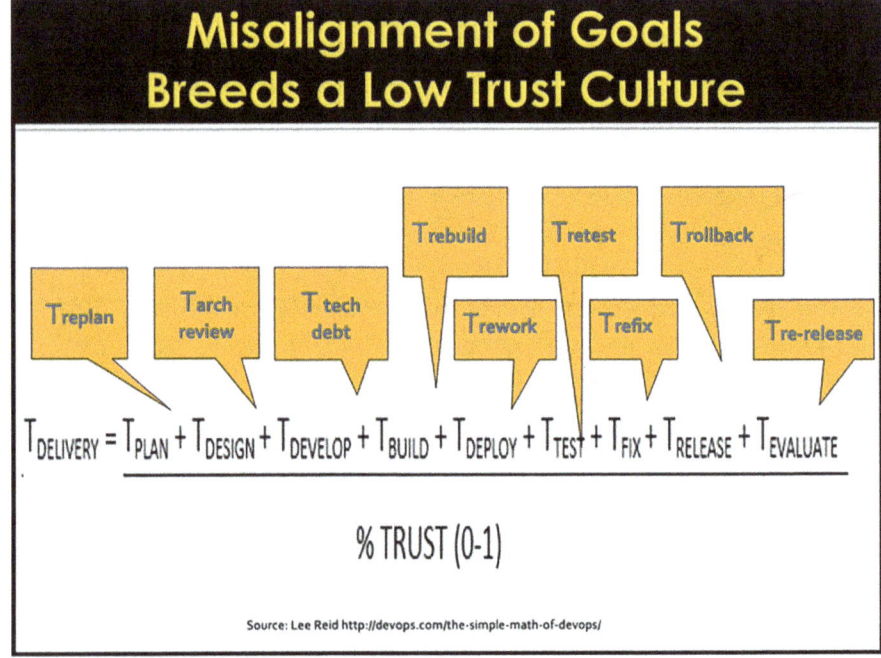

Figure 9-3. Misalignment of goals' impact on culture and delivery timeline

"Good news: it doesn't have to be this way! Let's take a look at the four industry-recognized metrics known as 'Accelerate metrics' that are used to measure software delivery and operational performance."

Display the slide from Figure 9-4 and introduce it with the following script:

"Notice the striking difference between the organizations at various levels of DevOps Evolution. Those companies that are at the Mid to High level of DevOps evolution can achieve both increased speed and increased stability. What differentiates the high performers from the rest of the pack is that they don't stop their DevOps journey at automation. They truly embrace the CALMS of DevOps: Culture, Automation, Lean, Measurement, and Sharing.

CHAPTER 9 BE THE GAMEMASTER

Let's hear from you now! Based on what you know about DevOps so far, how would YOU define it for your organization? I'd like to hear from three people in the room before I share my favorite one."

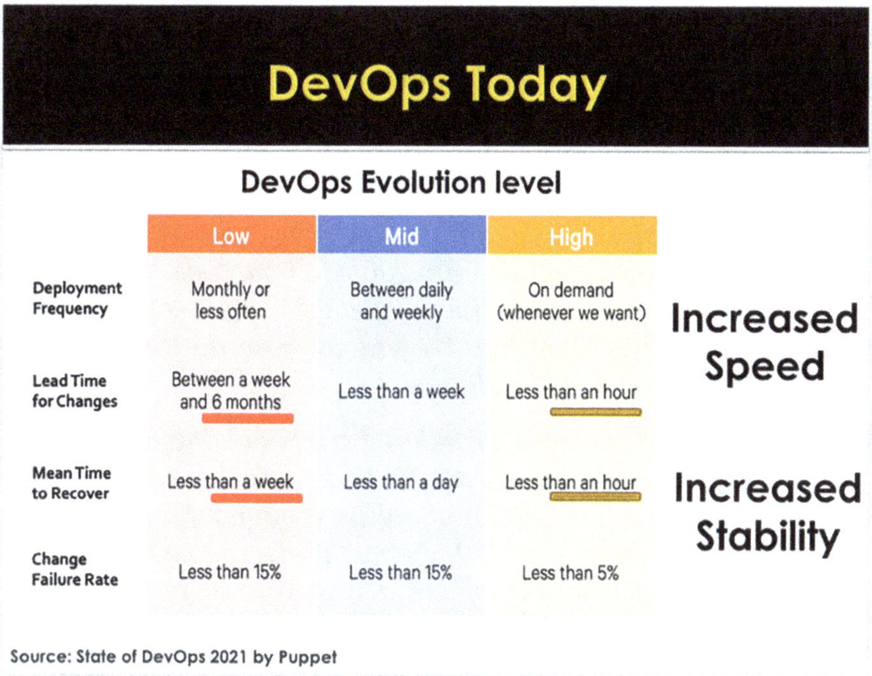

DevOps Today

DevOps Evolution level

	Low	Mid	High	
Deployment Frequency	Monthly or less often	Between daily and weekly	On demand (whenever we want)	**Increased Speed**
Lead Time for Changes	Between a week and 6 months	Less than a week	Less than an hour	
Mean Time to Recover	Less than a week	Less than a day	Less than an hour	**Increased Stability**
Change Failure Rate	Less than 15%	Less than 15%	Less than 5%	

Source: State of DevOps 2021 by Puppet

Figure 9-4. *DevOps success metrics based on the "State of DevOps" 2021 report by Puppet*

Invite three people from the audience to share their definitions of "DevOps" and then proceed with sharing your favorite one. You can also use this one by Michael Huttermann, the author of *DevOps for Developers*. He defines "DevOps" as follows:

> *"a mix of patterns intended to improve collaboration between development and operations. DevOps addresses shared goals and incentives as well as shared processes and tools."*

CHAPTER 9   BE THE GAMEMASTER

Introduce the brief history of DevOps, describe the early successes and groundbreaking results of DevOps unicorns (Flickr, Amazon, Spotify, LinkedIn, Etsy, etc.), and assert that by now DevOps has already been adopted by several large enterprises—the "workhorses" (Walmart, IBM, Microsoft, Barclay Capital, US Department of Homeland Security, and others). Explain how DevSecOps expands upon original ideas and brings Security further into the spotlight (see Chapter 3).

Introduce the *LEGO and Chocolate* simulation with the following script:

> *"Now that we've got the definition out of the way, and you've heard a few success stories, I am going to invite you to experience the benefits (and the challenges) that come with DevSecOps transformation. We are going to do it with the LEGO and Chocolate simulation.*
>
> *Go ahead and pick one of the role cards available at your tables. Imagine you have just joined a new organization, and this card is your 'New hire manual.' In a moment, I will start explaining the basic flow of this game. When you hear me call out the name of your role, please identify yourself by raising a hand. To get the most out of this simulation, I invite you to lean into playfulness. Embrace the name, gender, mindset, and behaviors of your selected character for the duration of this game.*
>
> *Take a minute to familiarize yourself with your 'job description' from your role card."*

Set a visible timer and give the group one minute to read through their cards.

CHAPTER 9　BE THE GAMEMASTER

Introduce the Flow of Sprint 1 (6 minutes)

Bring their attention to the slide and the handout (Figures 9-5 and 9-6). Use the script below to walk through the flow, prompting players to raise their hands when their roles are called.

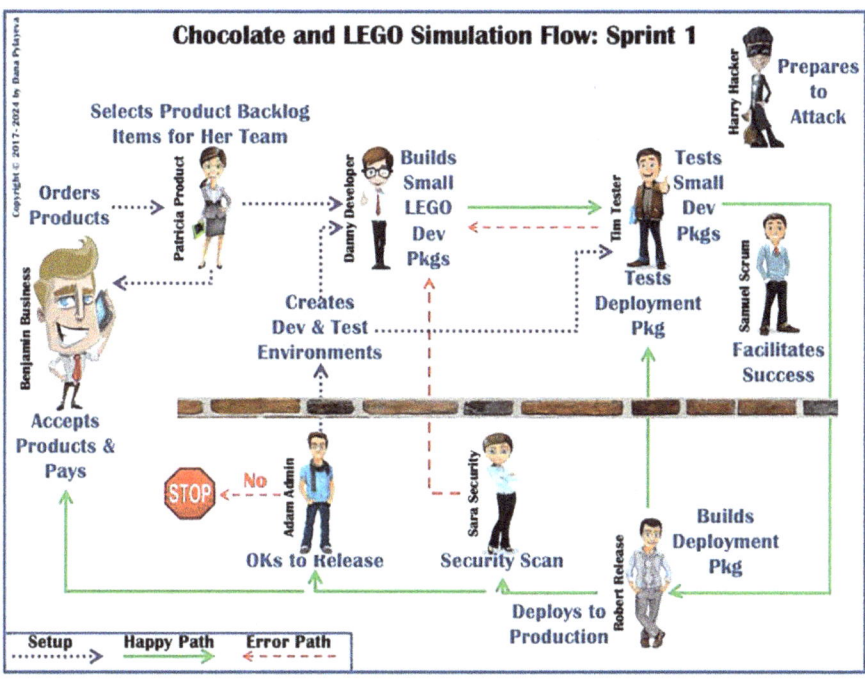

Figure 9-5. *Basic Game Flow slide (and the front side of the handout on players' tables)*

139

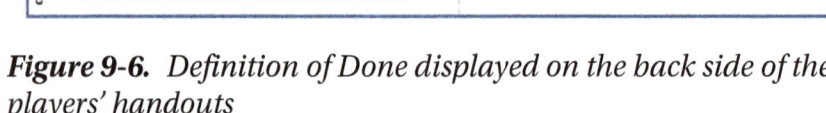

Figure 9-6. Definition of Done displayed on the back side of the players' handouts

"Welcome to the LEGO and Chocolate company! We are one of the oldest companies in the LEGO Animals market. Our development teams are using Scrum, while our Security and Operations are still operating as functional silos. You are joining us for three Sprints, with the intention to help optimize our processes and shift the organizational culture.

As I walk you through our current business operation, feel free to follow along using the handouts on your tables or the image you see on this slide. Remember to raise your hand when I mention your role!

CHAPTER 9   BE THE GAMEMASTER

*In our company, everything starts with the **Benjamin Business**. Benjamin knows what's hot on the market (he is using the Animal Exchange board for that). He knows exactly what needs to be built, in what quantity, and how much he is willing to pay for it. The only person who interacts directly with him is **Patricia Product**. From the start of the Sprint, Patricia works with Benjamin to understand his requirements for each of the product backlog items (PBIs) that she selects from the Animal Exchange board. Once she brings these PBIs to her development team, **Danny Developer** can start building the product, if and only if he has an individual development environment ready. The problem is, as a typical developer in our organization, Danny doesn't know how to provision the environment and needs **Adam Admin** to do it for him. Once the environment is ready, Danny will start building LEGO animals as explained by Patricia, ensuring that each development package meets our Definition of Done.*

Flip the instructions sheet to the other side to see our Definition of Done:

- *One LEGO animal per package*
- *One number label on each animal*
- *One candy*
- *The package is closed*
- *Content doesn't fall out when turned upside-down*

*This is what Danny is building and this is what **Tim Tester** is testing. Once all packages for these PBIs are created and tested, Tim is the one who will take it to the Operations team and give it to **Robert Release** for deployment packaging. In your instruction sheet you will see the Definition of Done for the deployment package:*

- *contains a PBI card and several development packages with a LEGO animal and a chocolate candy in each.*

CHAPTER 9   BE THE GAMEMASTER

> - *The types of animals and their quantity match the PBI card.*
> - *The package is closed and has a label with the team number and the Sprint number on it.*

*Once Robert creates the deployment package, he sends it to **Sara Security** for the final security scan. Sara uses her Security Issues catalog to see if any of the LEGO animals have numbers on their labels that match the numbers in her catalog. If she finds any, she sends the entire package back to the development team for remediation. If no issues are found, she gives it back to Robert for deployment. Robert checks in with Adam Admin for a deployment GO/no GO, and finally Benjamin Business gets his products. If Benjamin likes what he gets, he is going to pay for the products at the current market rate. And when I say 'pay,' I am not joking! Benjamin, can you open the green box from your table and show everyone what you have there? Here is the flow of our first Sprint! Now, our current process is very detailed and convoluted, so if you are not confused right now, it means you were NOT paying attention :) We will run this first round 'as is,' so you can experience the pain of our current process. We will debrief on it and see how we can optimize it, with your help, in the following two Sprints.*

I will take 3 questions from the group, and we will get started!"

Depending on the type of audience in your room, you may get a lot of questions or just a few. Your goal is to start the simulation as soon as you can, so address only a limited number of them. Feel free to share with the players that some of them will receive additional "secret instructions" that will modify the game (or skip this if you sense that there is already too much confusion in the room).

Assure everyone that you will be walking around the room and will help them individually if they get stuck! Just like learning a new board game, the sooner they start playing, the sooner they will understand the rules of the game. See Chapter 14 for the type of questions typically asked by the participants at this point of the game, and the suggested answers.

CHAPTER 9   BE THE GAMEMASTER

Sprint 1: Feel the Pain (18 min)

Display the next slide (see Figure 9-7), instruct Samuel Scrum to monitor the timeboxes, and start the 18-minute interval timer.

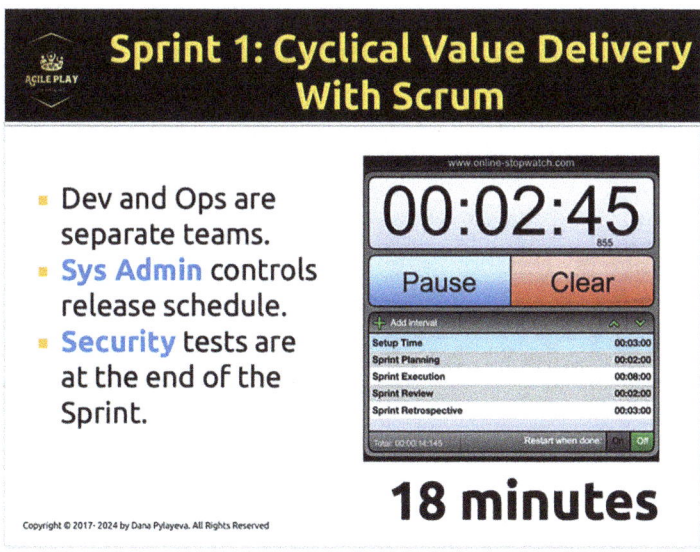

Figure 9-7. *Starting Sprint 1: Cyclical Value Delivery with Scrum*

Sprint 1 timeboxes are as follows:

- Setup time – 3 min
- Sprint Planning – 2 min
- Sprint Execution – 8 min
- Sprint Review – 2 min
- Sprint Retrospective – 3 min

Walk around the room and verify rules comprehension. Check in with Sara Security and ensure she understands how to set up the numbers in her security issues catalog. Confirm with Adam Admin, making sure he understands what it means to "provision the environment" using the masking tape. Ask him to wait until someone from a development team contacts him for help. Address questions as they come.

Watch the timer and the Operations table. When the first packages start showing up on the Operations table, or when there are about 5 minutes left in the game, give a special instruction card to Adam Admin: "We are in code freeze! No deployments are allowed for the remainder of the Sprint." Remind him that he can only share this information with Robert Release and only when Robert asks for a production deployment window. Continue monitoring the room for rules comprehension and dynamics. When the timebox ends, facilitate a debriefing.

THE GROUP NEEDS YOUR INTERVENTION WHEN . . .

1. Developers or testers are working without their dedicated environments. Call this out and instruct them to find Adam Admin.

2. Patricia Product is confused and not engaging with the business. Clarify the rules and expectations of the role.

3. Samuel Scrum is disengaged, not paying attention to the timer. Clarify the rules and expectations of the role.

4. Someone other than Robert Release is bringing packages to business. Bring Adam's attention—unauthorized deployments are not allowed.

First Debriefing (12 minutes)

The goal of this first debriefing is to reconstruct the picture of organizational dynamics in the first Sprint and highlight the dysfunctions and process bottlenecks. You can use your favorite debriefing techniques, experiment with debriefing tools from Chapter 12 of this book, or use the suggested debriefing outlined below.

Start with the Scrum teams and ask them to share what came up during their 3-minute retrospective. How many products were they able to develop in Sprint 1? It is very likely that at least one of the development teams will report that they successfully built several packages in Sprint 1. Acknowledge their successes and turn around to Benjamin Business with an observation and a question: "Benjamin, I hear that development teams managed to build a lot of products in this past Sprint. You must be really happy with how much got delivered to you!"

Watch the surprised developers' faces for a few seconds as Benjamin shares that he's got nothing! He is frustrated, and the Delivery Board is EMPTY! How can this be? The board is empty, as nothing got deployed into production—all packages are sitting at the Operations table. Ask Adam Admin to read out loud the Special Instructions card he received from you toward the end of this Sprint. We were in a code freeze! As our end-to-end process was slow, and the information wasn't shared across functional silos, we failed as an organization at delivering value to our customers.

Had any of the teams encountered security issues? If yes, ask them to share their experience with others. What was it like to receive the entire deployment package back for security issues remediation? Offer participants an opportunity to reflect on the dysfunctions/bottlenecks of the current process and share their suggestions for improvements in the next round.

CHAPTER 9   BE THE GAMEMASTER

Introduce the Next Topic: First Way of DevOps (7 minutes)

Start by introducing DevOps culture with the "Three Way of DevOps" slide (see Figure 9-8) and discuss some of the typical bottlenecks that organizations address during their DevOps transformations (see Figure 9-9).

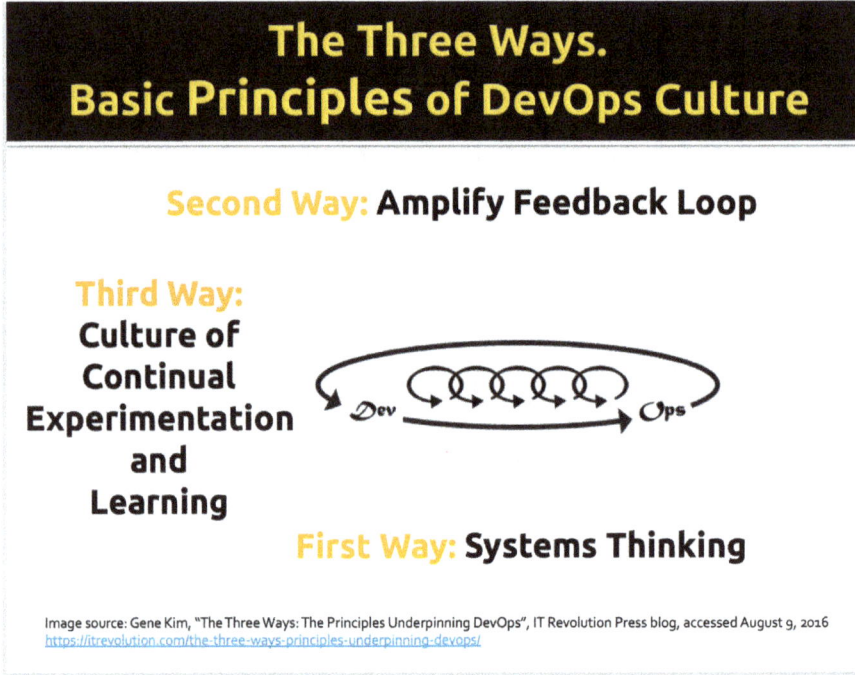

Figure 9-8. *Three Ways of DevOps*

Use the following script:

"Did you notice how the different goals of each team, lack of communication, and the presence of highly specialized roles of the players prevented us from delivering value to the business? That is exactly the problem space in which DevOps

can help! At the fundamental level, effective DevOps adoption patterns can be distilled down to the Three Ways of DevOps, introduced by Gene Kim in his seminal book The Phoenix Project.

Let's explore the first one—System Thinking. Largely inspired by the Theory of Constraints, the First Way invites us to broaden our perspective and take a system-level view (as opposed to seeking local gains) when trying to optimize our process. Tools, like values-stream mapping, can help us visualize the end-to-end process and understand how the planned work that delivers value moves through the organization. As we learn to optimize 'planned work,' we can then start seeking visibility into where the unplanned work causes the most disruption and how we can minimize its impact. What we are looking to gain because of this work is the clarity around process bottlenecks. Here are some of the typical bottlenecks that emerge through this analysis."

Display the bottlenecks slide (Figure 9-9) and ask the workshop participants to call out the ones that they've experienced in the first round of the game. Add on to their responses with examples of more nuanced bottlenecks from the game (and the real-world use cases).

CHAPTER 9   BE THE GAMEMASTER

Figure 9-9. *Typical bottlenecks slide*

Use the following script:

"That's right! Be aware of other kinds of bottlenecks at the tools, people, and policy levels. Lack of appropriate tools may limit the ability of the system to produce more. Mental models held by people or a lack of appropriate skills can cause behavior that becomes a constraint. There are many examples of this type of bottleneck. Front-end vs. back-end developers on a Scrum team is one of the examples. Another very common anti-pattern that we experienced in Sprint 1: Tim Tester was only doing 'testing tasks' and Danny Developer was only doing 'development.' Even though they were in a Scrum team, they acted based on their old 'functional team' mental model. Another example—a written, or unwritten, policy (segregation of duty) can impede the system's ability to deliver."

CHAPTER 9   BE THE GAMEMASTER

Introduce Process Modifications of the Second Sprint (2 minutes)

Distribute additional supplies and Mod Cards for Sprint 2 (see Chapter 6). Show the next slide (Figure 9-10) as you introduce the new process improvements.

Use the following script:

> *"Let's experiment with a few process modifications to address our biggest process bottlenecks. First, we are going to **'Shift-left on Security.'** We will ask Sara Security to start working (and sharing information) with her Scrum team from the very beginning, and even join them at their table! Second, we are going to increase the cross-functionality of our teams, moving away from the deep single specialization in one functional area ('I-shaped') to deep specialization in one area plus multiple complementary skills in other areas (**'T-shaped'**). On your tables, you have a set of multi-colored stickers. Each sticker is a metaphor for a specific functional skill: **Yellow** for development and testing, **Pink** for Security, **Orange** for Sys Admin skills, and **Green** for Release Engineering. Here is how we are going to simulate the cross-training in the first 3 minutes of the next Sprint.*
>
> *Once I finish explaining, you will*
>
> - *take the stickers with your current skill's color,*
> - *find someone in the room with skills different from yours,*
> - *explain what you do in your role in this game and learn about their role, and*
> - *exchange stickers to signify that you have finished cross-training.*

CHAPTER 9   BE THE GAMEMASTER

Make sure to prominently display your new stickers—they are a validation of your newly acquired skills. Now when Adam needs help with environment provisioning, anyone who got cross-trained as Admin can help. Same with deployment, security, or development skills. Those who got cross-trained with a variety of skills will be able to help with addressing the most significant process bottlenecks."

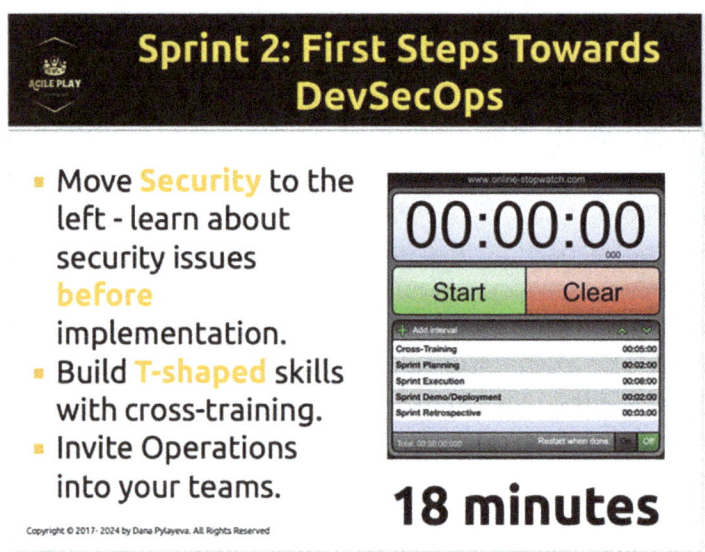

Figure 9-10. *Process modification for Sprint 2: first steps toward DevSecOps*

Sprint 2: First Steps to DevSecOps (18 minutes)

Remind Samuel Scrum to monitor the individual timeboxes and start the 18-minute interval time. Sprint 2 timeboxes are as follows:

- Cross-training time – 3 min
- Sprint Planning – 2 min

- Sprint Execution – 8 min
- Sprint Review – 2 min
- Sprint Retrospective – 3 min

Announce the start of Sprint 2. As the cross-training activity unfolds, walk around the room and encourage people to get cross-trained with as many people as possible. At the same time, verify that Benjamin Business is modifying the Animal Exchange board in response to the Mod Card he received from you prior to this Sprint: significantly reducing prices on all existing PBIs and creating new PBIs for more-expensive new animals.

Instruct Harry Hacker to enter the game. Now is the time to start hacking! As everyone is excited and distracted by the cross-training initiative, all development and testing environments are left unattended. Harry Hacker will walk around the room with a red marker and draw hearts on environment tapes to simulate the "Heartbleed bug" vulnerability. Once enough environments have been compromised, approach players in the Sara Security role and remind them about the Mod Card they received earlier. It is time to start checking all environments and stopping the development process to request emergency patching for any hacked environments.

As the group responds to the emergency patching request, watch out for Adam Admin becoming a bottleneck again. He doesn't need to be—anyone who was cross-trained by him earlier can now step in and help with patching. Continue observing players and their behaviors in the game.

CHAPTER 9 BE THE GAMEMASTER

| **THE GROUP NEEDS YOUR INTERVENTION WHEN . . .** |

1. Business hasn't changed the prices and has not asked for new animals. Remind them about this modified dynamic of Sprint 2.

2. Patricia Product still has her team working on the old PBIs. Call her attention to the higher price of the new animals.

3. The Delivery Board is not updated. Remind the business to keep track of how much they've paid to each team for the value delivered.

4. Development teams are forgetting to take the money from the business for the products delivered. Call their attention to it.

5. Development teams are working in environments with security issues (hacked)—call Sara Security. She must halt further work until the environments are patched.

6. Players are not using their new skills to elevate the process bottlenecks, so remind them of their new T-shaped skills.

7. Timid Harry Hacker—clarify the rules and encourage more hacking. You as a facilitator may need to step in to help with hacking as well.

After the first environment patching is completed, and patching is no longer a bottleneck, Adam will realize that he has more time available. Invite him to join you at the "Innovation Center" next to the "Known Good Environment Configuration" poster (see Chapter 7). Explain that now that he cross-trained others to perform some basic manual tasks, he has time to learn about new technology—Infrastructure as Code (see Figure 9-11). Show him how to build his first "Chef recipes" (simulated by a green painter's tape). He will be working ahead of the development team to enable automated environment provisioning in Sprint 3.

Figure 9-11. Adam Admin getting upskilled at the Innovation Center

Spring 2 Debriefing (15 minutes)

The goal of this second debriefing is to reconstruct the picture of organizational changes implemented in the second Sprint, highlight their impact on value delivery, and discuss what else is getting in the way. You can use your favorite debriefing techniques, experiment with debriefing tools from Chapter 12 of this book, or use the suggested debriefing approach with the 1-2-4-All Liberating Structure outlined here. Use the following script to introduce it:

> *"End of the second Sprint! What a difference in the room dynamic. Let's debrief on how your own role and your interactions with others were affected by the modifications we introduced in the second round. How did it feel to be a part of this organization in the second round? Let's use 1 minute of silent brainstorming to reflect on this. Take some stickies and markers from your table and in 1 minute or less write down a few of the "Aha!" moments that came up for you. One reflection per sticky. In silence, please."*

CHAPTER 9   BE THE GAMEMASTER

Give the group one minute, signal the end of the timebox, and follow up with the script for the next part of the 1-2-4-All activity:

> *"Now, pick up your stickies and listen carefully for the next step's instructions. Once I finish explaining, you will get up from your chair and find someone from a different table. Ideally, everyone finds a partner, but if you can't find one, join another pair to form a trio. In your pairs or trios, take 4 minutes to share your reflections, be succinct, and make sure everyone gets a chance to speak in this very short timebox."*

Give the group 4 minutes, then signal the end of the timebox, and follow up with this script to introduce the next part of the 1-2-4-All activity:

> *"Let's move on to the next step! Once I finish explaining, you will take your small group and merge it with another small group. In your group of 4–5 people, you will take another 4 minutes to share your reflections, now with the intention to distill them down to 1–2 most salient, most interesting ones that are worth sharing with the larger group. Select a spokesperson to share these items on behalf of the group in the final round."*

Give the group the final 4 minutes, then signal the end of the timebox. Ask each group to share 1–2 of their collective insights, and finish by adding all their stickies to the "Key Takeaways" poster. See Chapter 13 for a collection of "Aha!" moments from my previous workshop participants for your reference. Over time you will notice that this simulation generates consistent "Aha!" moments in a variety of organizations, countries, and cultures.

CHAPTER 9 BE THE GAMEMASTER

Optional Break (10 minutes)

You may want to offer a short break to your group at this point in the workshop. I typically offer one every 1.5–2 hours in my training. Feel free to skip it if the group doesn't need one.

Introduce the Final Topic (8 minutes)

Introduce the group to the key concept—the Second Way—and talk about technology and process changes that bring it to life in DevSecOps. Use the slide in Figure 9-12 and the following script:

> "The next concept you will learn about in this workshop is the Second Way of DevOps—Amplify Feedback Loop. We will briefly cover several technical practices, like containerization, microservices, Continuous Delivery (CI/CD), and telemetry, that support flow optimization and enable faster feedback loops for all teams involved in the end-to-end value stream.
>
> What is **containerization**? It is a process of packaging software code with all associated libraries, dependencies, and configurations so that it can be isolated in its own lightweight and portable container. Docker was the first one to introduce this technology in 2013. You can think of **microservices** as a modern version of Service Oriented Architecture. It is an approach to application development, where every service is isolated and only communicates with other services through lightweight APIs."

CHAPTER 9 BE THE GAMEMASTER

The Three Ways.
Basic Principles of DevOps Culture

Second Way: **Amplify Feedback Loop**

1. Small Batches

2. Implement CI/CD

3. Live Production Monitoring by Teams

Image source:
https://pixabay.com/photos/speed-car-limit-danger-gas-auto-164063/

Figure 9-12. *The Second Way of DevOps slide*

*"When applied to the deployment of microservices, and used with **CI/CD** pipeline, it can become a true illustration of optimizing flow with 'small batches'—the First Way of DevOps. Continuous Delivery is an approach to developing/deploying software that relies on a set of automated processes for moving a change (new feature, configuration change, bug fix, etc.) through each stage of the software development lifecycle in a safe, fast, predictable, and repeatable way. As the change gets promoted through the CI/CD pipeline, developers receive immediate feedback on the quality of their code. Only if the automated tests are passing will the change be promoted to the next step. Another example is the 'Shift-left on security' practice, which enables faster feedback about potential secu-*

rity issues, and suboptimal code quality with static code analysis tools in developers' IDE. It is important to recognize, and make available, a variety of upstream and downstream feedback:

- *implementing telemetry and collecting feedback on the server load, stability, and performance of the application under production load, making it visible to all*

- *collecting feedback on the new feature adoption from A/B testing*

- *sharing on-call rotation with the entire team (including developers and architects) to amplify the upstream feedback loop on the architecture, design, and coding decisions they've made.*

If some of these practices sound too radical for your organization, and you are thinking that amplifying the feedback loop or implementing the CI/CD pipeline is not a priority for you today, think again.

Even if your customers can wait a month or two for a new feature, the intruders of the world will not be so gracious in giving you time to roll out a security patch for the newly discovered vulnerability."

Display the following slide (Figure 9-13) and continue with this script:

CHAPTER 9   BE THE GAMEMASTER

Image source: https://pixabay.com/photos/hacker-attack-mask-internet-2883632/

Figure 9-13. *The time from vulnerability discovery to exploit is shrinking rapidly*

> "This is the world we live in today. The time from vulnerability discovery to exploit is shrinking rapidly. Your organization must be ready to reliably deploy fixes into production in a matter of minutes, not weeks or months. Implementing the CI/CD pipeline and embracing DevSecOps culture at all levels of the organization must be your number one priority now. Let's get to work, welcome to Sprint 3!"

Introduce Process Modifications for the Final Sprint (4 minutes)

Distribute additional supplies and Mod Cards for Sprint 3 (see Chapter 6). Show the next slide (Figure 9-14) as you introduce the new process improvements.

CHAPTER 9   BE THE GAMEMASTER

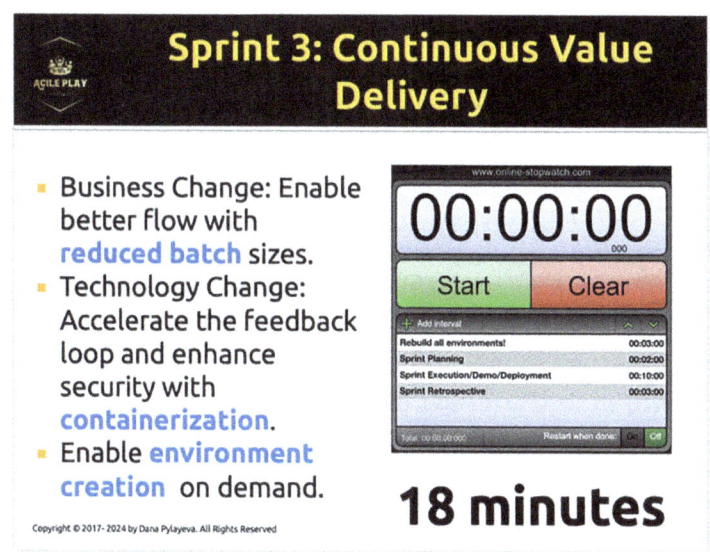

Figure 9-14. Process modification for Sprint 3: Continuous Value Delivery

Use the following script:

*"Let's experiment with amplifying the feedback loop and further improving our flow with a 'one-piece flow' approach. **First**, we will make modifications on the business side. We will educate the business and get their agreement to stop asking for large batches and **drop the batch size to 1** on all new animals. Patricia will help the teams **split any remaining large PBIs**. For example, if you get a card from the business that's still asking for 5 Dogs, Patricia will split it into 5 small PBI cards with 1 Dog each.*

***Second**, we will upskill our technology teams in **containerization** and **Continuous Delivery** as well as double down on security. On your tables, you will find the new green packages. These are super-secure Docker containers. When you build your LEGO animals into these packages, no additional packaging is required for deployment. The package still needs to contain the individual PBI card and have a label*

159

with the team name/Sprint number. With this change, each individual LEGO animal will be deployable directly into production by anyone on the team (automated CI/CD pipeline). The **third change** *is related to the new skill that Adam Admin has acquired already. As he cross-trained several of you during the last Sprint, he was able to find the time to learn about automated environment provisioning on-demand. Now when someone needs to provision a new environment, they can do it with a 'push of a button'—or a push of a green tape. All these new environments have a Total Security Suite built in and cannot be hacked!*

Just in time for what we need to do in the next Sprint! As our environments became brittle and inconsistent due to the numerous patchings last Sprint, we need to **reprovision all environments***! Follow Adam to the Innovation Center and let's get started!"*

Sprint 3: Continuous Value Delivery (18 minutes)

Remind Samuel Scrum to monitor the individual timeboxes and start the 18-minute interval time. Sprint 3 timeboxes are as follows:

- Rebuild All Environments – 3 min
- Sprint Planning – 2 min
- Sprint Execution/Review/Deployment – 10 min
- Sprint Retrospective – 3 min

Continue observing players and their behaviors in the game.

CHAPTER 9 BE THE GAMEMASTER

THE GROUP NEEDS YOUR INTERVENTION WHEN . . .

1. Business continues to ask for (or accept) the LEGO animals in large batches. Remind them about the modified dynamic of Sprint 3.

2. Patricia Product has her team working on lower-priced LEGO animals. Remind her to monitor the LEGO Animal Exchange board and respond to changes in the business demand.

3. The Delivery Board is not updated. Remind the business to keep track of how much they've paid to each team for the value delivered.

4. Development teams are still "batching" (waiting for multiple green packages before taking them to business, using the old deployment process. Remind them about the modified dynamic of Sprint 3.

Introduce the Final Debriefing Activity (3 minutes)

The goal of the final debriefing is to connect the learning from the entire simulation and inspire change in the real environments in which the groups operate today. How can the benefits from process optimization and DevSecOps practices experienced in the simulation be achieved in the "real life" of the participants? What needs to happen next?

You can use your favorite debriefing techniques, experiment with debriefing tools from Chapter 12 of this book, or use the suggested debriefing outlined here.

CHAPTER 9 BE THE GAMEMASTER

Bring out five empty chairs and arrange them in a semi-circle at the back of the room in preparation for this debriefing.

I find that the User Experience Fishbowl Liberating Structure works well for this final debriefing. This is how you can introduce it to the participants:

"Sprint 3 is over! We will take the time now to reflect and respond to the following question:

What have we learned from this simulation and how might we bring these ideas to life to influence change?

We will use a special format for this discussion—a User Experience Fishbowl. Our group will be split into two types of participants—the fishes (people in the fishbowl) and the observers. The five chairs you see at the back of the room are the physical boundaries of the fishbowl. Fishes will sit in the fishbowl and have a conversation with each other, responding to the question. Everyone else will be listening to their conversation. If any observer wants to make a comment or add something to the conversation, they would have to jump into the fishbowl and become one of the fishes.

Important!

The rule of the fishbowl: a maximum of four fishes in the fishbowl at any given time and one empty chair as an invitation for a new fish to join. When the last chair is taken, one of the older fishes must jump out of the fishbowl and create one empty chair again. The rule applies to everyone, even the facilitator. When I want to add something to the conversation, I must jump into the fishbowl. Let's take about a minute now for a silent brainstorming. You already know how to do it. Take a sticky, and a marker and (in silence) jot down what's coming up for you in response to this question:

CHAPTER 9   BE THE GAMEMASTER

What have we learned from this simulation and how might we bring these ideas to life to influence change?"

Give the group about a minute and then invite them into the fishbowl.

Final Debriefing: User Experience Fishbowl (27 minutes)

Simply state that the fishbowl is open, and then wait for people to start coming into the fishbowl. This structure requires minimum facilitation from your side as it is self-organizing by design. Listen to the reflections and ideas that people share in the fishbowl. This is your immediate feedback loop, allowing you to validate that the participants are taking away the right message about the DevSecOps culture.

If the group is engaged and actively joining the fishbowl, give them as much space as possible, only joining the fishbowl if you hear a statement that contradicts the learning objectives of this workshop. If the group is generally quiet, join the fishbowl to share your own observation about this dynamic of the group that you have observed through the three rounds of the game. As the flow of people in and out of the fishbowl dries out, come in to summarize the message and invite everyone to add their stickies to the "Key Takeaways" poster and close the workshop.

Facilitation Script for a Standalone Version of the LEGO and Chocolate Game (90 minutes)

This version assumes that you will either run the *LEGO and Chocolate* simulation as primarily a team-building activity or will incorporate it into your own training. It also assumes that you have no access to a projector or similar equipment and no ability to display the slides for the participants.

CHAPTER 9   BE THE GAMEMASTER

You will rely primarily on the physical role cards, materials, handouts, and room posters for communicating the rules of the game. You will need to use a tablet or phone timer to manage the timeboxes, and potentially supplement with additional noise makers to get the groups' attention.

Introduce the Game (8 minutes)

Use the following script to introduce the game:

> "Welcome to the LEGO and Chocolate company! We are one of the oldest companies on the LEGO Animals market and you are joining us as new hires. Go ahead, take a role card from your table and read the description—I will give you one minute for that."

Pause for one minute, give a signal at the end of the timebox, and continue with the script:

> "As I walk you through our current business operation, follow along using the handouts on your tables and raise your hand when I mention your role!
>
> In our company, everything starts with **Benjamin Business**. Benjamin knows what's hot on the market (he is using the Animal Exchange board for that). He knows exactly what needs to be built, in what quantity, and how much he is willing to pay for it. The only person who interacts directly with him is **Patricia Product**. From the start of the Sprint, Patricia works with Benjamin to understand what he needs and to select one of the work cards from the Animal Exchange board. Once she brings these work cards to her development team, **Danny Developer** can start building the product, if and only if he has an individual development environment ready. The problem is, as a typical developer in our organization, Danny doesn't know how to provision the environment and needs **Adam Admin** to do it for him. Once the environment is ready,

Danny will start building LEGO animals as explained by Patricia, ensuring that each development package meets our Definition of Done.

Flip the instructions sheet to the other side to see our Definition of Done:

- *One LEGO animal per package*
- *One number label on each animal*
- *One candy*
- *The package is closed*
- *Content doesn't fall out when turned upside-down.*

*This is what Danny is building and this is what **Tim Tester** is testing. Once all packages for this work card are created and tested, Tim is the one who will take it to the Operations team and give it to **Robert Release** for deployment packaging. In your instruction sheet you will see the Definition of Done for the deployment package:*

- *contains a work card and several development packages with a LEGO animal and a chocolate candy in each*
- *The types of animals and their quantity match the work card.*
- *The package is closed and has a label with the team number and the Sprint number on it.*

*Once Robert creates the deployment package, he sends it to **Sara Security** for the final security scan. Sara uses her Security Issues catalog to see if any of the LEGO animals have numbers on their labels that match the numbers in her catalog. If she finds any, she sends the entire package back to the development team for remediation. If no issues are found, she gives it back to Robert for deployment. Robert checks in with Adam Admin for a deployment GO/no GO, and finally Benjamin Business gets his products.*

If Benjamin likes what he gets, he is going to pay for the products at the current market rate. And when I say 'pay,' I am not joking! Benjamin, can you open the green box from your table and show everyone what you have there?

Here is the flow of our first Sprint, and if you are not confused right now, it means you were NOT paying attention :) We will run this first round 'as is' and see how we can simplify it for the next rounds. I will take 3 questions from the group, and we will get started!"

Sprint 1: Feel the Pain (15 minutes)

Have this timeline written on the poster (or a whiteboard), and instruct Samuel Scrum to keep these timeboxes in mind as the round progresses.

- Setup – 2 min
- Sprint Planning – 2 min
- Sprint Execution – 7 min
- Sprint Review – 2 min
- Sprint Retrospective – 2 min

Ask all players in Samuel Scrum's role to pull out their phones, set their countdown timer to 15 minutes, and simultaneously start it on your signal. (Don't forget to start your own countdown timer.)

Walk around the room and verify rules comprehension. Check in with Sara Security and ensure she understands how to set up the numbers in her security issues catalog. Confirm with Adam Admin, making sure he understands what it means to 'provision the environment' using the masking tape. Ask him to wait until someone from a development team contacts him for help. Address questions as they come.

CHAPTER 9   BE THE GAMEMASTER

Watch your timer and the Operations table. When the first packages start showing up on the Operations table, or when there are about 5 minutes left in the first round, give a special instruction card to Adam Admin: We are in code freeze! No deployments are allowed for the remainder of the game. Remind him that he can only share this information with Robert Release and only when Robert asks for a production deployment window. Continue monitoring the room for rules comprehension and dynamics. When the timebox ends, facilitate a debriefing.

THE GROUP NEEDS YOUR INTERVENTION WHEN . . .

1. Developers or testers are working without their dedicated environments. Call this out and instruct them to find Adam Admin.
2. Patricia Product is confused and not engaging with the business. Clarify the rules and expectations of the role.
3. Samuel Scrum is disengaged. Clarify the rules and expectations of the role.
4. Someone other than Robert Release is bringing packages to business. Bring Adam's attention—unauthorized deployments are not allowed.

First Debriefing (10 minutes)

Use your favorite debriefing techniques, experiment with debriefing tools from Chapter 12 of this book, or use the suggested debriefing outlined here.

Start with the Scrum teams and ask them to share what came up during their 3-minute retrospective. How many products were they able to develop in Sprint 1? It is very likely that at least one of the development teams will report that they successfully built several packages in Sprint 1. Acknowledge their successes and turn around to Benjamin Business with an observation and a question:

> "Benjamin, I hear that development teams managed to build a lot of products in this past Sprint. You must be really happy with how much got delivered to you!"

Watch the surprised developers' faces for a few seconds as Benjamin shares that he's got nothing! He is frustrated, the Delivery Board is EMPTY! How can this be? The board is empty, as nothing got deployed into production—all packages are sitting at the Operations table. Ask Adam Admin to read out loud the Special Instructions card he received from you toward the end of this Sprint. "We were in a code freeze! As our end-to-end process was slow, and the information wasn't shared across functional silos, as an organization we failed at delivering value to our customers.

Had any of the teams encountered security issues? If yes, ask them to share their experience with others. What was it like to receive the entire deployment package back for security issues remediation? Offer participants an opportunity to reflect on the dysfunctions/bottlenecks of the current process and share their suggestions for improvements in the next round.

Introduce Process Improvements and Modifications for the Second Round (2 minutes)

Distribute additional supplies and Mod Cards for Sprint 2 (see Chapter 6) and introduce the new process improvements using the following script:

"Let's experiment with a few process modifications to address our biggest process bottlenecks. **First**, we are going to **'Shift left on Security.'** We will ask Sara Security to start working (and sharing information) with her Scrum team from the very beginning, and even join them at their table! **Second**, we are going to cross-train the team and build some T-shaped skills. On your tables you have a set of multi-colored skills stickers: **Yellow** for development and testing, **Pink** for Security, **Orange** for Sys Admin skills, and **Green** for Release Engineering. Here is how we are going to simulate the cross-training in the first 2 minutes of the next Sprint.

Once I finish explaining, you will

- take the stickers with your current skill's color,

- find someone in the room with skills different from yours,

- explain what you do in your role in this game, and learn about their role, and

- exchange stickers to signify that you have finished cross-training.

Those who got cross-trained with a variety of skills will be able to help with addressing the most significant process bottlenecks in the next Sprint."

Sprint 2: First Steps to DevSecOps (15 minutes)

Update your poster/whiteboard with the following timebox breakdown for Sprint 2:

- Cross-training activity – 2 min
- Sprint Planning – 2 min
- Sprint Execution – 7 min
- Sprint Review – 2 min
- Sprint Retrospective – 2 min

CHAPTER 9   BE THE GAMEMASTER

Call your Samuel Scrums and again synchronize the start of their 15-minute countdown timers with the start of your own timer. Announce the start of Sprint 2.

As the cross-training activity unfolds, walk around the room and encourage people to get cross-trained with as many people as possible. At the same time, verify that Benjamin Business is modifying the Animal Exchange board in response to the Mod Card he received from you prior to this Sprint: significantly reducing prices on all existing work cards and creating new work cards for more expensive new animals.

Instruct Harry Hacker to enter the game. Now is the time to start hacking! As everyone is excited and distracted by the cross-training initiative, all development and testing environments are left unattended. Harry Hacker will walk around the room with a red marker and draw hearts on environment tapes to simulate the "Heartbleed bug" vulnerability. Once enough environments have been compromised, approach players in the Sara Security role and remind them about the Mod Card they received earlier. It is time to start checking all environments and stop the development process to request emergency patching for any hacked environments.

As the group responds to the emergency patching request, watch out for Adam Admin becoming a bottleneck again. He doesn't need to be—anyone who was cross-trained by him earlier can now step in and help with patching. Continue observing players and their behaviors in the game.

CHAPTER 9 BE THE GAMEMASTER

THE GROUP NEEDS YOUR INTERVENTION WHEN . . .

1. Business hasn't changed the prices and has not asked for new animals. Remind them about this modified dynamic of Sprint 2.

2. Patricia Product still has her team working on the old work cards. Call her attention to the higher price of the new animals.

3. The Delivery Board is not updated. Remind the business to keep track of how much they've paid to each team for the value delivered.

4. Development teams are forgetting to take the money from the business for the products delivered. Call their attention to it.

5. Development teams are working in environments with security issues (hacked)—call Sara Security. She must halt further work until the environments are patched.

6. Players are not using their new skills to elevate the process bottlenecks; remind them of their new T-shaped skills.

7. Timid Harry Hacker—clarify the rules and encourage more hacking. You as a facilitator may need to step in to help with hacking as well.

After the first environment patching is completed, and patching is no longer a bottleneck, Adam will realize that he has more time available. Invite him to join you at the "Innovation Center" next to the "Known Good Environment Configuration" poster (see Chapter 7). Explain that now that he cross-trained others to perform some basic manual tasks, he has time to learn about new technology—Infrastructure as Code (see Figure 9-15). Show him how to build his first "Chef recipes" (simulated by a green painter's tape). He will be working ahead of the development team to enable automated environment provisioning in Sprint 3.

171

CHAPTER 9   BE THE GAMEMASTER

Figure 9-15. Adam Admin getting upskilled at the Innovation Center

Spring 2 Debriefing (10 minutes)

What have participants observed in each group? Take 10 minutes to debrief with the group. Use your favorite debriefing techniques, experiment with debriefing tools from Chapter 9 of this book, or use the suggested debriefing with 1-2-4-All Liberating Structure outlined here. Use the following script to introduce it:

> *"End of the second Sprint! What was different about the Sprint 2 experience? Let's debrief on how your own role and your interactions with others were affected by the modifications we introduced in the second round. How did it feel to be a part of this organization in the second round? Let's use 1 minute of silent brainstorming to reflect on this. Take some stickies and markers from your table and in 1 minute or less write down a few of the "Aha!" moments that came up for you. One reflection per sticky. In silence, please."*

Give the group one minute, signal the end of the timebox, and follow up with the script for the next part of the 1-2-4-All activity:

"Now, pick up your stickies and listen carefully for the next step's instructions. Once I finish explaining, you will get up from your chair and find someone from a different table. Ideally, everyone finds a partner, but if you can't find one, join another pair to form a trio. In your pairs or trios, take 2 minutes to share your reflections, be succinct, and make sure everyone gets a chance to speak in this very short timebox."

Give the group 2 minutes, then signal the end of the timebox, and follow up with this script to introduce the next part of the 1-2-4-All activity:

"Let's move on to the next step! Once I finish explaining, you will take your small group, and merge it with another small group. In your group of 4–5 people, you will take another 4 minutes to share your reflections, now with the intention to distill them down to one most salient, most interesting one that is worth sharing with the larger group. Select a spokesperson to share this insight on behalf of the group in the final round."

Give the group 4 minutes, then signal the end of the timebox. For the remaining time in this timebox, ask each group to share their most salient insights, and finish by adding all their stickies to the "Key Takeaways" poster. See Chapter 13 for a collection of "Aha!" moments from my previous workshop participants for your reference. Over time you will notice that this simulation generates consistent "Aha!" moments in a variety of organizations, countries, and cultures.

CHAPTER 9   BE THE GAMEMASTER

Introduce Process Improvements and Modifications for the Final Round (2 minutes)

Distribute additional supplies and Mod Cards for Sprint 3 (see Chapter 6) and introduce the new process improvements. Use the following script:

> *"Let's experiment with a few additional modifications that can help us get to the 'one-piece flow.'* **First***, on the business side. We will educate the business and get their agreement to stop asking for large batches and* **drop the batch size to 1** *on all new animals. Patricia will help the teams* **split any remaining large PBIs***. For example, if you get a card from the business that's still asking for 5 Dogs, Patricia will split it into 5 small PBIs with 1 Dog each.*
>
> **Second***, we will upskill our technology teams in* **containerization** *and* **Continuous Delivery** *as well as double down on security. On your tables, you will find the new green packages. These are super-secure Docker containers. When you build your LEGO animals in these packages, no additional packaging is required for deployment. The package still needs to contain an individual work card and have a label with the team name/Sprint number. With this change, each individual LEGO animal will be deployable directly into production by anyone on the team (automated CI/CD pipeline). The* **third change** *is related to the new skill that Adam Admin acquired already. As he cross-trained several of you during the last Sprint, he was able to find the time to learn about automated environment provisioning on-demand. Now when someone needs to provision a new environment, they can do it with a 'push of a button'—or a push of a green tape. Additionally, these new environments have a Total Security Suite built in and cannot be hacked!*

*Just in time for what we need to do in the next Sprint! As our environments became brittle and inconsistent due to the numerous patchings last Sprint, we need to **reprovision all environments**! Follow Adam to the Innovation Center and let's get started!"*

Sprint 3: Continuous Value Delivery (15 minutes)

Update your poster/whiteboard with the following timebox breakdown for Sprint 3:

- Rebuild all environments – 2 min
- Sprint Planning – 2 min
- Sprint Execution/Review/Deployment – 9 min
- Sprint Retrospective – 2 min

Continue observing players and their behaviors in the game.

THE GROUP NEEDS YOUR INTERVENTION WHEN ...

1. Business continues to ask for (or accept) the LEGO animals in large batches. Remind them about the modified dynamic of Sprint 3.

2. Patricia Product has her team working on lower-priced LEGO animals. Remind her to monitor the LEGO Animal Exchange board and respond to changes in the business demand.

3. The Delivery Board is not updated. Remind the business to keep track of how much they've paid to each team for the value delivered.

4. Development teams are still "batching": waiting for multiple green packages before bringing them to business or using the old deployment process. Remind them about the modified dynamic of Sprint 3.

CHAPTER 9   BE THE GAMEMASTER

Final Debriefing (13 minutes)

Finish the game with a 13-minute debriefing. Use your favorite debriefing techniques, experiment with debriefing tools from Chapter 9 of this book, or use the suggested debriefing with 1-2-4-All Liberating Structure outlined here. Use the following script to introduce it:

> *"End of the game! What was different about the Sprint 3 experience? What are your takeaways from this experience? Take a sticky again and write down a few of the takeaways in 1 minute or less. One reflection per sticky. In silence, please."*

Give the group 1 minute, signal the end of the timebox, and follow up with the script for the next part of the 1-2-4-All activity:

> *"Now, just like in the previous debriefing, pick up your stickies and find a new partner. Take 3 minutes now to share your takeaways with each other."*

Give the group 3 minutes, then signal the end of the timebox and follow up with this script to introduce the next part of the 1-2-4-All activity:

> *"Let's move on to the next step! With your partner, join another group. In your small group, take 4 minutes to discuss your takeaways and distill them down to 1–2 most interesting ones that are worth sharing with the larger group. Select a spokesperson to share your insights on behalf of the group in the final round."*

Give the groups 4 minutes, then signal the end of the timebox. For the remaining time in this timebox, ask each group to share their most salient insights, and finish by adding all their stickies to the "Key Takeaways" poster. See Chapter 13 for a collection of "Aha!" moments from my previous workshop participants for your reference. Over time you will notice that this simulation generates consistent "Aha!" moments in a variety of organizations, countries, and cultures.

CHAPTER 9   BE THE GAMEMASTER

Summary

This chapter concludes the *LEGO and Chocolate* simulation part of the book. Starting with the brief history of DevOps and DevSecOps (Chapter 3), I covered key learning concepts that are modeled in the simulation. Feel free to go back to Chapter 4 for a quick refresher in preparation for your training session. Rules of the game (Chapter 5) introduced you to the cast of characters and their interactions through the three rounds of the simulation. I also included several images from my previous workshops to clarify a few less trivial elements of the game. Chapter 6 was there to help you assemble all the game components and pack the right number of them for the size of your group. Chapter 7 offered you several options for setting up the space for this simulation. Unlike other workshops, this simulation's effectiveness depends on the balance of roles and groups in the room. Allow more players in the Operations role and you may miss out on the opportunity to showcase a bottleneck. Put too many people in the Business role and you can have participants sitting idle, getting bored in the first Sprint. The core of the book—two session plans and two facilitation scripts (Chapters 8 and 9)—gave you everything you need to successfully facilitate this gamified simulation and get your group excited about DevSecOps.

As you may have noticed already, the *LEGO and Chocolate* simulation stops without covering the Third Way of DevOps. In the following two chapters of this book, I will introduce you to my other coaching games, created to supplement learning and bring focus to this important topic.

In the next chapter, you will get to meet a group of Fear monsters from the *Fear in the Workplace* coaching game. These playful characters and real-life scenarios will help to carry out conversations about organizational dysfunctions, signs of pathological or fear-ridden culture, and signs of disengagement in teams and organizations at large. In Chapter 11 I will describe the *Safety in the Workplace* coaching game—a collection of 32

CHAPTER 9   BE THE GAMEMASTER

psychological safety practices (for individuals, teams, and leadership) that can positively influence organizational culture and start shifting it from pathological or bureaucratic cultures to a generative culture of experimentation and learning[2]—the Third Way of DevOps.

---

[2] Westrum, R. A typology of organizational cultures. https://www.ncbi.nlm.nih.gov/pmc/articles/PMC1765804/pdf/v013p0ii22.pdf

CHAPTER 10

Fear in the Workplace Coaching Game

As you already know from Chapter 1 of this book, I initially created the *Fear in the Workplace* game as a coaching tool for facilitating my work with culture dysfunctions in a technology group of an international retail brand. As I started sharing the game at conferences and meetups, I discovered that the game had a broader application as it resonated with people from various organizations and industry sectors.

However, it was the "State of DevOps" report (see the "Refocusing on Culture" section of Chapter 3) that inspired me to explore a potential link between this game and the *Third Way* of DevOps. Ultimately, I've augmented my DevSecOps workshops with additional content and introduced *Fear in the Workplace* as the concrete practice for enabling fearless conversations and paving the way toward a culture of experimentation, innovation, and learning.

In this chapter, I will share with you several important concepts highlighted by this game. You will get to meet various "Fear Monsters"—a collection of playful characters that represent miscellaneous signs of toxic culture in the workplace. We will review several anonymized real-life scenarios that I've collected in my engagements with corporate clients in the United States, United Kingdom, Ireland, Canada, and Japan. I will also share a suggested facilitation plan for a one-hour deep dive into the Third Way of DevOps with this game applied as a concrete practice.

CHAPTER 10   FEAR IN THE WORKPLACE COACHING GAME

Finally, I will describe a variety of ways that this coaching tool can be leveraged to facilitate conversations about toxic culture. It has proven to be instrumental in bringing the fears of the group "out in the open" so that the group can address them together in a playful and effective exploration. The versatility of this coaching tool will allow you to use it as an add-on to the *LEGO and Chocolate* workshop or offer it as a stand-alone session for diagnosing teams' dysfunctions. You will find that it can be helpful as a part of a change management strategy, where it can bring focus to the human side of change. By anticipating organizational fears that can be triggered by the upcoming changes, as well as selecting potential safety-enhancing actions from the *Safety in the Workplace* extension, you will be able to lead change with empathy and reduce the disruptive impact of change.

DISCLAIMER

As an ICF Credentialed Professional Certified Coach (PCC), I've been trained in multiple coaching styles (Co-Active, Positive Intelligence Coaching, Executive Coaching, ORSC). However, I do not have a background in therapy. The coaching game I am sharing with you in this chapter is a useful tool for teaching DevOps culture concepts as well as facilitating conversations on sensitive topics—the "elephants in the room."

However, it is neither a therapy tool nor a tool for trauma-informed coaching or counseling. Please use your judgment and situational awareness when introducing it to a new group.

CHAPTER 10   FEAR IN THE WORKPLACE COACHING GAME

When DevSecOps and Organizational Culture Collide

Take a minute to reflect on the current culture of the organizations you are in. If culture is defined by a set of values and observable behaviors, what is important in your culture? What do you see? Does your culture expect perfection, or does it invite sharing half-baked ideas that can be expanded upon? Is it risk-averse or open to experimentation? Does it respond to failures with finger-pointing and heavy management oversight, or with blameless postmortems, inquiry, and emphasis on organizational learning? Do you rely on informational backchannels, or do you have access to the information you need via a variety of self-service repositories, communities of practice, and cross-functional forums? If the majority of your answers align with pathological or bureaucratic cultures as defined by Ron Westrum,[1] you have a lot to do!

Being intentional about creating a culture of experimentation and learning is essential to the success of your DevSecOps initiative. Your organization may bring in new automation tools and cloud infrastructure, but if you see a long-lived DevOps team on your org chart—it missed the point. A short-lived DevOps team may be OK as an interim strategy with a "train-the-trainer" learning model (a.k.a. "enabling team" in the Team Topologies[2] terms). However, creating a long-lived DevOps team only perpetuates departmental silos and further limits the flow of information across internal boundaries of an organization.

According to Ron Westrum's studies, the quality of information flow is tightly linked to a level of safety in the culture of the organization. Through the lens of the first two Ways of DevOps, one can observe how adopting new practices for amplifying the feedback loop and attempting to facilitate

---

[1] Westrum, Ron. (2014). The study of information flow: A personal journey. *Safety Science*. 67. 58–63. 10.1016/j.ssci.2014.01.009.
[2] Skelton, M., & Pais, M. (2019). *Team Topologies: Organizing Business and Technology Teams for Fast Flow*, IT Revolution Press

cooperation between development and operations can often collide with existing organizational culture. This is where the Third Way of DevOps comes into play, putting emphasis on the following cultural change:

> *"The Third Way is about creating a culture that fosters two things: continual experimentation, taking risks and learning from failure; and understanding that repetition and practice is the prerequisite to mastery."*
>
> —Gene Kim, "The Three Ways: The Principles Underpinning DevOps"[3]

It is worth noting that the negative impact of a risk-averse culture on the progress of DevOps implementations was called out in the 2021 "State of DevOps" report by Puppet (see Figure 10-1). According to this research, the percentage of highly evolved DevOps organizations stating that their culture discourages risks was two times lower than that of the low-evolution respondents.

The Third Way of DevOps describes precisely what Ron Westrum calls the "generative culture"—a highly cooperative, performance-oriented culture in which the risks are shared and transparency about problems is welcomed and encouraged. If this is your starting point for DevSecOps implementation, you are in luck (and in the minority). For the rest of us, the cultures of our organizations are far from the ideal. Often, our current cultures have various degrees of a phenomenon that gave the name to this chapter—fear in the workplace. What could go wrong with the presence of fear in your organizational culture? What if in your organization fear is not only tolerated but also perceived as an effective way to drive up performance? I've met several managers in my career who truly believed that fear was a great motivator for their direct reports . . . Sigh.

---

[3] https://itrevolution.com/articles/the-three-ways-principles-underpinning-devops/

Symptoms and Impact of Fear in Organizations

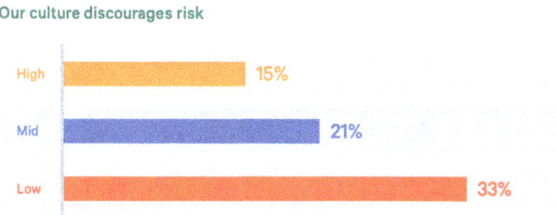

Figure 10-1. *Percentage of risk-discouraging cultures in organizations with high, mid, and low levels of DevOps evolution. Source: 2021 State of DevOps report by Puppet*

As noted in Ron Westrum's study, fear cripples the flow of information in an organization. This effect is known under many lovely nicknames ("success theater," "watermelon status," "Mum effect," etc.). It shows up as the tendency of subordinates to distort the information that they convey to their superiors, communicating upward in a way that minimizes the severity of the information shared.

On an individual level, fear blocks our ability to think strategically, consider other people's ideas, collaborate, or expand our circle of trust. Instead, it heightens our senses and conditions us to respond with a limited range of actions: fight, flight, freeze, or fawn. Daniel Goleman, in his book *Emotional Intelligence: Why It Can Matter More than IQ*, coined this effect the "Amygdala Hijack." He used this term to describe the emotional, physical, and chemical reactions triggered in our body and our brain in response to a real physical danger, or under a perceived psychological threat. How might these four fear responses show up in the workplace? Here is my attempt to map out these four responses to some of the typical dysfunctions in organizational culture (see Figure 10-2).

CHAPTER 10　FEAR IN THE WORKPLACE COACHING GAME

Figure 10-2. How four Fs of fear show up as dysfunctions in organizational cultures

Acting out the *fight response* are the *Brilliant Jerks*[4]—always right, constantly interrupting others during group discussions. People feel bad after interacting with these domineering, competitive, and intimidating team members. As brilliant as they might be, they are toxic to their teams and the organization.

The *freeze response* at work shows up as *Disengagement*, doing a bare minimum. According to the 2022 "State of the Global Workplace" report by Gallup, 79% of global workers are emotionally disengaged at work. The *flight response* shows up when the most skillful and most talented people in the organization begin to turn in their resignation notices in response to the negative changes in organizational culture. The *fawn response* of *Conflict Avoidance* is seen when people don't feel safe to voice their divergent opinion and instead choose to "go with the flow."

---

[4] https://www.inc.com/jim-schleckser/why-netflix-doesn-t-tolerate-brilliant-jerks.html

CHAPTER 10   FEAR IN THE WORKPLACE COACHING GAME

Here are a few additional examples of the symptoms of fear in the workplace (see Figure 10-3):

- *Gossip and rumors* – information mostly flows through the backchannels.

- *Risk avoidance* – running a pre-meeting before the meeting, rejecting new ideas, clinging to "we've always done it this way."

- *Success theater* – every project is "Green," and bad news seldom travels up the hierarchy.

- *Over-functioning* – consistently working extra hours, skipping lunch, responding to non-emergency work emails/messages during family time, etc.

- *Blaming and finger-pointing* – always looking for a culprit.

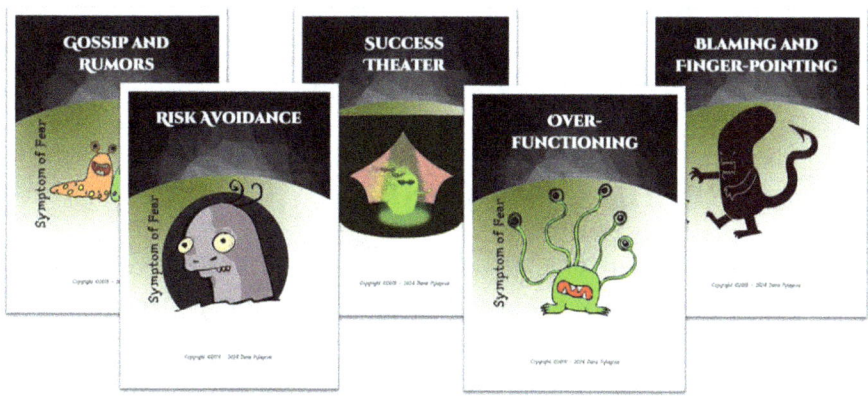

Figure 10-3. *More symptoms of fear in organizations*

185

How many of these symptoms have you observed at your current or former employer? If your count is anywhere between three and five, you are not alone! These symptoms are so widespread that one of them even showed up in the 2018 "State of DevOps" report by Puppet. In this report, the same questions related to the penetration level of DevOps practices were given to team members, management, and C-level executives. The difference in perception was startling! There was on average a 58% gap between what the teams on the ground knew and what was reported to the C-level executives. Welcome to the Success Theater!

Fear-Inducing Organizational Changes

Up to this point, I've shared with you examples of several fear symptoms that can be observed in organizations with various degrees of pathological or bureaucratic cultures. What do you think happens when these organizations begin a large-scale transformation initiative, execute a re-org, or acquire or merge with another organization? Aside from the most obvious—the Fear of Change—what are some of the other organizational fears that can emerge in the process, and potentially get in the way?

DevSecOps Transformations

Let's take a DevSecOps transformation example (see Figure 10-4). There are several potential fears that can show up for the individual contributors involved in this change. A few fundamental shifts in the ways of working that DevSecOps brings are a necessity of collaboration across the functional silos, as well as a preference for moving away from a narrow, specialized skillset of team members to a broader T-shaped skills model.

CHAPTER 10   FEAR IN THE WORKPLACE COACHING GAME

Figure 10-4. *Common fears in DevSecOps transformations (individual contributors)*

For starters, there is a steep learning curve associated with DevSecOps. The DASA DevOps Competence Model[5] deems four skills areas and eight knowledge areas essential for a DevSecOps team's success. If team members are expected to upskill on their own, and under a tight deadline, they are likely to feel overwhelmed by the *Fear of Lack of Expertise* and the *Fear of Failure*, and even be concerned about *Losing their Jobs*.

For mid-level management, DevSecOps (or even Agile) transformations can be associated with some of the fears featured in Figure 10-5. Empowering the teams and creating space for them to self-organize are some of the ways that management is expected to show up differently in Agile and DevSecOps, potentially heightening managers' own *Fear of Losing Control, Fear of Losing their Circle of Influence,* or even *Fear of Obsolescence*. Hiring new team members with cutting-edge DevSecOps skills can often mean hiring from Gen Z, learning to manage a very different generation of workers, and triggering a *Fear of Gen Z*.

---

[5] https://www.devopsagileskills.org/dasa-competence-model/

CHAPTER 10   FEAR IN THE WORKPLACE COACHING GAME

Figure 10-5. Common fears in Agile or DevSecOps transformations (management)

Mergers and Acquisitions

The next collection of Fear cards (see Figure 10-6) describes a scenario that had unfolded in front of my eyes and became an unfortunate inspiration for creating the first version of this game. A small successful startup with a generative company culture had been acquired by a large traditional organization with a bureaucratic culture. The leadership team of the startup was excited about the idea of a "reverse cultural takeover," envisioning a real possibility to inspire a positive culture change in the larger organization.

Figure 10-6. Common fears during post-merger and acquisition restructuring

When I joined this organization six months after the acquisition, the first thing that struck me was the very strong presence of the remains of each individual company's culture (the *Company Ghosts*). Just like oil and balsamic vinegar in one bottle, the two cultures were not mixing. Developers from the former startup were afraid of *Losing their Autonomy* and felt like they were *Not Being Heard* by the new management. Across the board, the *Lack of Transparency* and the *Fear of Major Layoffs* were impacting morale and the company culture.

Reorgs and Layoffs, Is There a Better Way?

Coincidentally, as I was working on this chapter, two of the organizations I've been closely connected with have undertaken major restructuring and eliminated several Agile roles. As I was processing this heartbreaking news, I started reflecting on all the layoffs I witnessed over the course of my career. Some of them were carried out with careful planning, in a more humane and empathetic way.

CHAPTER 10   FEAR IN THE WORKPLACE COACHING GAME

What if there were a way to include an open conversation about fears as one of the steps in a change management approach? How might a proactive conversation about fears that can be triggered because of a change potentially influence the approach to executing this change?

I brought these questions and a deck of the *Fear in the Workplace* cards with me to the Agile Coach Camp in Raleigh, North Carolina, and proposed an Open Space session to experiment. My hypothesis was that by opening conversations about potential future fears from an upcoming organizational change, it would become possible to bring in more empathy toward those affected by it.

We split the session participants into two groups and asked them to imagine that they were in charge of introducing an organizational change. The first group was asked to think about potential fears that can show up as a response to introducing Agile. The second group was asked to explore fears that can be triggered by reorgs or layoffs.

What I observed at the coach camp was promising! Participants engaged in deep discussions, eventually shifting from uncovering fears to strategizing how to minimize their impact. Here are a few quotes from their feedback:

> *"Having the cards on the table makes the process of dealing with them much more concrete."*
>
> *"Putting people at the center of change."*
>
> *"This is great for equitable decision-making. People come first."*
>
> *"Playing the card game draws attention to multiple fears for situations that I had not thought of."*
>
> *"The Fear cards created a human connection to the change and influenced the approaches we would take."*
>
> *"Increased my vision of fear-based empathy building (scope, impact, nature)."*

CHAPTER 10   FEAR IN THE WORKPLACE COACHING GAME

You can see the results of this experiment in Figures 10-7 and 10-8.

Figure 10-7. *Exploring potential fears from introducing Agile (Agile Coach Camp, Sep. 2023)*

Figure 10-8. *Exploring potential fears when planning a reorg (Agile Coach Camp, Sep. 2023)*

The results of this first experiment left me optimistic and excited to continue experimenting. As you read this chapter, I hope it will inspire you to experiment with bringing more empathy into the organizational changes you are about to drive. Good or bad, a change will trigger fears. Explore them proactively and plan careful interventions to mitigate their impact on those affected by change.[6]

---

[6] To learn more about change management, check out Kotter (https://www.kotterinc.com/methodology/8-steps/) and ADKAR (https://www.prosci.com/methodology/adkar) models.

CHAPTER 10   FEAR IN THE WORKPLACE COACHING GAME

Team-level Fears

The final collection of fears and fear symptoms I'd like to share with you in this chapter are the ones I observed in teams with low levels of psychological safety. As the team members don't feel safe to share their ideas, speak up, or to ask questions, they are affected by a *Fear of Ridicule* or a *Fear of being Invalidated*. These fears can be present if the team is still new, the team members haven't had a chance to get to know each other, or haven't yet gelled as a team. These fears can also show up because of some "lessons learned" or "scars" from the past (either on this team or on the previous one).

When team members experience (or observe) that *Initiatives Are Squashed,* over time they become less inclined to take them, developing protective behavior known as *Learned Helplessness.* At the same time, if the learning opportunities are low, team members may also experience the *Fear of Stagnating* in their careers.

Figure 10-9. *Fear and Fear Symptoms in a team with low psychological safety*

193

CHAPTER 10   FEAR IN THE WORKPLACE COACHING GAME

Facilitating the Fear in the Workplace Game

In addition to *Fear* and *Fear Symptoms* cards, the deck contains sixteen *ClassifyMe* cards with anonymized real-life quotes of the statements made by employees of organizations with toxic cultures (see Figure 10-10). Some of these may sound very familiar to you. That is the intent.

These selected scenarios sound "close enough" to be relevant and generic enough to not be personal or painful to explore. I usually ask the team to pick a first example at random, play a sample round to understand the dynamic of the game, and to "meet the monsters." When using the game to address a particular team's dysfunction, I instruct the team to then flip these *ClassifyMe* cards face up and vote on the card that they collectively would like to explore in the next round.

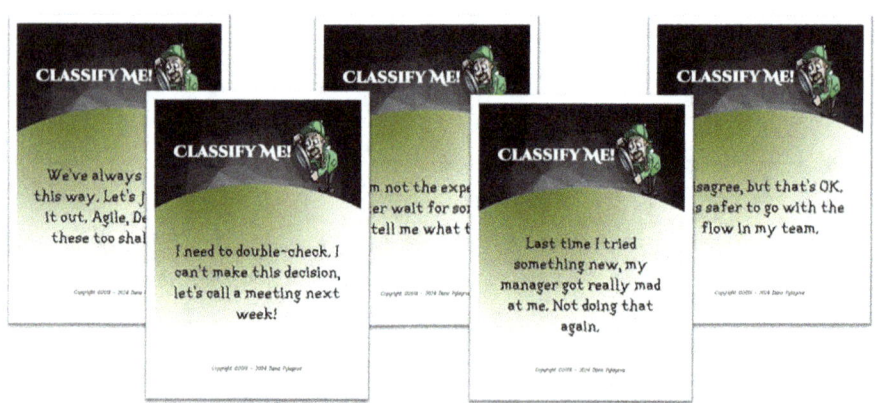

Figure 10-10. *Example of ClassifyMe cards included in the game*

Option One: A Competitive Game

`Group size: small`
`Duration: 15 min`

CHAPTER 10   FEAR IN THE WORKPLACE COACHING GAME

One of the easiest ways to start the conversation about fears is by playing a simple game with your team (based on the "Cards Against Humanity" dynamic):

1. Deal the *Fear* and *Fear Symptoms* cards to all players. Place the *ClassifyMe* cards in the middle (face down).

2. Have one player (the Reader) read a *ClassifyMe* card and others select the best matching *Fear* or *Symptom* card from their hands.

3. Have a conversation about each match and have the Reader pick the best match for their *ClassifyMe* card.

4. The player with the best match wins the *ClassifyMe* card. Discard all other Fear cards proposed in this round. Continue the game, rotating the role of the Reader.

5. Do a debrief with the group after the game is over. Help them reflect on the connections they've made with their own workplace.

Option Two: A Collaborative Game

Group size: small
Duration: 15-30 min

Less dynamic than the first option, the collaborative version of the game works as a fear-diagnostic activity. Many teams will prefer to use the collaborative version of this game for two main reasons.

First, there are always several fears or symptoms that can be traced back to a selected *ClassifyMe* card. In fact, a conversation becomes richer as the team proceeds to build a full story. Cards codify a variety of fears/fear symptoms and help the team explore their potential causation.

In these discussions, while fighting against "fear monsters," the team comes together, develops empathy, and starts to open up for deeper conversations. As one of the participants noted in his feedback: "Looking at fears like this puts the problem before us vs. between us. Unites vs. divides."

Second, this version makes all fears offered by each player valid, as players don't discard the *Fear/Symptoms* cards (as they do in the competitive version of the game. Instead, each player adds a card and adds to the story constructed by the team.

Option Three: A Short Activity for an Extra-large Group

Group size: extra large
Duration: 5 min

What if your group is large and the timebox is short? That was exactly my challenge in the lightning keynote at Agile + DevOps East 2018! I used this deck to lead 400 people through their first discussion about fears—in just 5 minutes! Here is what worked for me:

1. Distribute a fear/fear symptom card to every other participant.

2. Briefly introduce the impact of fear on our ability to innovate and connect Third Way of DevOps with Psychological Safety (2 min).

3. Invite them to form pairs or triads and ask each other three questions (2 min):

- What is your name?
- What is your role?
- How often have you observed this fear in your workplace?

4. In the last minute, invite them to continue this conversation with their partners from the exercise, or bring the conversation back to their workplace.

Teaching the Third Way of DevOps with the Fear in the Workplace Game

When using *Fear in the Workplace* as a coaching tool for introducing the Third Way of DevOps, use Table 10-1 as your guide and adjust the timeline based on your group's level of engagement and overall timebox.

Start with introducing the basic concepts. Pay attention to the energy of the group. If people are engaged in fear-diagnostic activities and curious about each scenario, offer them extra time as an opportunity to deepen the conversations. Encourage them to consider each scenario from multiple perspectives: the person who is vocalizing the concerns, their manager, their peers, etc. If energy and engagements are low, advance the group to the final activity—25/10 Liberating Structure with the following invitation: *"If You Were 10 Times Bolder, What Big Ideas Would You Experiment With in Your Organization?"*

CHAPTER 10 FEAR IN THE WORKPLACE COACHING GAME

Table 10-1. *Session Plan for a 1-hour Third Way of DevOps Training with Fear in the Workplace Game*

Starting Time (Duration)	Description	Goal of This Activity
0:00 (5 min)	**Turn and Talk** Invite participants to find a new partner and share with them the answers to the following two questions: 1. What is your name/role? 2. How is psychological safety important in the work that you do?	C1: Connection: Connect participants with each other and the topic.
0:05 (8 min)	**Introduce the topic.** Introduce the participants to the fundamental ideas from the Third Way of DevOps, Ron Westrum's typology of organizational cultures, and give examples of organizations with pathological, bureaucratic, or generative cultures (see Chapter 3). You may choose to use the slides from Figure 10-11. Describe the findings from the 2019 "State of DevOps" report that connected psychological safety with software delivery and operational performance. Share a quote from the "Unicorn Project" that positions it as a Fourth Ideal of work. Bring everyone's attention to the "absence of fear" that is required for solving problems (see Figure 10-12).	C2: Concept: Present the key learning concepts

CHAPTER 10 FEAR IN THE WORKPLACE COACHING GAME

0:13 (4 min)	**Setup** Introduce the *Fear in the Workplace* game. Invite participants at each table to do the following: • distribute evenly all *Fear* cards and place *ClassifyMe* cards in the middle of the table, face down. • Ask one player (the Reader) to read a *ClassifyMe* card out loud. • Invite participants to work together at their tables as one coaching team, and using the cards in their hands, identify observable fear symptoms, as well as select the fears that they feel are the most relevant to the current *ClassifyMe* card scenario. • Instruct participants to make a hypothesis about the collection of *Fears* at play for this scenario (for the person in the scenario, their peers, and their manager).		Game onboarding
0:17 (10 min)	**Fear in the Workplace Game round** Start a ten-minute timer and walk around the room, observing the groups as they engage in the first round of the coaching game. When the group feels they've explored a scenario, they can discard the *ClassifyMe* card, take back the *Fear* cards from their table, and continue with the next *ClassifyMe* scenario.		C3: Concrete practice:

(continued)

199

CHAPTER 10   FEAR IN THE WORKPLACE COACHING GAME

Table 10-1. (*continued*)

Starting Time (Duration)	Description	Goal of This Activity
0:27 (12 min)	**Debriefing** Apply your favorite debriefing approach, 1-2-4-All or W3 Liberating Structures (see Chapter 12). Help the participants reflect on their experience of the game. What surprised them? What has the game enabled? Where do they see an opportunity to connect the discussion to their own workplaces?	C4: Conclusion: Share individual reflections and connect learning to the scenarios that may play out at their workplace.
0:39 (16 min)	**Finish on the high note – 25x10 Liberating Structure** Invitation: *"If You Were 10 Times Bolder, What Big Ideas Would You Experiment With In Your Organization?"* Distribute index cards and explain the next activity – 25x10: *"When I finish explaining, you will take one minute to write your best idea on your index card in response to the invitation provided. I will give you a signal, and you will start passing your index cards to other people in the room, exchanging the cards without reading.*	C4: Conclusion: Inspire action and identify the most impactful ideas from the group.

CHAPTER 10   FEAR IN THE WORKPLACE COACHING GAME

	When I say 'STOP,' you will read the index card that is in your hand now, flip the card to the other side, and rate it on a scale from one to five: one – not feeling it, don't think it will be impactful five – WOW! I am all in, would love to see this happen! When I say 'SHUFFLE,' you will start passing the cards again without reading again, until I say 'STOP.' Then you will read and rate the cards again. We will do it five times."	
	Facilitate the five rounds of the shuffle and rate activities and then provide the following instructions:	
	"You should all have a card with five ratings now. Go ahead: add them up, write the result on the card, and circle it. We are going to hear the top ten ideas from this group now! These ten ideas belong to the entire group now! Someone came up with them, but you all as a group reviewed it, and provided your rating.	
	Do we have anyone with the card that was rated as 25? Please join us at the front of the room! 24? . . . "	
	Continue inviting people with their index cards to the front of the room, until you have 10 people selected. Ask them to read out loud the ideas that are written on their cards.	
0:55	**Buffer time**	Buffer Time
5 min	Use the buffer time to expand a debriefing, if needed	

CHAPTER 10   FEAR IN THE WORKPLACE COACHING GAME

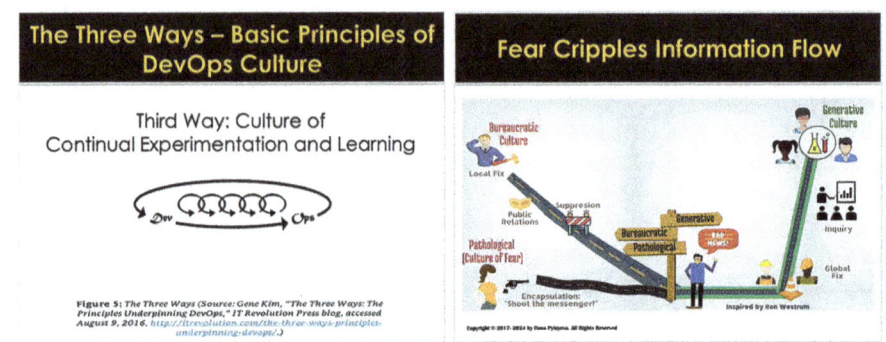

Figure 10-11. *Third Way of DevOps slide and Ron Westrum's typology of organizational culture*

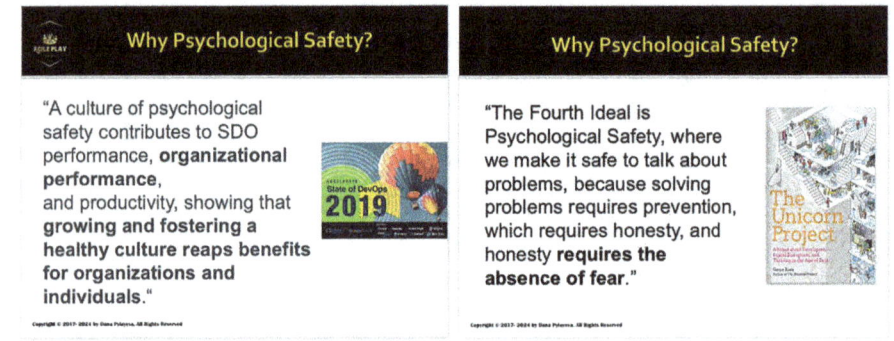

Figure 10-12. *Slides for connecting psychological safety with DevSecOps*

Summary

In this chapter, I introduced you to my *Fear in the Workplace* coaching game and shared a few examples of facilitating fearless conversations with teams of individual contributors, change agents, and a wide audience of conference participants. I shared a sample facilitation plan for using this game in the context of the *Third Way of DevOps* training, where it can enable open conversations about the "elephant in the room" and pave a path toward creating a culture of experimentation, innovation, and learning.

CHAPTER 10　　FEAR IN THE WORKPLACE COACHING GAME

In the following chapter, I will share with you the *Safety in the Workplace* collection of psychological safety enhancers that can be used as an action-focused follow-up to the diagnostic dialog initiated by the *Fear in the Workplace* game.

CHAPTER 11

Safety in the Workplace Coaching Game

In this chapter, I will introduce you to the *Safety in the Workplace* coaching game—a collection of ideas, practices, and tools that have proven to be effective at enabling the culture of experimentation and learning essential to the success of the DevSecOps initiatives. Designed as an action-oriented extension to the *Fear in the Workplace* game, this set includes the tried-and-true practices from my own experience coaching teams and leaders in organizations internationally as well as ideas and inspirations from the work of Amy C. Edmondson, Brené Brown, Jim and Michele McCarthy, Heidi Helfand, Keith McCandless, Henry Lipmanowicz, and many others.

I don't expect you to read this chapter in one go. Instead, refer to it when playing the *Safety in the Workplace* game and coming across a safety enhancer that you don't recognize from your own coaching practice. All safety enhancers in this set are split into three categories: *individual*, *team*, and *leadership*. These category names suggest the primary owner for each of the safety enhancers. You will find them by their **intense emphasis** style in the text of this chapter and by a corresponding icon on each card in the deck.

CHAPTER 11   SAFETY IN THE WORKPLACE COACHING GAME

As you continue to inspire actions with coaching conversations using the *Safety in the Workplace* card deck, you will discover that, over time, the area of direct control over the implementation of each individual safety practice will start expanding. Inspired by the successes of their previous experiments, people will become more willing to "poke the system," stepping into informal leadership roles, applying leadership safety enhancers from this deck, and shifting the culture toward the generative culture of learning. Let's dive right into it!

How to Use This Game

As you discovered in the previous chapter, the *Fear in the Workplace* game offers a safe and playful way to facilitate open conversations about a toxic culture that might be present in an organization or a team. It acts as a diagnostic tool, helping participants to uncover the fears/fear symptoms that drive the dysfunctional behaviors in their environments, and to brainstorm the way forward. And this is exactly where many less experienced teams get stuck, having access to only the actions and ideas that they've tried before! The *Safety in the Workplace* extension deck serves as a mini catalog of practices that can be applied by individuals, teams, and leaders. Think of it as a buffet of choices that can expand one's range of interventions to experiment with in the situation at hand.

When used as an add-on to *Fear in the Workplace*, it allows you to continue the collaborative nature of the exploration, inviting the entire team to participate in an action-selection process, driving the collective ownership of change. You may want to use a Lean Coffee style of discussion, focusing the conversation on one fear/symptom at a time (see Figure 11-1).

CHAPTER 11   SAFETY IN THE WORKPLACE COACHING GAME

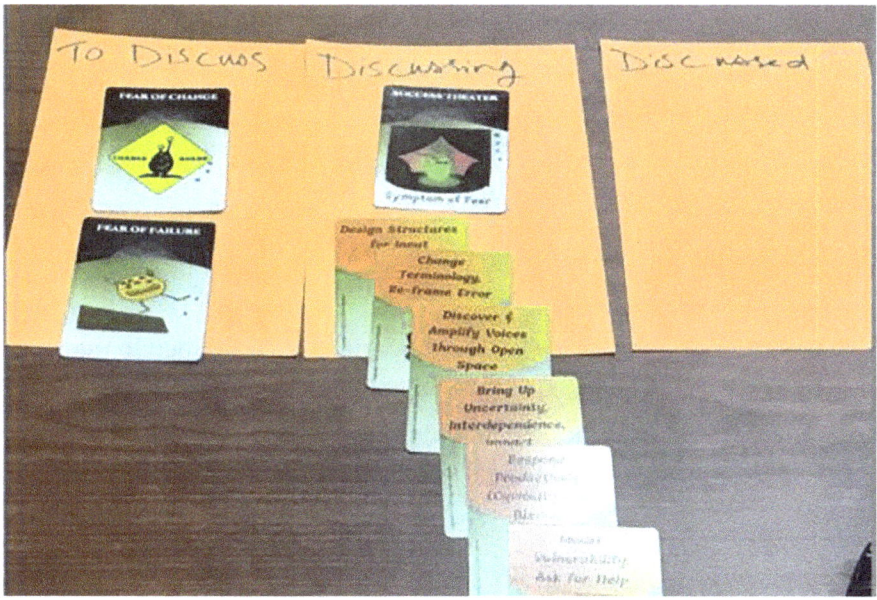

Figure 11-1. Facilitating discussion—Lean Coffee style

1. Use your favorite prioritization technique to order Fear cards for discussion and place them into the "To Discuss" column.

2. Move the topmost Fear card into the "Discussing" column and invite everyone on the team to select a safety enhancer that they feel would help to alleviate this specific Fear. Invite everyone to share their perspective about the selected safety enhancers and agree on one or two specific actions that the group would be willing to experiment with as the next step.

3. Reflect as a team: Is this action in our control, or do we need to find a way to influence/persuade someone? Who will be driving this experiment? By when? How would we know this experiment was successful?

4. Move the Fear card to the "Discussed" column and continue with the next card in your "Fear backlog."

Consider using one of the Liberating Structures described in the appendix (1-2-4-All or Conversation Cafe, for example) to further improve the engagement of the group and create space where both the introverts and the extraverts can equally contribute their perspectives.

Safety Enhancers Collection

While some of the safety enhancers in the collection are self-explanatory, others may be unfamiliar to your group. The rest of this chapter will run through each individual safety enhancer card to help you understand the practice or idea that can help increase the likelihood of a positive outcome in the group of people you coach. Don't think of these practices as silver bullets; instead, treat them as an inspiration, and an invitation to run an experiment with the group. While a deep dive into each practice is beyond the scope of this book, I will point you to additional available reading when referencing a practice described elsewhere.

SCARF® model

When creating this coaching game, I chose to organize all safety enhancers roughly around the five domains of the SCARF model. Created in 2008 by Dr. David Rock, the co-founder of the Neuroleadership Institute, this model describes five social domains that activate the same threat or reward responses in our brains that we rely on for physical survival.

"SCARF" is an acronym that stands for Status, Certainty, Autonomy, Relatedness, and Fairness. According to Dr. Rock's research, when any of the five models' domains are affected in a positive way, our brain triggers a reward response. We feel good about the situation, and are open to exploring alternative points of view, ready to experiment with new ideas, and ready to build new connections (also called out in the broaden-and-build theory[1]). Every time these domains get affected in a negative way, our brain triggers a threat response and causes us to experience the "amygdala hijack" with the infamous Fight, Flight, Freeze, or Fawn reactions. You've already read about these threat responses in the previous chapter.

Being aware of these social domains is a must for anyone who works with people. The SCARF model and *Safety in the Workplace* game can help us proactively seek out tools and practices to raise the possibility of activating the brain's reward responses for ourselves, our teams, and the leaders we work with.

As you continue learning more about these safety enhancers, don't get hung up on the specific domain I aligned them with in this book. Some of them may have the ability to impact more than one domain! I will be calling out a secondary (or tertiary) domain as we go and will encourage you to reflect on their application outside of the domains I aligned them with.

Status

What kind of status are we talking about here? The first kind that comes to mind is the relative seniority of one's position in an organization. In addition to the formal status, one may be concerned about their status as an expert, an authority on a specific topic, their social standing, etc. One of the most common examples of "status preservation" behavior in

---

[1] Fredrickson BL. The broaden-and-build theory of positive emotions. Philos Trans R Soc Lond B Biol Sci. 2004 Sep 29;359(1449):1367-78. doi: 10.1098/rstb.2004.1512. PMID: 15347528; PMCID: PMC1693418.

a workplace is holding back a question, driven by an assumption that everyone else already knows the answer. Another common example—struggling with a particular assignment and not asking for help, assuming that someone competent in this role "should" already know how to do it. Sounds familiar? I know, I've been there! Let's look at several practices that can help generate positive responses in this domain (see Figure 11-2).

Model Asking Clarifying Questions

To this day, I remember the first time I felt the importance of this *individual* practice when working with an experienced product manager. She made a point to ask questions about anything that sounded even remotely vague in our team's discussions. Most of the time, others would chime in as well after her clarifying question with, "Yes, I was confused about that too!" Initially, people simply appreciated her for asking the questions. Over time, the culture of the team started to shift, and more team members started asking questions as they felt safe to do so.

Figure 11-2. Psychological Safety Enhancers related to Status

Ask For & Provide Candid Feedback

Everyone knows how status-crashing and threat-triggering the feedback we get during annual performance appraisals can be. Many years ago, I was introduced to a very sad acronym, describing an employee's typical reaction to 360 feedback - an anonymous feedback collection tool, commonly used for performance management in large corporations. This reaction is known by the acronym SARA (Shock, Anger, Resistance, Acceptance). Unlike the traditional feedback process, *Ask for & provide Candid Feedback* **individual** safety enhancer describes a drastically different approach. Instead of pushing the feedback on someone once a year, the feedback is invited by the recipient with the intent to help improve on a specific action, a behavior, or an artifact.

This safety enhancer is very effective in a peer-to-peer feedback exchange and can be very powerful when modeled by a more senior member of the group. I've experienced this when coaching a team of leaders and observing the tribe lead often asking his direct reports in a Slack channel: "I'd like your feedback on this, please" immediately after delivering a speech at the all-hands meeting, iterating on the strategy, etc. Seeing this relentless focus on improvement, others (me included) felt safe to ask for frequent feedback on their work as well.

Model Vulnerability: Ask for Help

I have observed this ***individual*** practice to be especially difficult to embrace for highly technical team members who take pride in being experts in their field. However, as there is a steep learning curve associated with DevSecOps, not asking for help can significantly impede the overall progress of the initiative. This safety enhancer is an invitation to lean into a beginner's mindset, pairing up with peers from your group, as well as your counterparts from other departments, reaching across the functional silos. "Ask for Help" is also known as one of the Core Protocols, introduced by Jim and Michele McCarthy as the set of guiding principles for a high-performing team culture.[2]

Another useful facilitation technique that supports asking for help at scale is a Liberating Structure called WINFY[3] ("What I need from you"). This facilitation technique enables people from different functions to clearly articulate the support they need and receive commitment, clarification, or refusal to help in a transparent, respectful, and unambiguous way. You may want to experiment with this approach in your organization, especially while dealing with DevSecOps transformation challenges.

---

[2] https://thecoreprotocols.org/protocols/askforhelp
[3] https://www.liberatingstructures.com/24-what-i-need-from-you-winfy/

Manage by "Not Knowing"

This ***leadership*** practice has a lot in common with the spirit of the previous three safety enhancers; however, this one requires a certain level of vulnerability from a leader employing it. Eileen Fisher, the founder of a famous women's clothing brand, describes her leadership style as a "Don't Knower."[4] You might have also heard about another great example of this practice from David Marquet's book *Turn the Ship Around*,[5] in which he described how he had no choice but to rely on the knowledge and experience of his crew when he found himself appointed as a captain of a submarine which he knew nothing about.

When leaders can let go of their own "expert mindset" and trust the experience and knowledge of their people, they become a true catalyst of change, creating a culture where people feel appreciated, invited to contribute their ideas, and inspired to work toward a common goal. According to fifteen members of the Forbes Coaches Council,[6] admitting to not having all the answers and actively seeking input from others can lead to a higher level of innovation and creativity in the group.

While I aligned these four safety-enhancers mentioned above with the Status domain, you can argue that they can also positively influence Relatedness by enabling collective learning and knowledge sharing, and promoting uninhibited information exchange in the group.

Speak Candidly about Ambiguous Threats

The next ***individual*** safety enhancer deals with an obstructed information flow in an organization, specifically in the case of potential failure, someone's hunch, uncertainties, or easily dismissed observations. It is

---

[4] https://www.huffpost.com/entry/be-a-dont-knower-one-of-e_b_7242468

[5] Marquet, D.L. (2013) Turn the Ship Around!: A True Story of Turning Followers into Leaders (Portfolio; 1st edition)

[6] https://www.forbes.com/sites/forbescoachescouncil/2021/03/09/how-to-get-comfortable-with-not-knowing-15-leadership-tips

a reminder to individual team members to share "weak signals" about potential problems that they may have come across in their work.

One of the teams I worked with embraced the "See something, say something" motto as part of their team norms to remind, encourage, and make it safe for the team members to speak up about potential issues. Not surprisingly, this norm was added after the team had experienced one of the (preventable) release failures. This turned into a great reminder for more junior team members, who otherwise felt more threatened by the prospect of "losing status" if their observations turned out to be wrong.

Share Concerns Cross-Hierarchy

This ***team*** practice expands on the previous one by encouraging the entire team to be aware of the need to raise issues, embrace transparency, and seek help with impediment removal early and often. This practice is especially important in DevSecOps transformations, where as an organization we recognize the need to challenge existing functional silos and reshape the flow of information so that we can collectively optimize the end-to-end flow of value.

As a coach working with a team, or as a more experienced member of the group, you can help the team embrace this practice by modeling it, by inviting others to think about potential issues, or by applying the safety enhancer, described next.

Amplify Signal ("Helpful Cassandras")

As you may recall from Greek mythology, Cassandra had the ability to predict the future and was cursed to have no one believe in her prophecies. How many times have you been in a meeting, trying to say something, or hearing someone trying to bring everyone's attention to a specific issue, only to be ignored by the rest of the group? This is one of the examples of Cassandra's effect.

Depending on the power dynamic of the group, you may need to pay closer attention to ideas and voices in the discussion that need to be amplified. Newer members of your group and introverts in the room may need help getting the airtime to add their ideas to the group discussion, or to have their ideas acknowledged and heard by the group. Strong facilitation as well as the use of Liberating Structures can be instrumental in bringing this *leadership* safety enhancer to life.

Certainty

Have you ever felt overwhelmed by a large new effort when you didn't know the exact steps involved in getting it done (DevSecOps transformation, anyone?) How about when you started a new job or joined a new team?

Our brains crave predictability; we feel safer when we know what to expect. The practices in this section (see Figure 11-3) can help with increasing certainty by clarifying the organizational norms around collaboration, information flow, and level of transparency as well as a level of tolerance toward failure, ambiguity, experimentation, and empirical learning.

Figure 11-3. *Psychological Safety Enhancers related to Certainty*

Practice Heavy Transparency

This ***leadership*** practice becomes critical in times of uncertainty and organizational change. In my career, I've been through several re-orgs. While all of them introduced some level of anxiety about the future, several of them were carried out better than others. In the less painful ones, leaders approached the re-orgs with extreme consideration and carefully crafted, compassionate, and transparent communication.

Another example I can share is from the times I was working at a Japanese company, one well-known in the e-commerce space. The founder of the company had been hosting a 30-minute all-company meeting every Monday sharing strategy and company financials as well as inviting important updates from various parts of the organization (good and bad). This level of transparency was beneficial to the organization for increasing certainty at all levels as well as demonstrating a lot of trust from the leadership team. As Bridgewater Associates founder Ray Dalio, who's been known for his "radical transparency" culture noted in his *Principles*[7] *book:*

> *"Giving people the right to see things for themselves is better than forcing them to rely on information processed for them by others."*

Bring Up Uncertainty, Interdependence, Impact

This ***individual*** safety enhancer can be applied by a team member when faced with a situation or effort they feel unclear about, or when dealing with potential blocking dependencies that others are unaware of. It can also be applied by a leader to ease the discomfort or fear of failure in

---

[7] Dalio, R. (2017). Principles: Life and Work. (Avid Reader Press / Simon & Schuster)

a group at the beginning of a new initiative. I've read about it in Amy Edmondson's book and had an opportunity to experience the power of it first-hand in my recent community work.

A well-known international conference I was leading had to start using a brand-new submission system. The team was nervous and was feeling the pressure to do it right from the get-go. When I noticed that, the first thing I did was to recognize the team's feelings and acknowledge that we were about to lean into uncertainty and experimentation. I invited everyone to be patient with their teams, with the leadership team, and with themselves as we were going to figure this out together. Even this simple acknowledgment and reassurance was enough to ease the initial concerns of the group, reducing the threat response that was flooding their brains. In addition, it opened a conversation about the support they needed from me to move forward with confidence and led to a creative solution—running a review Hackathon.

Host Failure Parties (Fail–Learn–Move on)

Focused on destigmatizing failure and turning it into a learning opportunity, this *team* practice also increases certainty for team members, making it clear that they will not be punished for making genuine mistakes. A few of the organizations I've been a part of have hosted regular internal failure parties to develop a habit of speaking openly about failures and sharing learning outside of the immediate team affected by them.

There have also been several industry-wide events (Fail Festival,[8] FailFest[9]) that celebrate failure as a "mark of leadership, innovation, and risk-taking in pushing the boundaries of what is possible." Etsy, the global online marketplace, is one of the organizations well knows in the DevSecOps culture circuits for its experiments with cultivating blameless

---

[8] https://failfestival.org/
[9] https://failfest.us/

culture. To this day, the company continues a tradition of giving out the annual "three-armed sweater" award to an engineer or a team that turned the biggest failure into innovation and a learning opportunity.[10]

Frame Silence as an Unethical Choice

This is another **leadership** practice from Ray Dalio's culture of radical transparency. As a leader, you have an opportunity to increase certainty for people in your organization about the type of behavior that will/will not be tolerated. Your teams need to know that their voices and opinions matter—and even more so, that they are expected to bring in their dissenting views and their observations about what's working or not working "on the ground." Make it very clear—"success theater" is not welcomed in an organization with a generative culture.

Uncouple "Fear" from "Failure"

This *leadership* idea is inspired by the following quote:

> "The goal, then, is to uncouple fear and failure—to create an environment in which making mistakes doesn't strike terror into your employees' hearts."[11]
>
> Ed Catmull, co-founder of Pixar Animation

This approach aims to increase certainty around risk-taking and emphasizes that both success and failure are viable outcomes of an experiment. If you want to dive deeper into this topic, check out Amy

---

[10] https://www.linkedin.com/posts/etsy_etsys-three-armed-sweater-2023-winners-activity-7064279455413727233-LWCW/

[11] Catmull, E., Wallace, A. (2023). *Creativity, Inc (The Expanded Edition): Overcoming the Unseen Forces That Stand in the Way of True Inspiration.* (Random House; 1st edition)

C. Edmondson's new work[12] on failure. On the spectrum of causes for failure (sabotage, inattention, inability, challenge, uncertainty, or experimentation) she asserts that only sabotage is truly blameworthy. The other ones require further root cause analysis, which often would reveal causes outside of one's control. In the case of experimentation, the failure may even be praiseworthy, as evidence that the team (or an individual) didn't settle for a "safe" solution, a derivative of what's been used before—as long as we learn from this failure and don't fail twice in the same exact way.

Change Terminology, Reframe Error

This **leadership** practice resonates strongly with me as it reminds me of the times I, as a leader, had to reframe my own response to error. This happened when I was a DBA manager, leading a group of in-house and off-shore DBAs (when we still had physical data centers, and a mission-critical Oracle Exadata instance was under 2TB in size).

One of the production deployments ran into several issues, lasted longer than expected, and eventually ended in a rollback to the previous code version. I was very eager to find out whose fault it was and take action as I had no doubt that the failed release was a result of someone's incompetence. I was unfamiliar with the concept of "blameless postmortem" and at first was very unhappy when the team came back with all sorts of findings but didn't give me the name of a *specific person* who messed up!

Fast forward to 2023. A different team, in a different organization I was coaching, had their first failed production deployment. Just like me, 15 years ago, they didn't know about blameless postmortem—a process of reflecting on a failure with the intent to learn about the complexity of the environment, assumptions that were made, and the sequence of steps that led to the incident, *without* looking for a culprit. This is another practice

---

[12] Edmondson, A.C. (2023). *Right Kind of Wrong: The Science of Failing Well.* (Simon Element / Simon Acumen)

introduced to the world by Etsy[13] in 2012. Determined to learn from their incidents, and to help others avoid making the same mistakes, Etsy has been maintaining a public repository of their blameless postmortem reports.

Guiding my current team through their first blameless postmortem, I was able to reframe error for them, shifting the focus away from finger-pointing and toward methodical, level-headed learning. We were able to reconstruct the full picture of the event (without drama), uncover factors that led to or contributed to the incident, agree on the action items, and come out stronger as a team!

Good news, if you are working in a Scrum team, you have already experienced a different style of conversation in your team's Sprint Retrospectives. Many teams like to start them with re-emphasizing safety by reciting Norman L Kerth's Prime Directive:

> "Regardless of what we discover, we understand and truly believe that everyone did the best job they could, given what they knew at the time, their skills and abilities, the resources available, and the situation at hand."[14]

Reframe the Role of the Boss

This **leadership** practice is crucial for increasing safety as it helps clarify for individuals what to expect from their bosses and how to show up in the relationship with them to be successful. Amy C. Edmondson offers a side-by-side comparison of two different ways to frame leadership.[15] A default frame we have about the role of the boss is mostly based on Frederick

---

[13] https://www.fastcompany.com/3064726/what-etsy-does-when-things-go-wrong-a-7-step-guide
[14] https://www.oreilly.com/library/view/project-retrospectives-a/9780133488753/
[15] Edmondson, A. C. (2018). *The Fearless Organization: Creating Psychological Safety in the Workplace for Learning, Innovation, and Growth.* (Wiley; 1st edition)

Taylor's management theory: the boss is the one with all the answers, who gives orders, and who assesses others' performance. Subordinates are mostly the "order-takers" and must do what they are told.

An alternative frame (or a way to reframe) is to view the boss as someone who sets the vision, invites input from the employees to improve clarity, and creates the conditions for the employees to develop as professionals, learn, grow, and contribute their critical insights. As you may recall from David Marquet's story, this is exactly the reframing that he was able to do with the crew of the submarine he was on. Instead of command-and-control leadership, he introduced intent-based leadership, enabling the knowledge and experience of the crew to emerge in the most effective and powerful way.

Adopt an Experimental (vs. Operational) Mindset

This ***leadership*** safety practice brings clarity (and certainty) around an organizational focus on an experimental mindset (adapting to new information; risk-taking for the sake of innovation) as opposed to an operational mindset (strict adherence to budgets, plans, and schedules; striving for efficiency). This mindset allows the group to move forward, avoiding "analysis-paralysis," running frequent experiments, and knowing that failing and succeeding are both parts of the process. And that is exactly what makes a difference:

> *"As companies try to scale up their online experimentation capacity, they often find that the obstacles are not tools and technology but shared behaviors, beliefs, and values. For every experiment that succeeds, nearly 10 don't—and in the eyes of many organizations that emphasize efficiency, predictability, and 'winning,' those failures are wasteful."*[16]
>
> Stefan Thomke, Harvard Business School

---

[16] https://hbr.org/2020/03/building-a-culture-of-experimentation

CHAPTER 11   SAFETY IN THE WORKPLACE COACHING GAME

Autonomy

All safety enhancers included in this section are practices and ideas that will be most effective when either driven by or supported by the leadership (Figure 11-4). They are shifting the culture away from micromanagement and instead creating a space for people and teams to try out new ideas, share their opinions without hesitations or filters, and even exercise their choice of what project to work on or which team to join.

Figure 11-4. Psychological Safety Enhancers related to Autonomy

Success through Course Correction: "Early, Often, Ugly"

This *leadership* idea is inspired by an interview with Christa Quarles, the CEO of OpenTable, published in the *New York Times*.[17] Sharing one of the surprises from her first years as a CEO, Quarles noted:

> *"Teams were trying to perfect something before they would show it to me, and they'd waste a ton of time trying to get it to be perfect to show to the C.E.O. So I said, "Early, often, ugly. It's O.K. It doesn't have to be perfect because then I can course-correct much, much faster."*

Ironically, I had the opportunity (or misfortune) to work with several organizations where leaders believed that fear is an effective motivator, that excruciating perfection is worth spending time and effort on, and that information can only be shared up the hierarchy via polished and perfect PowerPoint decks. The level of micromanagement (under the disguise of feedback) that was involved in perfecting these decks was soul-crushing! As someone who values autonomy and freedom in my work, I felt completely demoralized, unmotivated, and suffocating from this talent- and time-wasting activity.

When I came across this quote, it resonated with me strongly. I wish the leaders I was working with embraced the "Early, often, ugly" mantra!

---

[17] https://www.nytimes.com/2016/08/14/business/christa-quarles-of-opentable-the-advantage-of-early-often-ugly.html

Practice Inclusive Leadership

This *leadership* style supports autonomy, first and foremost, by treating everyone respectfully and fairly, creating a culture where people feel that they belong and that their insights and opinions matter. Amy C. Edmondson's research[18] identified the following behavioral attributes of inclusive leadership:

1. Being approachable and accessible.
2. Acknowledging one's own fallibility.
3. Proactively inviting input from others (staff, direct reports, etc.).

Experiment with Dynamic Reteaming[19]

Inspired by the work of Heidi Helfand, this *leadership* safety enhancer refers to a set of patterns for enabling teams' evolutions toward their high performance despite fluctuations in the team structure. Instead of resisting disruptions in the stability of a team, Heidi shows how to embrace change and guide the teams through their growth, splitting, and re-birthing again as autonomous high-performing teams. Related to this practice is another technique, known by the name of Self-Selection.[20] Introduced by Sandy Mamoli and David Mole, Self-Selection is an approach to designing (or restructuring) teams in which the individuals (not their managers) are given the opportunity to choose a team they want to be a part of.

---

[18] Edmondson, A. C. (2018). *The Fearless Organization: Creating Psychological Safety in the Workplace for Learning, Innovation, and Growth* (Wiley; 1st edition)

[19] Helfand, H. (2020). *Dynamic Reteaming: The Art and Wisdom of Changing Teams.* (O'Reilly Media; 2nd edition)

[20] Mamoli, S., Mole, D. (2015). Creating Great Teams: How Self-Selection Lets People Excel. (Pragmatic Bookshelf; 1st edition)

I've experimented with Self-Selection during my work with a technology team of a Canadian retailer[21] in New York, a software company in Chicago, and a few others. The transparency of the approach, the clarity of the process, and the autonomy of selecting the work (and the team) that aligned with the individual's career aspirations was a powerful and rewarding outcome for the participants!

Abandon "Trust-Destroying" Practices

This *leadership* safety enhancer refers to another case study from Amy Edmondson's book, now from the world of manufacturing. According to this study, Bob Chapman, the CEO of Barry-Wehmiller, developed a well-documented set of values and methods for "establishing a psychologically safe workplace where learning and growth thrive." When reviewing the "Guiding Principles of Leadership" with the front-line workers, Chapman learned from them about the "time clocks, break bells, and locking inventory in cages" practices that inhibited the trust that the company was trying to instill. Chapman ordered to immediately get rid of what he called the "trust-destroying and demeaning practices, inappropriate for responsible adults."[22]

Discover & Amplify Voices through Open Space

Another way a *leader* can dial up autonomy is by running the next large meeting (an all-hands meeting, an off-site, or a strategy session) with Open Space Technology[23] (OST). Invented by Harrison Owen, this format allows the participants to generate their agenda ad hoc—at the beginning of their

---

[21] https://www.agileplayconsulting.com/post/let-s-run-an-experiment-self-selection-at-hbc-digital
[22] Edmondson, A. C. (2018). *The Fearless Organization: Creating Psychological Safety in the Workplace for Learning, Innovation, and Growth.* (Wiley; 1st edition)
[23] https://openspaceworld.org/wp2/hho/papers/brief-users-guide-open-space-technology/

gathering, based on the topics that are "top of mind" for them at the time. With no management pre-approval and no vetting, anyone can propose a topic for discussion.

As multiple parallel sessions find their way to the agenda, participants are then invited to make their own selections and join those discussions that are most relevant to them. They are also invited to leave and switch to a different topic (without hesitation) if the discussion is no longer relevant: if you are neither learning nor contributing, go to a different discussion where you will.

I have participated in and facilitated over 100 Open Spaces of different sizes, durations, or formats, and the magic of the OST never failed to impress me. One of the virtual ones I ran using Mural recently was hosted to follow up on the results of a company-wide employee survey with a department I was coaching at a well-known music company. The leadership team and the squads' members alike jumped in at the opportunity to propose their topics for discussion and to go deep into what was hiding behind the survey results. Moving at their own will between breakout rooms in Zoom, they were able to participate in a variety of candid and open conversations, generating ideas and committing to take several concrete steps toward improving the organizational culture.

Design Structures for Input

Just like Open Space Technology can enable information flow across the hierarchy and functional silos, there are several other ways ***leadership*** can unblock communication channels and create space for organizational learning. From internal communities of practice, conferences, and book clubs to peer-to-peer coaching and mentoring programs—these learning structures facilitate autonomous idea exchanges across departments and business units. As people connect with their peers and hear about similar challenges, they are also able to increase relatedness. Additionally, these opportunities to expand their network and share their knowledge with others can also positively impact their status.

CHAPTER 11   SAFETY IN THE WORKPLACE COACHING GAME

A few other examples of this practice: running skip-level meetings, focus groups, fire-side chats with the leadership team, and bringing in an experienced facilitator who can help with creating a safe and engaging space for employees to speak openly about their challenges. In remote meetings, leaders can use tools like Sli.do, Mentimeter, or Poll Everywhere to solicit feedback and gather questions.

Relatedness

This group of safety enhancers (Figure 11-5) is my personal favorite! I've applied them often in my own coaching practice and have seen their impact on increasing safety in teams, and as a result, have seen the team's performance take off to the next level.

Figure 11-5. Psychological Safety Enhancers related to Relatedness

CHAPTER 11   SAFETY IN THE WORKPLACE COACHING GAME

Practice Speaking about Feelings

This **team-level** safety enhancer is surprisingly difficult for a typical team of software engineers, and yet starting your team meeting with a quick "atmosphere" check-in will help with planting the first seed of relatedness and empathy. Here are a few of my favorite ways to talk about feelings at check-in.

If your current mood was a weather pattern, how would you describe it?

This question invites a bit of playfulness and creativity, reducing a barrier to having a "touchy-feely" conversation. After hearing all the team members' responses, as a facilitator you may want to bring it all together into a shared "current weather" update. If you used this check-in to start their retrospective, you may find it useful to go deeper into these team-generated metaphors during the rest of the retrospective.

What version of you is showing up here today?

This question requires a bit of "modeling" with a group that is new to speaking about feelings. I may hold space for the first person to jump in, or step in after 10 seconds with: "Here is how I would answer a question like that: The version of me that is here today is a curious, excited, and a little apprehensive version. I am trying something new with you here and I don't know yet how it will land. Who would like to share next?"

Check-in with "I feel . . . (Mad |Sad |Glad |Afraid). I am In."

This approach is taken directly from the Core Protocols[24]—the set of practices for operating as a high-performing team created by Jim and Michele McCarthy. Check-in protocol is a great starting point for new teams as it offers a small practice "vocabulary of feelings" to use in a conversation. In this

---

[24] https://liveingreatness.com/core-protocols/

approach, each individual team member uses a specific pattern to check-in by saying: "I feel…" followed by one or more words from only the four options (mad, sad, glad, or afraid). They finish their turn by saying "I am in". The group responds with: "Welcome!" The turn then moves on to the next team member for them to check in with the same pattern. As every team member gets their turn, this "check-in" ritual creates a shared commitment to being fully present and to giving undivided attention to the work the team is doing.

Take Team Outside (Share Experiences Together)

This *team* practice enables relatedness by creating shared team experiences outside of their day-to-day work-related interaction. When it was originally included in the Safety in the Workplace set, I was referring to "outside of the office." When COVID-19 made all teams distributed and dispersed, this practice took on a brand-new meaning.

From 2021 to 2023, I was coaching an organization that, at that time, cared deeply about strengthening relatedness among the team members in a fully remote environment. The teams had been encouraged to create the space and time for creating a shared experience "outside of the work context." Each team had their own cadence and their own preference for the variety of shared virtual experiences. Teams have increased relatedness over building a mini-terrarium, hosting a cheese tasting, learning how to make a mocktail together, building a mini-LEGO sculpture, etc.). We've hosted monthly virtual game hours (Drawphone, Codenames, baby pictures Bingo, and others), learned about each other's favorite holidays and food, practiced a "word of the day" in a foreign language, and so much more!

Create & Share Your User Manual

User Manual is a *team* practice introduced by Atlassian, in which each team member creates a set of written instructions on the best way for others to interact with them. The team starts by creating a set of questions (or selecting one of the existing templates), for example:

- I work best when . . .
- Under stress, I tend to . . .
- The best way to communicate with me . . .
- The way I like to receive feedback is . . . and the type of feedback I find useful . . .
- I learn best by . . .
- I don't have patience for . . .

The team reviews each member's responses together and may follow up with creating a team working agreement, team norms, etc. User Manuals are then stored in a shared team document repository, can be added to team members' email signatures, and can be shared more broadly. When a new member joins this team, they have an opportunity to learn more about each team member as well as add their own user manual.

Increase Communication Frequency in the Team

This *team* practice is especially important in DevSecOps transformations for increasing relatedness as well as for breaking the old patterns of containing information within one's functional silo. The key to this practice is to be intentional about creating space and channels for meaningful communication while minimizing potential communication overload. Meeting hygiene, a balance between synchronous and asynchronous communication as well as a team working agreement can help make this practice effective.

Run Frequent Retrospectives

Another *team* practice that requires no introduction. One of the five Scrum Events, a Sprint Retrospective creates space for a team to reflect on their last Sprint and "plan ways to increase quality and effectiveness."[25]

---

[25] https://scrumguides.org/scrum-guide.html#sprint-retrospective

One element of a well-facilitated retrospective that helps with amplifying relatedness and safety is the Retrospective Prime Directive is as follows:

> *"Regardless of what we discover, we understand and truly believe that everyone did the best job they could, given what they knew at the time, their skills and abilities, the resources available, and the situation at hand."*
>
> Norm Kerth[26]

While Scrum teams have a built-in cadence for running their Sprint Retrospectives, the teams that follow a different way of working will benefit from the consistency and increased frequency of this team-leaning event.

Introduce & Use Core Protocols

I already mentioned **Check In** protocol earlier in this chapter. Building on that, the "Introduce and Use Core Protocols" *team* practice invites you to explore the other commitments and protocols from this collection. The protocols increase relatedness and safety by codifying a set of norms and behaviors exhibited by the best teams. Introduced by Jim and Michele McCarthy and later popularized by Richard Kasperowski,[27] the Core Protocols create space for positive bias, connection, self-awareness within the group, and effective decision-making, and define ways of course correction should the team go off track. Some examples of the Core Protocols I've used with various groups are Check In, Check Out, Decider, Ask for Help, Intention Check, and Perfection Game.

---

[26] Kerth, N. L. (2001). *Project Retrospectives: A handbook for Team Reviews.* (Addison-Wesley Professional; 1st edition)

[27] Kasperowski R. (2015). *The Core Protocols: A Guide to Greatness.* (With Great People Publications)

Fairness

Fairness, in the context of teams, describes an individual perception of unbiased, objective, and fair treatment of people within an organization. In this section, you will find several team and leadership practices that can help you increase the sense of fairness in your group (Figure 11-6).

Figure 11-6. *Psychological Safety Enhancers related to Fairness*

Embrace Sustainable Pace

This **team** safety enhancer is an homage to Agile Manifesto[28] principle number eight. When a sustainable pace is not respected by an organization, it causes team members to experience burnout.

---

[28] https://agilemanifesto.org/principles.html

While overworked and under stress, the team is likely to start pulling back from collaboration and withholding their contributions to the shared success of the team. You may even discover that team members engage in a "sandbagging"—a strategy of creating an impression of being less capable, less skilled than they truly are.[29] If an organization rewards "heroics" and pulling all-nighters, not only will it continue to experience more quality issues, but it will also reinforce the environment where people feel pressured to prioritize work over their family commitments. Not surprisingly, this will have a negative effect on the sense of fairness in this team.

Co-Create Team Norms

Implementing this *team* practice can help the team embrace a sustainable pace and clarify what's acceptable and what isn't in this team. Also known as team working agreements, this concise team artifact documents a shared understanding of how the team is to work together to achieve the most desirable outcome and the most desirable team culture. Each working agreement is unique to the team needs. It helps the team clarify the rules of engagement as well as assists in navigating conflicts if/when they arise. (The Core Protocols that you learned about earlier in this chapter can be viewed as a special type of team norms.)

In addition to increasing fairness, this practice can positively influence certainty and relatedness. Co-creating the norms (as opposed to being presented with the norms created by the management) can also increase the sense of autonomy in the team.

In the typical team maturity life cycle, the norms get created at the beginning of team formation, or when a new team member is added to an existing team. Periodically, a team will choose to validate their adherence

---

[29] Gibson, B. (2000). *Sandbagging as a Self-Presentational Strategy: Claiming to Be Less than You Are.* Personality and Social Psychology Bulletin, 26(1), 56–70.

to team norms, and the norms' applicability to the current team needs in their regular retrospective.[30]

Negotiate Boundaries with Delegation Poker

Introduced by Jurgen Appelo in 2010, as part of this Management 3.0 model,[31] this *leadership* safety enhancer has a positive influence on the fairness domain by clarifying (and negotiating) upfront the boundaries and expectations between the team and their leader. The model introduces seven levels of delegation: tell, sell, Consult, agree, advise, inquire, delegate. Often used together with a delegation board,[32] it facilitates conversations around typical decisions that need to be made in the context of this team and creates a shared understanding of the extent of management involvement expected. In addition to fairness, this safety enhancer has a positive impact on the autonomy, certainty, and status domains.

Measure Team's Health & Safety

This *team* safety enhancer helps to bring attention to the team's psychological safety and the health of their practices. There are several commercial and community tools that you can leverage for this. You can also create your own! The true value of this practice is in its ability to take an anonymous "temperature reading" across the team, learn about the patterns and outliers in the team's health, and then use it to drive conversation with the team members.

---

[30] https://www.agileplayconsulting.com/post/every-team-needs-a-working-agreement

[31] Appelo, J. (2010). *Management 3.0: Leading Agile Developers, Developing Agile Leaders*. (Addison-Wesley Professional; 1st edition)

[32] https://management30.com/practice/delegation-poker/

Leadership can also use the data collected across the entire organization to reflect on patterns from multiple teams. However, for this practice to have a positive impact on fairness, it must be carried out in a very specific way. What I learned from my first experience running the Team Health Checks for 22 teams at a Canadian retailer[33] is it is critical to avoid comparing the teams to each other. Instead, when sharing the aggregated data with the leaders, guide them to explore the common teams' challenges that can benefit from the support of the leadership team.

Go After the "Things that Suck"

I picked up this *leadership* practice when working with the same Canadian retailer referenced earlier in this book. While this practice has the same intention as "removing impediments" and "addressing organizational growth items," the less formal language of it carries empathy for people affected by these "things that suck." When a leadership team is relentless in improving the environment and creating a space where their people can be successful, you will see fairness, certainty, and autonomy flourish.

Anti-Gossip Rule: "Fire Slimy Weasels"

While this *leadership* practice is inspired by Ray Dalio's *Principles*[34] that are embraced at Bridgewater Associates, many other organizations implement "anti-gossip policies." An explicitly stated position on gossip (and gossipers) makes it clear: evaluative talk about others (when they are not present) will not be tolerated in an organization. In addition to emphasizing formal communication channels for information exchange, this practice positively affects a sense of fairness by negating

---

[33] https://www.agileplayconsulting.com/post/would-you-rather-be-awesome-or-deadly

[34] Dalio, R. (2017). *Principles: Life and Work*. (Avid Reader Press / Simon & Schuster)

an interpersonal power dynamic associated with gossip. According to the model developed by Nancy B. Kurland and Lisa Hope Pelled in their research,[35] gossip has the ability to influence the degree of power that the gossiper gains over the gossip recipient. From coercive or reward powers (the ones that emerge from a gossip recipient's belief that the gossiper can punish or provide a desired outcome), to expert power (in which the gossip recipient believes that the gossiper has special expertise or knowledge that can benefit the recipient), to referent power (belief that being in the "trusted circle" with the gossiper can be an advantage for the recipient), gossip-rich culture can wreak havoc and undermine your DevSecOps initiative.

Respond Productively (Curiosity over Blame)

Another **leadership** practice associated with blameless culture is a great reminder about a downward spiral dynamic that leaders can prevent. Tricia Broderick and Diana Larsen write about it in their book:

> *"When we feel blamed by others or shamed by ourselves, we cripple our ability to perform well. We become incapable of innovative, creative thought. Movement in a new direction comes with too much threat. Faultfinding, judgments, blame, and shame work together to prompt a negative downward spiral."*[36]

Guess what? A DevSecOps implementation is all about moving in a new direction, breaking old patterns, and taking on a steep learning curve. It will be more successful when supported by leaders who can shift away from seeking "who to hold accountable" (a.k.a. blame) in case of

---

[35] Kurland, N.B., Pelled, L. H. (2000). *Passing the Word: Toward a Model of Gossip and Power in the workplace. The Academy of Management Review, 25(2), 428–438*

[36] Larsen, D., Broderick, T. (2022). *Lead Without Blame: Building Resilient Learning Teams.* (Berrett-Koehler Publishers; 1st edition)

inevitable setbacks along the way. Responding productively means, among other things, tailoring the response to the type of failure at hand. Was it preventable? Was it caused by complexity? Was it a result of an experiment the team was running?

Responding with curiosity means assuming positive intent, leaning into the spirit of the Retrospective Prime Directive, and asking a different type of question:

- What was present (and what was lacking) in the system that caused the team to make a decision that has been made?
- What barriers, impediments, and old processes prevented the team from reaching the intended outcome?
- What have we uncovered now that wasn't known at that time?
- What can the team (and the organization) learn from this failure so that the likelihood of its happening again will be diminished in the future?

Emphasize the Goal

This last *leadership* practice helps amplify fairness by reminding the teams about the shared goal they are after. DevSecOps is a long game. As organizations attempt to shift culture, break through functional silos, learn a new technology stack, and migrate their databases and servers from physical data centers to a cloud, they are going to face a high degree of uncertainty. At times they will feel like they are taking one step forward, just to fall two steps back. Celebrating small wins along the way, supporting the teams in times of failure, enabling a generative learning culture, and re-emphasizing the meaningful goal can all help in increasing the safety and resiliency of the team.

CHAPTER 11 SAFETY IN THE WORKPLACE COACHING GAME

Summary

In this chapter, we ran through the 36 safety practices that I chose to include in the *Safety in the Workplace* game. As you start using this set in your team and leadership coaching practice, I'd love to hear what resonates the most in your organizational culture. What practices inspire action? Which ones are your groups shying away from? What other practices have you discovered that positively influence the domains of the SCARF model?

CHAPTER 12

Master Your Debriefing

A few years ago, at one of the Play4Agile coach camps, I heard a phrase that stuck with me: "Every game is an excuse to debrief." It surprised me. It made me stop and reflect on my own experience using simulations and Agile games in my training, as well as the experience of being in a participant's shoes during simulations facilitated by other trainers. What distinguished an insightful learning experience from a fun game we played that wasn't clearly connected to the material we'd been learning?

You guessed it! The time we took after the game to debrief the experience, reflect on our feelings and behavioral patterns, and connect what we learned from the game to the "real life" application made a significant difference. When there was enough time built into the agenda for "reflection-in-action, reflection-on-action, and reflection-beyond-action,"[1] the session participants had a more meaningful learning experience.

Over time, as I came to appreciate the value of a good debriefing and played around with various approaches to it, I collected several techniques that I'd like to share with you in this chapter. You will also find here several existing models that can improve the effectiveness of your next debriefing session. How will you know if your debriefing was successful? According

---

[1] Kristina Thomas Dreifuerst, Getting Started With Debriefing for Meaningful Learning, Clinical Simulation in Nursing, Volume 11, Issue 5, 2015, Pages 268–275

to Scott Nicholson, a professor of game design and development at Wilfrid Laurier University, it is when "both the learner and also the instructors gain much more out of the original exercise."[2]

Why Is Debriefing Important?

As I alluded to earlier, playing a game, or taking part in a simulation experience without a proper debriefing, may leave an adult learner confused, disconnected, and even frustrated: "What did you learn in the class? I don't know... How to build paper airplanes, I guess..." Debriefing helps to make sense of the experience, process emotions that might've arisen during the simulation, deepen the intended learning outcomes of the session, and help create a connection with participants' "real life" situations.

Another important aspect of debriefing is that it allows the participants to "reflect upon the experience, identify the mental models that led to behaviors or cognitive processes, and then build or enhance new mental models to be used in future experiences."[3]

In the case of the *LEGO and Chocolate* simulation, the goal of a debriefing is to inspire change and lessen the anxiety that people may feel about the upcoming DevSecOps transformation. Since this simulation serves as a metaphor for an organizational change, debriefing allows us to reconstruct the experience through the eyes of each role, reflect on the organizational dynamic and the current mental models of the participants, discuss potential obstacles for introducing the change in participants' organizations, as well as debunk the myths and assumptions related to DevSecOps transformations.

---

[2] Nicholson, S. (2012). Completing the Experience: Debriefing in Experiential Educational Games. In the Proceedings of The 3rd International Conference on Society and Information Technologies. Winter Garden, Florida: International Institute of Informatics and Systemics. 117-121

[3] Jason J. Zigmont, Liana J. Kappus, Stephanie N. Sudikoff, The 3D Model of Debriefing: Defusing, Discovering, and Deepening, Seminars in Perinatology, Volume 35, Issue 2, 2011, Pages 52-58

CHAPTER 12   MASTER YOUR DEBRIEFING

When describing the elements of an effective learning experience, Sharon Bowman, the author of the popular *Training from the Back of the Room*[4] model, talks about "collaborative interdependence and individual accountability." Debriefing helps to tap into both! As each participant experiences the simulation from the perspective of their individual role, the debriefing creates a space for everyone to share these experiences. As they collectively add nuances, a comprehensive picture of the complex simulation experience emerges in the debrief, deepening the experience and cross-pollinating the insights. As Dr. Nicholson noted:

> *"One of the powerful aspects of debriefing is that it allows each participant to take what he or she internalized from the activity, share it with others, and learn from others."*

If you are still not convinced, there is one more reason why you need to allocate enough time for several debriefing moments during the *LEGO and Chocolate* simulation. These debriefing moments serve as a feedback loop for you, providing an opportunity for you as a facilitator to course-correct the experience if the simulation isn't going as planned. Yes, occasionally the debriefing will reveal a gap between the designed experience of the simulation and the actual experience of this particular group going through it. After all, you have humans playing it, not AI bots!

My favorite story about a human-inflicted variation is from the time I ran it in Canada and all my players in the Operations team decided to go "on strike." I discovered it during our debriefing, and we turned it into a learning moment about dealing with resistance to change.

---

[4] Bowman, S.L. (2008). *Training from the Back of the Room!: 65 Ways to Step Aside and Let Them Learn.* Pfeiffer.

CHAPTER 12   MASTER YOUR DEBRIEFING

Debriefing Models

There are several well-known debriefing models that offer a very structural approach to stimulate reflection, thinking, and learning. The Debriefing for Meaningful Learning© (DML)[5] model uses six distinct phases for debriefing: engage, explore, explain, elaborate, evaluate, and extend. The 3D Model of Debriefing, referenced above, has three main parts—Defusing, Discovering, and Deepening—as well as an introduction (Pre-briefing) and a closing (Summary of Lessons Learned) activities. Both models are used extensively in healthcare for experiential learning in clinical settings.

Another debriefing model will sound very familiar to you if you've ever facilitated, attended, or read about an Agile Retrospective[6]: Set the Stage, Gather Data, Generate Insights, Decide What to Do, Close. While typically used for reflecting on a longer experience (from a few days to a few weeks) it has a similar intent of helping the participants to collectively reflect on, process, and learn from their experience.

If you are a big fan of Bloom's Taxonomy (see Figure 12-1), you will be pleased to know that there is even a model that suggests approaching the debriefing process in the order of the cognitive processing or thinking levels outlined by Bloom. Larry K. Quinsland and Anne Van Ginkel, professors at Rochester Institute of Technology (RIT) and the authors of this approach,[7] suggest starting a debriefing session from the most basic level by asking the participants to recall the sequence of activities that they engaged in the simulation, then proceeding with questions related

---

[5] Kristina Thomas Dreifuerst, Getting Started With Debriefing for Meaningful Learning, Clinical Simulation in Nursing, Volume 11, Issue 5, 2015, Pages 268-275.

[6] Derby, E., & Larsen, D. (2006). Agile Retrospectives: Making Good Teams Great. (Pragmatic Bookshelf; 1st edition)

[7] Quinsland, L. K., & Van Ginkel, A. (1984). How to Process Experience. Journal of Experiential Education, 7(2), 8-13.

to understanding of the simulation by all the participants. Methodically proceeding further up in the taxonomy to application, analysis, and evaluation, according to their research, will enable deeper learning and make the processing of the experience much less jarring for the participants.

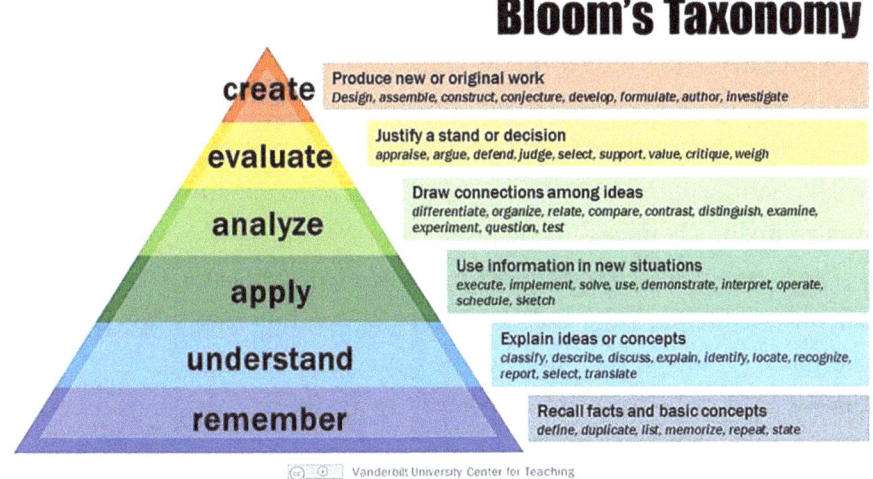

Figure 12-1. Bloom's Taxonomy

While this section is not indented as an exhaustive coverage of debriefing models, I do want to mention two more models that are worth checking out: the Six Phases of Debriefing[8] by Dr. Sivasailam "Thiagi" Thiagarajan and the Debriefing Cube[9] by Julian Kea and Chris Caswell.

---

[8] https://thiagi.net/archive/www/pfp/IE4H/february2004.html#Debriefing
[9] https://www.kilearning.net/TheDebriefingCube_CC-BY_v20.pdf

CHAPTER 12   MASTER YOUR DEBRIEFING

Debriefing Tips for DevSecOps Games

As you may recall from the earlier chapters of this book, the *LEGO and Chocolate* simulation was designed to support experiential DevSecOps training. It is based on the 4C framework, in which each Content segment is followed by a Concrete Practice (a round of simulation) and a Conclusion segment (a round of debriefing). With this approach, the group can weave in the learning from the shorter rounds of reflection throughout the simulation. The workshop then finishes with a longer round of synthesizing the learning from the entire experience, connecting it to the "real life" application, beyond the classroom, and evaluating the options for introducing change.

I have also discovered through trial and error that using Liberating Structures to facilitate these debriefs creates the most powerful learning experience for the participants. As the name implies, these facilitation techniques introduce just enough structure to liberate learning and engage everyone equally in the discussion. Table 12-1 describes my current approach to debriefing this workshop.

CHAPTER 12   MASTER YOUR DEBRIEFING

Table 12-1. Debriefing Approach for DevSecOps Training Workshop

Sprint	Game	Goal	Liberating Structure in Debriefing	Time
One	LEGO & Chocolate	Rebuild a system-level view based on the individual reflections, highlight bottlenecks, and apply learning to the next Sprint.	W3: What? So What? Now What?[10]	15 min
Two	LEGO & Chocolate	Build empathy and connectedness by debriefing the experience with participants from different tables. Gain a system-wide perspective, explore feelings, and highlight mental models.	1-2-4-All[11]	15 min
Three	LEGO & Chocolate	Synthesize learning from 3 rounds of the simulation in a self-organized group discussion format. Evaluate application beyond the classroom. Amplify the mental models shift. Collect written reflections for further analysis.	User Experience Fishbowl[12]	30 min
Four	Fear in the Workplace	Draw connections between scenarios in the game and the real-life challenges that exist in participants' workplaces. Explore options and inspire change.	1-2-4-All, W3 and 25/10 Crowd Sourcing[13]	30 min

---

[10] https://www.liberatingstructures.com/9-what-so-what-now-what-w/
[11] https://www.liberatingstructures.com/1-1-2-4-all/
[12] https://www.liberatingstructures.com/18-users-experience-fishbowl/
[13] https://www.liberatingstructures.com/12-2510-crowd-sourcing/

CHAPTER 12   MASTER YOUR DEBRIEFING

Debriefing Sprint 1

The goal of this first debriefing is to connect all the puzzle pieces of the experiences of each role and each table into a comprehensive full-picture view of the simulation. After all, the first round is designed to highlight the disconnect, confusion, and departmental silos in an organization "before DevSecOps." Debriefing is there to expose the bottlenecks in the end-to-end process flow and inspire thinking about potential change for Sprint 2.

When debriefing this round of simulation, I like to use the approach loosely based on the What? So What? Now What? structure. Here is how you can run it with your group:

1. **What?** Invite people to reflect on and then discuss with others: *What happened in the first Sprint? What have they noticed? What observations stood out from their perspective?* (no judgment, simply stating the facts, just like a video camera would record it).

    a. 1 min – write down individual reflections

    b. 2 min – discuss at their tables

    c. 5 min – share the most salient insights with the entire group. When asking the groups for their share-outs, please start by inviting input from the Development teams, then the Business team, followed by the Operations and Security teams. Instruct players to make public the "secret instructions" that they received from you in Sprint 1.

2. **So What?** Next, help the group to make sense of the facts. *Why is that important? What hypotheses can they make about our way of working in Sprint 1?*

a. 1 min – write down individual reflections

   b. 2 min – discuss at their tables

   c. 3 min – share the most salient insights with the entire group. When asking the groups for their share-outs, please start by hearing from the Development teams, then the Business team, followed by the Operations and Security teams.

3. ***Now What?*** Ask participants for a few suggestions on what can be done differently in Sprint 2. *Based on what we explored, what changes make sense now?* While you will not be applying all of them in Sprint 2, it will be useful to connect to their ideas when you start introducing modifications for Sprint 2.

Debriefing Sprint 2

By the time you are ready to kick off the Sprint 2 debriefing, your participants have already created a new level of connectedness and safety in the room. Having gone through the T-shaped-skills cross-training activity as well as engaged in a newly discovered collaboration for the Ops, Security, and the Development teams, the energy in the room is palpable! You want to carry this positive energy forward into the next debriefing. I like using a simple 1-2-4-All structure for that. Here is how you can run it with your group:

1. 1 min (solo) – Invite people to reflect on their experience in Sprint 2 and write down the biggest "Aha!" moments that came up for them.

2. 3 min (pairs) – Ask people to form a pair with someone from a different table and share with each other the insights they wrote in step 1.

3. 5 min (in quads) – Next, instruct them to keep the same partner, and merge with another pair to review all "Aha!" items. Select one that is worth sharing with a larger group and pick a spokesperson to represent this quad.

4. *All* 6 min (entire group) – Go around the room, hear one insight from each quad, and acknowledge feelings, changes in perspectives, and shifts in the group's mental models that emerge during debriefs. Collect all the written insights in one visible place. I like using an "Key Takeaways" poster for that.

Debriefing Sprint 3

When facilitating a debriefing after Sprint 3, you will be inviting the group to reflect on the entire simulation experience and synthesize learning from all three Sprints. The participants will be evaluating the application of DevSecOps culture beyond the classroom. This will be the final opportunity to amplify their mental model shift, evoked by the *LEGO and Chocolate* simulation.

I like using the User Experience Fishbowl structure for this debrief. You will need to create a special physical container for it: five empty chairs arranged into a semi-circle (see Figure 12-2).

CHAPTER 12   MASTER YOUR DEBRIEFING

Figure 12-2. Five chairs prepared for a User Experience Fishbowl debriefing activity

Here is how you can run this debriefing with your group:

1. 1 min – Invite participants to reflect and write down responses to the following question: **What have we learned from this simulation and how might we bring these ideas to life to influence change?**

2. 2 min – Explain the dynamic of User Experience Fishbowl:

    a. "Our group will be split into two types of participants—the fishes (people in the fishbowl) and the observers. The five chairs you see at the back of the room are the physical boundaries of the fishbowl. Fishes will sit in the fishbowl and have a conversation with each other, responding to the question. Everyone else will be listening to their conversation.

b. If any observer wants to make a comment or add something to the conversation, they will have to jump into the fishbowl and become one of the fishes.

   c. The rule of the fishbowl: a maximum of four fish in the fishbowl at any given time and one empty chair as an invitation for a new fish to join.

   d. When the last chair is taken, one of the older fishes must jump out of the fishbowl and create one empty chair again. The rule applies to everyone, even the facilitator. When I want to add something to the conversation, I must jump into the fishbowl.

3. 27 min – Simply state that the fishbowl is open and wait for people to start coming into the fishbowl.

   a. Listen to the reflections and ideas that people share in the fishbowl. This is your immediate feedback loop, allowing you to validate that the participants are taking away the right message about the DevSecOps culture.

   b. Give people space; only join the fishbowl if you hear a statement that contradicts the learning objectives of this workshop.

   c. If the group is generally quiet, join the fishbowl to share your own observation about this dynamic of the group that you have observed through the three rounds of the game.

   d. As the flow of people in and out of the fishbowl dries out, come in to summarize the message, and invite everyone to add their stickies to the "Key Takeaways" poster and close the workshop.

CHAPTER 12   MASTER YOUR DEBRIEFING

Debriefing Sprint 4

Technically, there is no Sprint 4! Your group isn't running a *LEGO and Chocolate* simulation at this point in the workshop. They are still learning about DevOps culture; however, they are doing it now with a different tool—the *Fear in the Workplace* game. By the time you are ready to run this debriefing, the energy of the room has shifted to a more quiet, reflective mode. In the debriefing, you want to help your group to draw connections between scenarios in the game and the real-life challenges that exist in participants' workplaces. In addition, you want to finish the experience on a high note by crowdsourcing ideas and inspiring change.

For the first part of this debrief I like using 1-2-4-All, What? So What? Now What? structures or even offer a few open-ended questions for their reflection:

- What surprised them the most about this game?
- What has the game enabled?
- Where do they see an opportunity to connect the discussion to their own workplaces?

There are a few activities you can use to crowdsource ideas for organizational change. My favorite one is the 25/10 Crowdsourcing. Here is how you can run it with your group:

1. 1 min – Invite participants to write their best idea on an index card in response to the invitation: ***If you were 10 times bolder, what big ideas would you experiment with in your organization?***

2. 10 min – Instruct participants to start passing the cards to each other without reading.

251

a. Once they hear your signal, they will stop, read the card in their hand, and rate it on a scale from 1 (not feeling it) to 5 (best idea ever!).

   b. On your signal, the group will continue passing the cards without reading, then reading, and rating them on your signal for a total of five rounds.

   c. At the end of the last round, everyone will tally the ratings on the card in their hands and circle the total rating.

3. 10 min – Explain that now as a group you are going to discover the top 10 crowdsourced ideas and ask a person who is holding an idea with a 25 rating to step forward. Continue calling forward the participants with ideas rates as 24, 23, 22 . . . until you have 10 ideas at the front of the room.

4. Ask people to read out loud the ideas that are written on their top-rated cards.

5. Optionally, you can have the group explore these top-rated ideas further and identify a small next step to advance them forward.

Summary

I hope that this chapter inspired you to learn more about debriefing and experimenting with available models, and to find one that provides you and your group with the most impact. At the very least, it should have convinced you to never skip debriefing.

Curious to learn about the "Aha!" moments that have emerged in my previous debriefings? Keep reading! In Chapter 13, I will share with you the most salient insights I've collected over the years running these games internationally. They will help you get an idea of what to expect from your group, what to watch out for, and what messages to amplify for more insightful learning.

CHAPTER 13

Key Takeaways

In this chapter, you will find my collection of participants' insights from various DevSecOps workshops I facilitated over the years. Why am I sharing them with you? First, these soundbites can offer you a preview of what to expect in your own workshops. Second, they can help you spot deviations from the intended learning objectives and trigger a reflection on possible adjustments that can enhance the workshop delivery. Third, they can offer a glimpse into DevSecOps skeptics' perspectives so that you can be prepared to respond to them if/when they arise.

Finally, this collection can help you make a case for bringing this workshop to new organizations, highlighting the openness of discussions and the shift in perspectives instigated by the experiential nature of this workshop.

Visualizing Bottlenecks and Silos

One of the big highlights of this workshop has always been the opportunity to start from a bottleneck-heavy, locally optimized process of the first Sprint, and then experience first improvements in the overall flow of value. Here are a few of my favorite insights:

> "Work around the bottlenecks & improve around them."

> "Bottlenecks must be visible for teams to flow to them."

> "Remove bottlenecks, not just local optimize."

"Focus on bottlenecks"

"Seeing silos in action"

"Silos suck!"

Benefits of Cross-training

Another topic that regularly comes up in debriefing is the benefit (and fun) of the cross-training (or T-shaped skills-building) activity (see Figure 13-1). Here are a few additional comments:

"Understanding all the roles in DevOps makes it easier to be productive."

"Cross-training helped connect with the team as opposed to ordering them."

"Cross-training enabled teams to grow and interchange skills."

"Share what you know, cross-train!"

"Cross-training in development, operations, and security reduced stress and chaos."

"Sharing knowledge leads to innovation."

"T-shaped skills help the team move faster/take pressure off individuals."

CHAPTER 13 KEY TAKEAWAYS

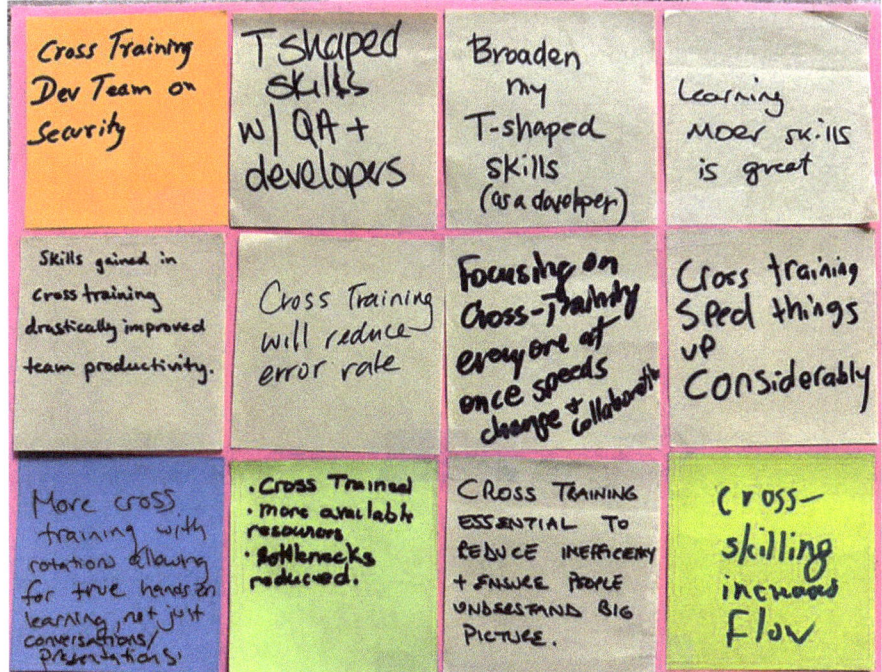

Figure 13-1. Participants' insights about cross-training

Concerns about the Cross-training

While the majority of participants love the effect of cross-training in the game, occasionally you will have a player or two who will comment on several potential side effects of it. There might be an initial confusion about the new process, or some teams will find it hard to let go of the old roles, while others will happily drop the old roles and the team will "skip" a step or two as a result:

> "Cross-training, while beneficial, initially impacts the throughput of the team."

> "Cross-trained, but not interested/ready to work for that skill. Need time to become a part of the team after cross-training. Fear of change."

CHAPTER 13 KEY TAKEAWAYS

You may also hear concerns from those players in "operations" roles related to job security. Some of these are captured in Figure 13-2.

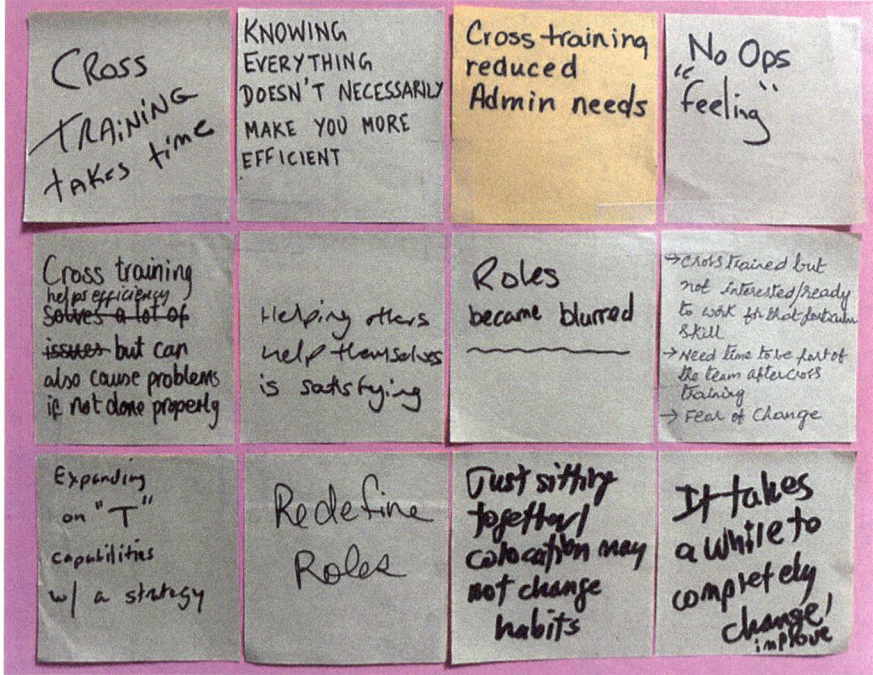

Figure 13-2. *Participants' concerns related to cross-training*

"Shift-left" on Security

One of the key learnings that this simulation is designed to invoke is the changing role of security in DevSecOps:

"Secure verification at the beginning"

"Shift left!"

"Having security work with developers is key!"

"Trust is central to progress as a group"

You can see the validation of this learning through the reflections captured in Figure 13-3.

Figure 13-3. Participants' reflections on the role of Security

DevSecOps' Impact on Business

I want to bring your attention to this brand-new insight. At the time of writing the first edition of this book, it hadn't yet come up in the reflections. However, in the last couple of years, this insight became another consistent learning for the participants: DevSecOps will change the dynamic of the interaction between business and technology in an organization. The business team needs to be aware and ready for it. In fact, they may really benefit from being invited to learn about DevSecOps in this gamified, non-techie-friendly format!

CHAPTER 13   KEY TAKEAWAYS

Here are some relevant insights (see Figure 13-4 for more):

"Releasing small increments increases the workload of business/PO."

"Having business continuously check and provide feedback helped the team a lot!"

"Smaller packages = more scope for quick feedback and improvement"

"Communication up and down the org is very important."

"Collaboration and willingness to work together + have fun is key!"

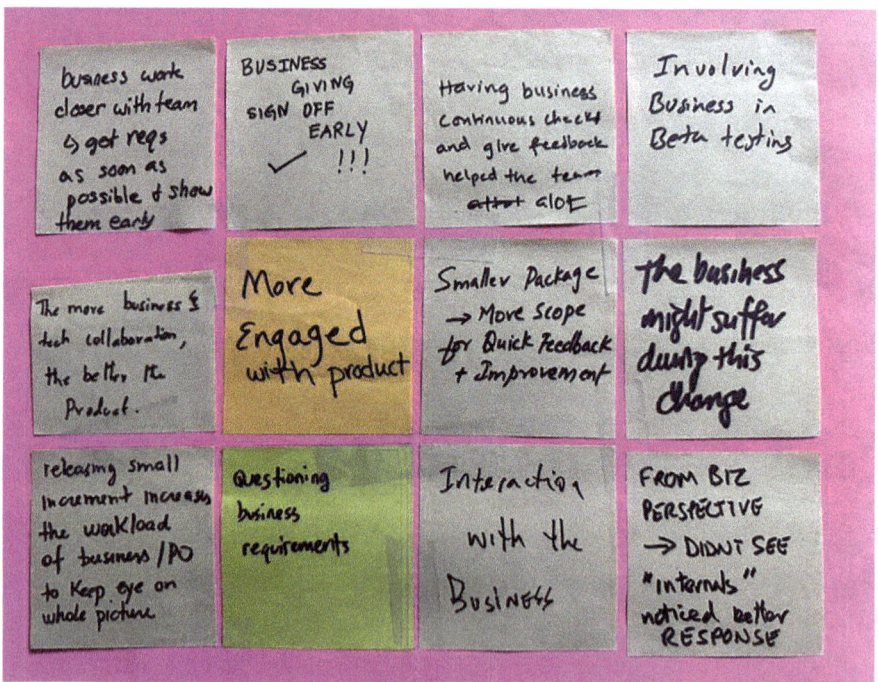

Figure 13-4. *Participants' reflections on DevSecOps impact on Business team*

Fearless Culture

Finally, in this section, I collected insights from the conversations enabled by the *Fear in the Workplace* and *Safety in the Workplace* coaching games. Most of the participants are surprised at the ease with which they can engage in conversations about fear using these coaching games:

> *"Great to hear that organizational fears can be managed in a safe, creative way."*
>
> *"Fear resonates differently for everyone, and it is all about discussions."*
>
> *"The third exercise (fear + safety enhancers) was very interesting. I loved the images and how they naturally opened good discussions."*
>
> *"There are more fears than I could ever articulate. It helps to have a set of solutions/tools to discuss and choose from."*
>
> *"Fun helps to reduce fears."*
>
> *"Collaborate and discuss fears."*
>
> *"Fear cripples information flow."*
>
> *"The game made it easier to recognize fear symptoms, and learn about ways to eradicate it through self, team, and leadership approaches."*

See additional insights in Figure 13-5.

CHAPTER 13   KEY TAKEAWAYS

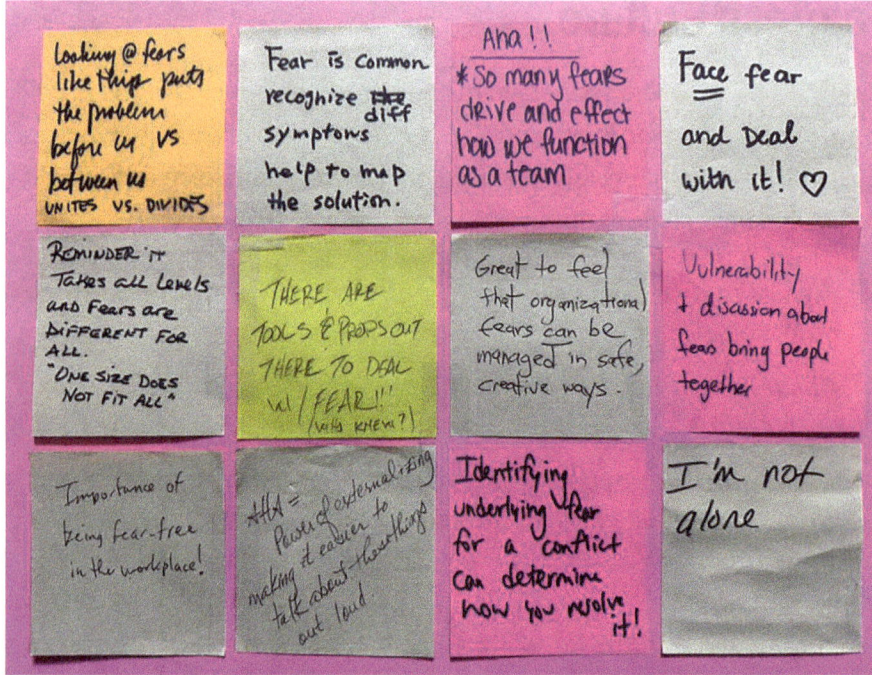

Figure 13-5. *Participants' reflections from Fear in the Workplace game*

Summary

In this chapter, you got to hear the voices of the participants from many of the workshops I facilitated. Different countries, different audiences, different depths of technical experience, yet very consistent takeaways.

As you start facilitating these games in your own workshops, the benefit of collecting these "Aha!" moments will become even more apparent. The sheer act of inviting your group to think and write makes their learning stronger. Collecting their thoughts and putting their takeaways on paper helps the participants to internalize their learning. Taking the time for reflection allows them to draw new parallels from the "magic circle" of the game to their real-life experiences.

Keep an eye on what works best in your setting and what part of the game can be simplified further. Experiment with the game dynamic and try new props, share your discoveries, and pass on your feedback, as well as that gathered by the other facilitators of these games in the community.

Stay connected! Share your photos on LinkedIn and tag me @DanaPylayeva. Ask your questions, share your modifications, and post your participants' "Aha!" moment on the game's Facebook page: `http://bit.ly/chocolegogameconnect`.

CHAPTER 14

Frequently Asked Questions

This chapter will equip you with several handy answers to the most frequently asked questions. Overall, you can expect to hear questions about the applicability of the experience in these games to the participants' specific situations. There will be questions about overcoming resistance to change, influencing management and business, and running these games with remote teams. Feel free to use my responses—or create your own!

LEGO and Chocolate Simulation

Q: Why are there no assembly instructions provided for the LEGO animals in this game?

A: The lack of assembly instructions is intentional. The purpose of the game is NOT to build LEGO animals according to an existing specification (that would be analogous to a manufacturing process). Instead, the game simulates product development, where customer needs may shift in response to market demands, and the final version of the product will emerge in close collaboration with the customer through iterations and feedback cycles.

In fact, to emphasize the need for the Scrum team to collaborate with the business, players in Benjamin Business roles are instructed to reject the LEGO animals if they were built without any input from them.

CHAPTER 14   FREQUENTLY ASKED QUESTIONS

Q: I am a designer. Where would my role be in this game?

A: In one of the Scrum teams as a developer. According to Ken Schwaber and Jeff Sutherland, co-creators of Scrum and the authors of the *Scrum Guide*:

> *"Developers are the people in the Scrum Team that are committed to creating any aspect of a usable Increment each Sprint. The specific skills needed by the Developers are often broad and will vary with the domain of work."*

Q: Why is it that the Scrum team in the game has separate roles for a Developer and a Tester?

A: Good catch! Many traditional organizations, while adopting the Scrum framework, fail to embrace it in its entirety. Instead, they carry forward their pre-existing functional roles (frontend developer, backend developer, QA/QE tester, etc.). The separate roles (Tim Tester and Danny Developer) are intentional. They are designed to highlight a typical anti-pattern and explore (through the game) the impact of this inner silo on the overall team effectiveness.

Q: The cross-training (in Sprint 2) reduced the need for Adam Admin. Do I still have a job after DevSecOps?

A: Absolutely! By training others and reducing the bottleneck in your process area, you've created bandwidth for innovation and learning. Now you can invest the time into upskilling yourself, learning about AWS, containerization, automated environment provisioning, CI/CD, and the extensive DevSecOps technology stack. You have the opportunity to redefine your role from firefighting to fire prevention and teams-enablement.

Q: I got cross-trained as a developer (in Sprint 2) but found it hard to integrate into a new team.

A: This is another important insight that the game highlights: we need to be mindful of the impact of structural team changes on the team's dynamic. In the game, and in real life, those teams that take time to integrate their new members, revisit team norms, and clarify roles and responsibilities, have a shorter path to becoming a high-performing team.

Q: How does DevSecOps fit with a segregation of duty required in our organization?

A: The segregation of duty is typically implemented to control risk. Extensive logging of automated builds, deployment pipelines, and automated environment provisioning is much more effective at controlling risk than traditional segregation of duty. As part of your DevSecOps transformation, you may need to have a conversation with the groups in charge of audit, risk, and compliance to help clarify and document how DevSecOps enables organizations to control risk.

Q: How are we going to reduce the size of the batches (in Sprint 3) if the client is still requesting them in large batches?

A: This is a great question. For DevSecOps transformation to succeed, it must be able to instigate change in the Business processes as well.

Q: Our DevOps is a siloed team; they are working on AWS migration and CI/CD work. Can we benefit from this game?

A: Absolutely! While it sounds like your organization has made progress in adopting the technical side of DevSecOps, this game can offer them an opportunity to dive into the cultural aspect of it.

Q: In our organization, Operations are called <insert specific group name here>.

Is it better to change the name of the roles in the game to match the roles in our organization?

A: While it might be tempting to do this, I would advise against it. The beauty of the game is in its abstraction from the "real world" during the simulation rounds. This abstraction enables a safe learning environment as it reduces defensiveness, blame, and finger-pointing. This is especially critical at the beginning of the game when we simulate a "pre-DevSecOps" way of working, discussing bottlenecks and inefficiencies in the game.

CHAPTER 14   FREQUENTLY ASKED QUESTIONS

If you are not convinced, consider this additional point from Bernie Maloney, the technical reviewer of this book:

> "Games help participants dissociate from their lived situation, helping them get into (in coaching terms) '3rd position.' In fact, in the breakthrough work I do, there's a common pattern:
>
> - associate client to a problem (uplevel the problem)
>
> - dissociate client from problem
>
> - associate client to new resources
>
> Any game/simulation dissociates the participants from their current situation, enabling the facilitator to safely associate them to the problem (through the simulation)."

Q: I am an RTE (release train engineer) in my organization. Why doesn't this game provide instructions on how to correctly number releases? It also doesn't provide instructions on how to do <insert your favorite release engineering best practice>!

A: You are right. This simulation is designed to model the end-to-end development and operation lifecycle. As such, it intentionally doesn't include every single detail of the process. They are "roughly right" to support the learning objectives of the game. By "stepping back," the game enables visualization of the flow of value, and the bottlenecks in that flow at the level of an organization. The detailed responsibilities of any role, or a deep dive into their associated best practices, are beyond the scope of this simulation.

CHAPTER 14   FREQUENTLY ASKED QUESTIONS

Fear in the Workplace and Safety in the Workplace Games

Most of the questions I receive when facilitating coaching conversations with these tools are either about game dynamics, specific fears, or safety practices listed on these cards. You can access a catalog of *Fears in the Workplace* as well as facilitation instructions in Chapter 10 and a catalog of *Safety Enhancements* in Chapter 11 of this book.

Q: Is there a "right" way to match specific Fears to their specific Safety Enhancers?

A: No. This is not a matching game, nor do I claim to have a set of silver bullets for each situation. The point of the game is to enable conversation and offer a set of ideas, practices, and tools that have helped others elevate safety.

Facilitation with Remote Teams

Q: My team is remote. Do you have a version of the *LEGO and Chocolate* game that can be facilitated in a virtual space?

A: Unfortunately, no. I spent some time at the beginning of the pandemic experimenting with ways to bring it online using Zoom breakout rooms and the Mural collaboration platform. What I discovered was that while I could technically find a way to recreate the elements of the game, I couldn't recreate the energy and ease of the physical movement in the room.

Here are several challenges I ran into:

- Peer-to-peer interaction beyond one table. The logistics of moving from one Zoom room to another (for Patricia Product to interact with Business, and for the Scrum teams to interact with Adam Admin, Robert Release,

CHAPTER 14   FREQUENTLY ASKED QUESTIONS

and Sara Security) were too cumbersome. While the Zoom breakout rooms enabled the creation of space for parallel conversations at each "table," they also reenforced organization silos.

- Moving "packages" between participants. Even if I opted for sending a set of LEGO bricks to every participant, it wouldn't help with the original game dynamic. In this game, the animals needed to be packaged and passed from one table to another!

- The steep learning curve of online collaboration platforms. Using Mural (or Miro) for simulating LEGO and Chocolate package building turned the simulation into a game for learning various Mural features, not a game for learning DevSecOps.

Even for a very experienced Mural user, the fun and the excitement of the in-person learning experience were lost. Learning about DevSecOps became boring and mundane at best, and I couldn't let this happen!

Later, as I was interviewing several DevSecOps trainers for Chapter 16 of this book, I learned about their attempts at taking this game online. Check out that chapter to learn what was different about their approach and how you might leverage similar adaptation for your needs.

In addition, consider bringing your remote team together for an offsite. Running the *LEGO and Chocolate* simulation with this team will have an added benefit of team building. Exploring the current challenges and team dysfunctions with the *Fear in the Workplace* game will help to deepen trust and empathy among the team members.

Q: How about *Fear in the Workplace* and *Safety in the Workplace*? Do you have a remote-friendly version of these games?

CHAPTER 14   FREQUENTLY ASKED QUESTIONS

A: Yes! As these games are "card games" in the physical space, it was much easier to convert them to a Mural board without sacrificing the game dynamic (see Figure 14-1). I had to reduce the number of cards in each game to make them fit better into one screen, and modify the layout and some graphics on the cards to improve readability.

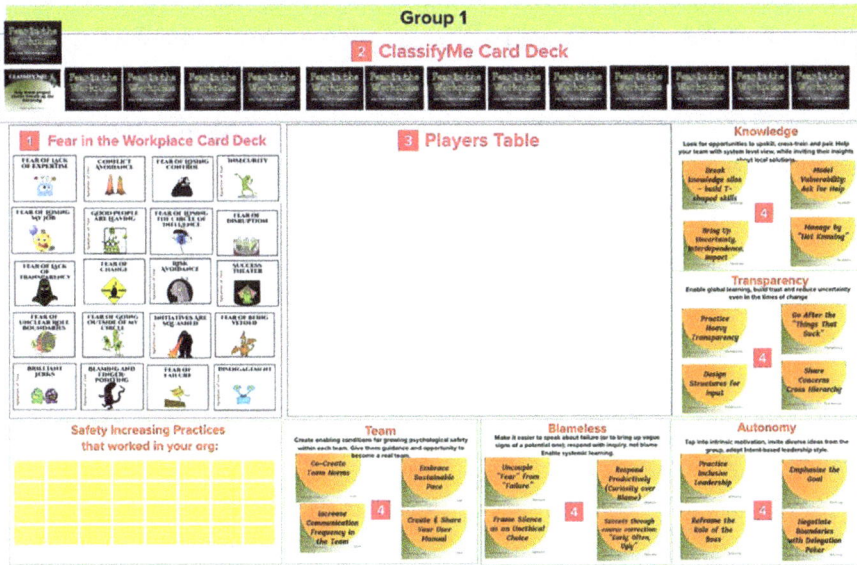

Figure 14-1. *Mural template of remote-friendly version of Fear in the Workplace and Safety in the Workplace coaching games*

While playing with a physical card deck still beats moving cards in Mural any day, the resulting coaching conversations are still powerful! The best part is that the simplicity of recreating and sharing boards in Mural (via Templates) makes it possible to offer them to the broader community with ease.

I have also experimented with a few playing card simulators. While the resulting dynamic was more engaging than Mural, these tools were not suitable for my corporate clients due to their restrictive "approved software" policies.

271

CHAPTER 14 FREQUENTLY ASKED QUESTIONS

> **Note** You can access my Mural template for *Fear in the Workplace* and *Safety in the Workplace* here: `http://tinyurl.com/FWBoardTemplate`

Q: Do you have a recommendation for additional ways to facilitate fearless conversations about culture in DevSecOps transformations?

A: There are several activities I found effective for this. One of them is TRIZ[1] Liberating Structure. It is designed to identify (and stop) counterproductive behaviors in a team dynamic, a business process, or an end-to-end workflow.

In this technique, the group is invited to come up with all possible ways to fail (instead of succeeding) with a desired outcome. Using the same dynamic as in 1-2-4-All,[2] the input is first created individually, then expanded upon in pairs, and then converged on in the groups of four.

As this first step is very playful, the group lets go of their inhibitions and typically lists out dysfunctions that they are familiar with. They may exaggerate them to make it more fun, and that is exactly the intent of this step.

In the second step, they are asked to select from the initial list those actions and behaviors that they are already doing. You finish by facilitating a discussion and inviting them to identify an item that they would be willing to STOP doing. You can check out the results of this activity from one of the groups I facilitated in Figure 14-2. I used Google Slides to enable remote collaboration in this example. You can also use Mural, Miro, or other collaboration tools.

> **Note** You can access my Mural template for facilitating TRIZ here: `http://tinyurl.com/TRIZBoardTemplate`

---

[1] https://www.liberatingstructures.com/6-making-space-with-triz/
[2] https://www.liberatingstructures.com/1-1-2-4-all/

CHAPTER 14   FREQUENTLY ASKED QUESTIONS

(LS) TRIZ Online Instructions

STEP 1: How can we reliably design a perfect way to fail a DevOps Transformation? List all the actions, behaviours and org design choices we can use to ensure it fails in the most spectacular way! Go Wild!

Compartmentalize info
Localize feedback
Create a DevOps Group but really make them a shared-service
Shoot the messenger
Announce DevOps transformation and make everyone figure out what that is.
Keep middle managers in the dark so they create Resistance to change
Don't include operations
Tell them they will be replaced by automation
Set a specific date to be DevOps, cancel it if we don't make the date
Dont' allow cross-functional teams
No budget for tools and no open source
Tools are the answer. Provide lots of them

STEP 2: Check the list again. Highlight the ones that you are already doing.

Figure 14-2. Sample output of TRIZ from one of the remote workshops, using Google Slides

Another activity popular with Liberating Structures practitioners is called **Tiny Monsters**. It is very effective at creating a safe space for conversations about fears. I was introduced to this activity by Nancy White, one of the LS maestros.[3]

In this activity, teams are invited to first write down their concerns and worries about the upcoming DevSecOps transformation. Then they are instructed to draw four simple shapes: a square, a circle, a spiky shape, and a random shape. Next, they are asked to add scary elements to their shapes (fur, horns, scary ears, teeth, etc.) to make them look like tiny monsters. Finally, they are asked to map their top four worries to their four

---

[3] https://fullcirc.com/2018/01/25/drawing-monsters-thanks-to-lynda-barry/

monsters and introduce their monsters to a random partner in a room (see Figure 14-3). Here is a small list of common fears that were uncovered through the Tiny Monsters activities with various groups:

- Fear of losing my job
- Fear of lack of expertise
- Fear of unicorns
- Fear of unclear role boundaries
- Fear of losing the circle of influence
- Fear of going outside of my circle
- Fear of failure
- fear of change

Figure 14-3. *Workshop participants sharing their DevSecOps concerns with each other using the Tiny Monsters activity*

CHAPTER 14   FREQUENTLY ASKED QUESTIONS

Summary

In this chapter, I shared with you several frequently asked questions that I encounter when running these simulation games. Workshop after workshop, it is the participants' questions that inspire me to reflect on the clarity of instructions, on having a balance between playfulness vs. learning, and continue to iterate on the games.

In the next chapter, I will share the play history and modifications of these DevSecOps coaching games that brought them to the state they are in today.

CHAPTER 15

Play History and Modifications: It's All about the Feedback!

I am writing this book as the *LEGO and Chocolate game* approaches its 10th anniversary. In this chapter, you will have an opportunity to learn about this game's evolution over the years. I've always looked at every conference, meetup, or private workshop with my clients as a chance to play-test it again, get more feedback, and continue improving it further. This chapter is the story of continuous improvement.

2013: Minimum Playable Version

As you may recall from the earlier chapters, this game originated as a small experiment for an internal meetup at Rakuten Marketing in November 2013 (see Figure 15-1).

CHAPTER 15   PLAY HISTORY AND MODIFICATIONS: IT'S ALL ABOUT THE FEEDBACK!

Figure 15-1. *Rakuten Marketing Thinkshare meetup, November 2013*

Inspired by *The Phoenix Project* and empowered by "gamification" training from Coursera, I designed a small activity with basic roles and rules to introduce DevOps "in plain language".

Since the meetup was scheduled right after Halloween, I had a lot of chocolate left in the house after my daughter's trick-or-treating and decided to use it at the meetup. In the first game, players were packing chocolate candies, and there was no LEGO in the game. Even though most of the current game dynamics hadn't been invented at that time, the game still turned out to be fun and helped the players broaden their views and learn a few things about DevOps. The game was far from perfect, but it had potential.

CHAPTER 15   PLAY HISTORY AND MODIFICATIONS: IT'S ALL ABOUT THE FEEDBACK!

2014–2015: First Public Workshops (v 1.0)

Right around the same time, the global Agile community was fascinated with LEGO games and training simulations. *LEGO4Scrum*[1] (aka LEGO City) by Alexey Krivitsky, and *TDD and Refactoring with LEGO*[2] by Bryan Beecham and Mike Bowler were the two simulations that inspired me to start learning more about the use of LEGO for training and coaching.

When I later described my game to Bryan, he helped me realize that by incorporating LEGO, I would have an opportunity to better simulate the dynamic of "knowledge work" (creating LEGO animals based on business needs) as opposed to the current "manufacturing" dynamic of the game (packing chocolates). He also convinced me to submit my first session proposal (as a co-speaker) to a public conference, and collaborated on the next version of the game, when the proposal got accepted at the Global Scrum Gathering New Orleans.

We called that session "Chocolate, LEGO, and Scrum Jambalaya[3]" as we were mixing several different ideas, topics, and materials in this workshop, just like a cook mixes ingredients in this famous New Orleans dish.

The game was evolving. We added role cards for the Scrum teams and Operations teams (Figure 15-2), solidified a story plot, and introduced the demand fluctuation idea with the Animal Exchange dynamic. We envisioned that the simulation would run in the second part of the 90-minute workshop, following a short lecture about Scrum, bottlenecks, change, gamification, and the Three Ways of DevOps. I also built the Prezi-style instructions to introduce the rules of the game we called "Treats4U."

---

[1] https://www.lego4scrum.com/
[2] https://www.infoq.com/presentations/tdd-lego/
[3] https://www.slideshare.net/danapylayeva/intro-todevops-chocolatelegoscrumjambalayasgnola

CHAPTER 15 PLAY HISTORY AND MODIFICATIONS: IT'S ALL ABOUT THE FEEDBACK!

Figure 15-2. *First role cards (version 1.0)*

Global Scrum Gathering New Orleans, May 2014

My first public speaking experience was nerve-racking, but when the workshop was over, I knew that I wanted to do it again! It was fascinating to see the game experience unfolding, and even more so, to play the role of the gamemaster in this simulation (Figure 15-3). The best part, of course, was the knowledge and experience of the workshop participants, and the feedback they shared at the end of the game.

How was this first public feedback? While everyone acknowledged the fun that they had in the sessions, several of them wondered whether the game had the right balance of learning versus fun and hoped for more learning. The other participants liked the game so much that they wanted to bring it to their organizations and wished for some facilitation instructions. The feedback from the former and interest from the latter inspired me to pursue further game development and to start working on the first facilitator guide on Leanpub.

I was now determined to seek more opportunities to play the game with an experienced audience by submitting several session proposals to various conferences, now as the main speaker. As I put my foot in the door of the exciting world of public speaking, I was also curious: where else can this game take me, if I make it more powerful, better balanced, and more robust?

In my wildest dreams, I couldn't have imagined that I would end up speaking at over 80 conferences and meetups in 16 countries after that first Scrum Gathering!

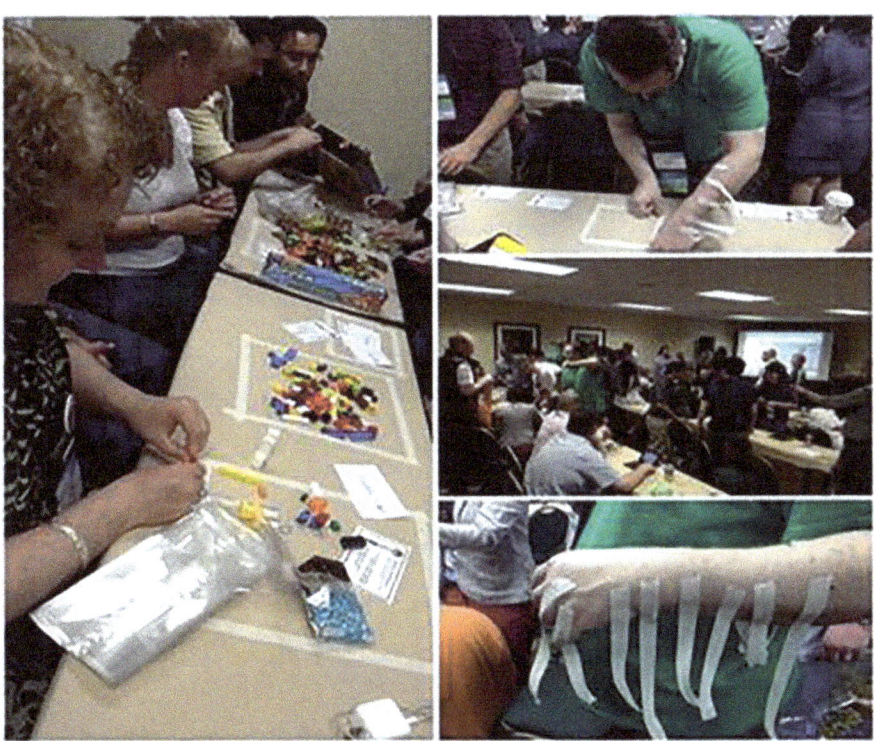

Figure 15-3. *Global Scrum Gathering, New Orleans, May 2014*

CHAPTER 15   PLAY HISTORY AND MODIFICATIONS: IT'S ALL ABOUT THE FEEDBACK!

Global Scrum Gathering Berlin, September 2014

This was my first international conference! I made a few incremental changes to the game and replaced confusing Prezi instructions with a simplified one-side version. I was also more confident in my ability to deliver this session at the public event. As I was walking the streets of Berlin mentally preparing for my workshop, I stumbled upon a stunning work of art at the Europa Center (Figure 15-4).

What can be a better metaphor for process bottlenecks? I included this photo in the slide deck[4] for my session (and kept it there till this day). Running this workshop in Berlin allowed me to tap into the experience and perspectives of participants from outside of the United States and validate that the game resonated with them as well. I received additional feedback on the role cards, requests for more instructions, and a suggestion to intermix the lecture segment of the workshop with the game's segments for a better flow.

---

[4]https://www.slideshare.net/danapylayeva/introduction-to-devops-with-lego-and-choco

CHAPTER 15   PLAY HISTORY AND MODIFICATIONS: IT'S ALL ABOUT THE FEEDBACK!

Figure 15-4. *The Flow-of-Time Clock by Bernard Gitton at Europa Center. Berlin, October 2014*

Toronto Agile and Software, November 2014

I modified the game again and brought it to a conference in Canada (see Figure 15-5). The workshop now had a better session flow, included rules of the game handout with seven pages of detailed instructions, and offered LevelUp stickers. I've also added plastic table covers for practical reasons—the break between my workshop and the next session was short, and I needed a way to simplify the clean up after my session.

CHAPTER 15   PLAY HISTORY AND MODIFICATIONS: IT'S ALL ABOUT THE FEEDBACK!

Figure 15-5.   *Toronto Agile and Software, Canada. November 2014*

Play4Agile in Rückersbach, February 2015

I got some valuable feedback from the workshop participants in Toronto, but I started to recognize that I needed a different type of feedback. If I wanted to make this game better, I needed to playtest it with agilists who were experienced in game design. Luckily, there was a group like that, and it gathered every year in a very special coach camp in Rückersbach, at the top of a mountain, in the middle of a German forest. This event was so popular, it had an admission lottery. I applied. I couldn't believe my luck when I got an email from them later, confirming that I was in!

I ran this game at Play4Agile with a group of 14 Agile game designers (Figure 15-6). This experience proved to be the most impactful for further game development. The detailed feedback and the new ideas inspired me

CHAPTER 15   PLAY HISTORY AND MODIFICATIONS: IT'S ALL ABOUT THE FEEDBACK!

to completely overhaul the game and create the next version (v2.0). Here are the most significant changes I introduced:

- two new characters (Benjamin Business and Harry Hacker)
- new avatars for Tim Tester, Robert Release, and Adam Admin
- complete redesign of all role cards with the addition of clear role dependencies
- retirement of Game Rules handouts—no one had the patience to read seven pages of instructions!

Figure 15-6. *Play4Agile. Rückersbach, Germany, February 2015*

CHAPTER 15   PLAY HISTORY AND MODIFICATIONS: IT'S ALL ABOUT THE FEEDBACK!

2016–2018: More Public Workshops (v2.0)

I loved this new version, and what's more important, conferences around the world loved it too! My session proposals were getting accepted now in more places, and this gave me the confidence to try something that had always scared me.

You see, my native language is Russian. I grew up in a Russian-speaking part of Eastern Ukraine, went to a university in Moscow, then came to New York when I was 25 years old.

As I started my professional life in the United States, I was using English exclusively for my business communication. When Agile and DevOps became popular, I learned about them in English. There were no words in my Russian vocabulary to describe either of them. It was driving me crazy that I was no longer capable of using my native language in a business context. I had to find a way to force myself to learn it, and I submitted my session proposal to a Russian-speaking conference in Moscow.

Agile Days 2015, March 2015

I created a completely new version of the slides for this conference, incorporated cultural references, and chose local names for the characters (see Figure 15-7), intentionally avoiding direct translation from one language to another.

CHAPTER 15   PLAY HISTORY AND MODIFICATIONS: IT'S ALL ABOUT THE FEEDBACK!

Figure 15-7.   Russian role cards created for Agile Days 2015, Moscow, Russia

At the same time, I was playtesting the game dynamic and the new card design of version 2.0 of this game. The feedback from the conference was positive and confirmed that the new card design was here to stay. The English version of these cards became the new standard for the workshops that followed (see Figure 15-8). After returning from this conference, I published the Russian version of the facilitation instructions for this workshop and the PDF of the role cards on LeanPub.[5]

---

[5] https://leanpub.com/chocolatelegoscrumgame_russian

CHAPTER 15   PLAY HISTORY AND MODIFICATIONS: IT'S ALL ABOUT THE FEEDBACK!

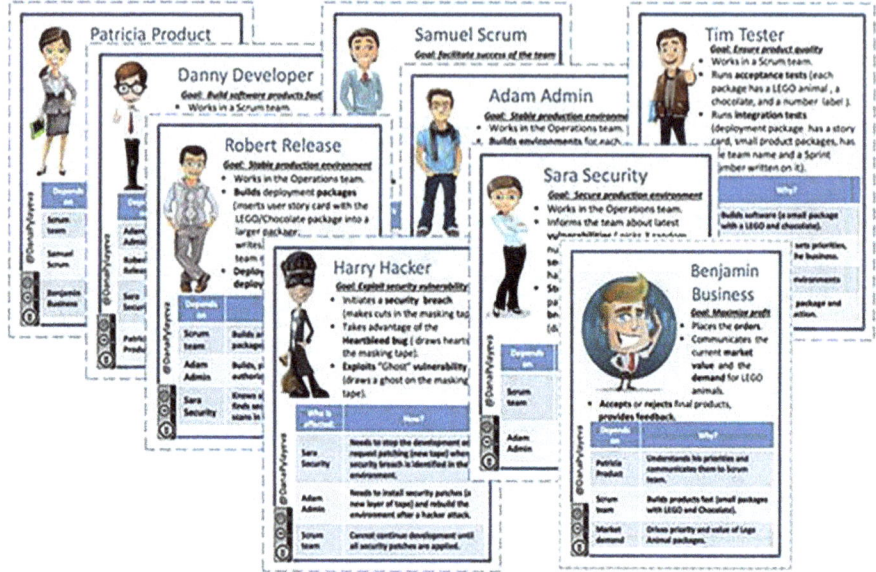

Figure 15-8. Role cards for version 2.0 of the game

I was ready for the next big challenge. It showed up as an opportunity to extend this game from its current 90-minute version to a half-day workshop as well as connect it with a subject of continuous delivery. If I could do it, the game would take me to Helsinki, Finland, in May!

XP2015, May 2015

Working with a half-day timebox allowed me to leave ample time for debriefing and, for the first time, experience the difference it can make for deepening participants' learning.

The version of the game that I brought to Helsinki had a better game dynamic for the Animal Exchange board as well. I discovered that by having an initial set of PBIs defined by the facilitator (myself), I could reduce the complexity for participants in Benjamin Business roles. These participants later embraced the opportunity to simulate market fluctuations, adjusting the prices and the demand up or down. I also introduced play money. Surprisingly, it had a major impact on people's engagement and increased their interest in building more complex products (Figure 15-9).

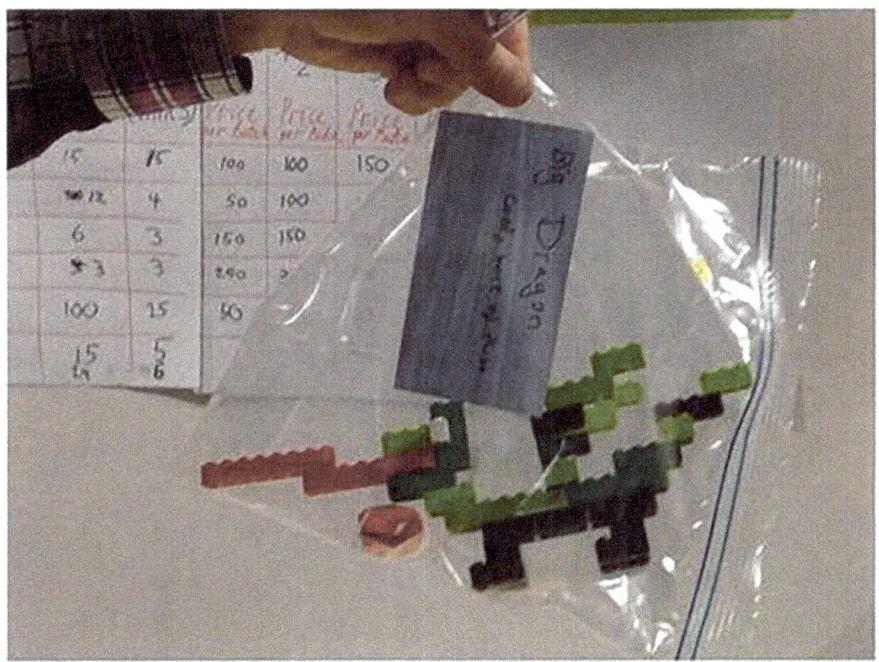

Figure 15-9. *One of the PBIs delivered by XP2015 participants: "A big dragon with a flame"*

This was also the first time that I introduced a cross-training simulation activity, using stickers of various colors to represent various skills of the players in the game. As I was describing each color-to-role mapping, one of the participants got up and wrote it down on an empty flipchart for everyone's reference. I later created a special in-room poster inspired by this impromptu one.

CHAPTER 15   PLAY HISTORY AND MODIFICATIONS: IT'S ALL ABOUT THE FEEDBACK!

Finally, I added the Total Security upgrade in Sprint 3 (simulated with a request to rebuild all the environments with a layer of green tape), introduced a "one-piece flow," and added the Continuous Delivery simulation in Sprint 4 (with individual green "secure" packages permitted for direct deployment into "production"). Again, another participant started tracking the number of packages he received at the business table (Figure 15-10). This later inspired me to add another in-room poster—the Delivery board.

The XP2015 experience was valuable and effective. Working with a small group of 30 people allowed for a lot of interaction, engaging discussions, and individual attention for each participant.

Figure 15-10. *XP 2015. Continuous delivery of value*

As I was running my game, I was also learning how to be a better facilitator, how to manage group dynamics, how to notice ideas worth building on for the future versions of the game, and how to accept feedback (both positive and constructive) as a gift.

Agile2015, August 2015

The Agile Alliance annual conference. The main stage. A dream for any aspiring Agile speaker. My workshop got accepted for Agile 2015 in Washington, DC, and I knew that this would be the most rewarding and the most challenging experience by far.

Unlike at the smaller conferences, there were no small rooms at Agile2015. I had to find a way to *scale the game up* to 100 players and at the same time *scale it down* to a 75-minute timebox. I had to find a way to engage a secondary facilitator to assist with the Animal Exchange Marketplace dynamic, divide the room for parallel facilitation of the game, and become really crisp with the timeboxing. Despite all these challenges, the workshop was successful and delivered clear learning for the participants (see Figure 15-11) and I even got selected to be interviewed by InfoQ.[6]

---

[6] https://www.infoq.com/interviews/dana-pylayeva-agile-scrum-lego-chocolate/

CHAPTER 15 PLAY HISTORY AND MODIFICATIONS: IT'S ALL ABOUT THE FEEDBACK!

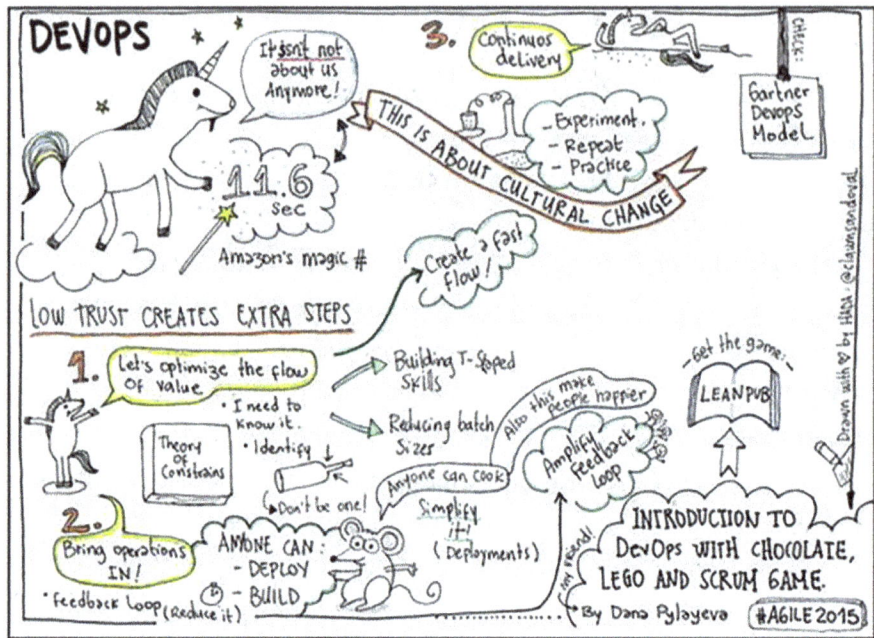

Figure 15-11. *A sketch note created by Claudia Sandoval during the workshop at Agile2015*

With all the feedback I gathered at Agile2015, the next modification was in order. The new iteration of the game included a one-page handout with a clear game flowchart as well as a new set of modification ("Mod") cards (Figure 15-12).

CHAPTER 15   PLAY HISTORY AND MODIFICATIONS: IT'S ALL ABOUT THE FEEDBACK!

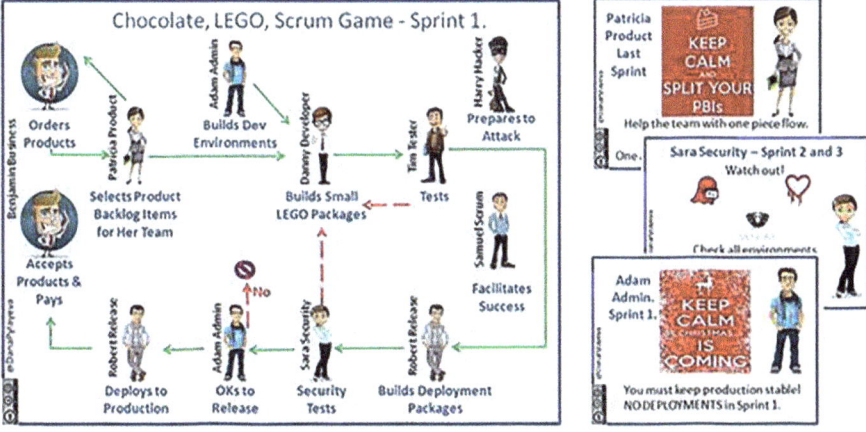

Figure 15-12. New game elements introduced after Agile2015

The Mod Cards formalized "surprise instructions" previously delivered verbally by the facilitator. In addition to improving the game, I've also improved the quality of content. Starting with Agile2015, I've included the latest findings from the "State of DevOps" reports, as well as the industry case studies about successful DevOps implementations. These changes proved to be beneficial and tested very well at the next two conferences in November of 2015.

Global Scrum Gathering Prague, November 2015

Back to a European conference, now with a much-improved version of the simulation! In this 90-minute workshop with 60 participants in the room, I confirmed the effectiveness of the new handouts (Figure 15-13) and met my future technical editor. I also observed a new dynamic in the Harry Hacker role. Though it was normally a secondary role reserved for a latecomer, this time around it became more visible. Due to the large size of the group in the workshop, we had a larger than usual number of Harry Hackers. They organized themselves very well and ended up planning their cyber-attacks like experienced cybercriminals.

CHAPTER 15   PLAY HISTORY AND MODIFICATIONS: IT'S ALL ABOUT THE FEEDBACK!

Figure 15-13. Global Scrum Gathering Prague 2015

Initially very disruptive, these attacks prompted the Development teams to become more creative and more vigilant in preventing and anticipating cyber-attacks.

Rakuten Technology Conference, November 2015

Can you guess what was the biggest surprise for me at the Rakuten Technology Conference in Tokyo, Japan? The 45 participants in my 90-minute workshop were not very comfortable with English! The main modification at that conference was running the game with a translator! I had to become very crisp with the instructions, trust the translator's experience with DevOps, and trust that the dynamic of the game would work, even with the language barrier hiccup (Figure 15-14).

CHAPTER 15   PLAY HISTORY AND MODIFICATIONS: IT'S ALL ABOUT THE FEEDBACK!

Figure 15-14. *Rakuten Technology Conference 2015 Tokyo, Japan*

US, Brazil, and Portugal Conferences in 2016

I continued speaking at conferences and gathering participants' feedback to fine-tune the game:

Agile & Beyond[7], Detroit, MI, US, May 2016
Regional Scrum Gathering Rio[8], Brazil, June 2016
Regional Scrum Gathering Porto, Portugal, December 2016

---

[7] https://www.slideshare.net/danapylayeva/bring-down-the-walls-for-confusion-agile-and-beyond-2016
[8] https://www.slideshare.net/danapylayeva/introduction-to-devops-with-chocolate-and-lego-game

CHAPTER 15   PLAY HISTORY AND MODIFICATIONS: IT'S ALL ABOUT THE FEEDBACK!

Content Delivery Redesign with TBR in 2017

In April 2017, I was able to join a training from The Back of the Room (TBR) workshop with Sharon Bowman. The brain-based learning principles of Sharon's approach to instructional design resonated with me and helped me rethink my style of teaching the DevOps Culture (see Figure 15-15).

Figure 15-15. Redesigning DevOps Culture workshop at training from the Back of the Room training with Sharon Bowman, April 2017

CHAPTER 15   PLAY HISTORY AND MODIFICATIONS: IT'S ALL ABOUT THE FEEDBACK!

Taking Sharon's training led to a redesign of the workshop delivery with the alignment to the 4Cs framework (Connection, Concept, Concrete Practice, Conclusion). I also enhanced it with several teaching techniques from TBR (checking for comprehension, teach-back, three-before-me, etc.).

The next two conferences confirmed the effectiveness of these improvements. DevOps with *LEGO and Chocolate* game workshops received rave reviews at both the Agile Alliance Technical Conference[9] (AATC2017) in Boston as well as at Regional Scrum Gathering South Africa[10] in Cape Town.

2018: The *Fear in the Workplace* Is Born!

Originally introduced under the working title of the "Fear Eradicated" game in my keynote[11] at the Agile Games 2018 conference (see Figure 15-16), both the *Fear in the Workplace* and the *Safety in the Workplace* games have gone through several iterations, improving the design of the game components and completely changing the dynamic of the games.

---

[9] https://www.slideshare.net/danapylayeva/aatc-gamifying-devops-with-lego-and-chocolate-game

[10] https://www.slideshare.net/danapylayeva/devops-game-at-sgza

[11] https://www.slideshare.net/danapylayeva/agile-games-2018-keynote-team-up-to-eradicate-fear

CHAPTER 15   PLAY HISTORY AND MODIFICATIONS: IT'S ALL ABOUT THE FEEDBACK!

Figure 15-16. Fear Eradicated game components as they appeared at the Agile Games conference. Boston, US, April 2018

The first version of the game was heavily inspired by two of my favorite board games: Pandemic[12] and Dragonwood.[13] However, participants at the Agile Games conference found the game dynamic confusing. They also wanted to spend more time discussing each of the fears and learning more about the psychological safety–enhancing practices, rather than rolling the dice and collecting the cards. While the original dynamic wasn't ideal, the conversations that these cards enabled surprised the participants. Everyone commented on the depth of the discussions and the ease with which they could engage in conversations about fears.

---

[12] https://www.amazon.com/Z-Man-Games-ZM7101-Pandemic/dp/B00A2HD40E

[13] https://www.amazon.com/Dragonwood-Game-Dice-Daring-Board/dp/B00UB7OV7K?th=1

CHAPTER 15 PLAY HISTORY AND MODIFICATIONS: IT'S ALL ABOUT THE FEEDBACK!

Fear-Focused Retrospective at HBC Digital

Inspired by the feedback, I continued experimenting. I brought the cards to an organization I was coaching at that time and used them to facilitate a "fear-focused retrospective" with a team and their manager (see Figure 15-17).

Figure 15-17. *Fear landscape identified in a fear-focused retrospective with a team*

In this version, every participant received a deck of fear cards and was asked to select the top five that they were experiencing in their current team. The selected cards were collected by the facilitator (face down), shuffled, and arranged at the table. The resulting fear landscape was further discussed by the team. The experiment produced the results in more ways than expected. First, I was able to identify and add new fears to this deck in preparation for this retrospective, and second, the team and their manager were able to have an open conversation about the dysfunctions that their relationship was struggling with.

AgileCamp2018 Conference, New York, September 2018

Next, I tried introducing a Lean Coffee-style dynamic at the AgileCamp2018 conference in New York City (Figure 15-18). The participants were asked to dot-vote on the fears that they observe most often in their organizations, prioritize them for discussion, and then spend 5-8 minutes discussing each fear and identifying one or more safety practices to add to their fear eradication strategy.

CHAPTER 15   PLAY HISTORY AND MODIFICATIONS: IT'S ALL ABOUT THE FEEDBACK!

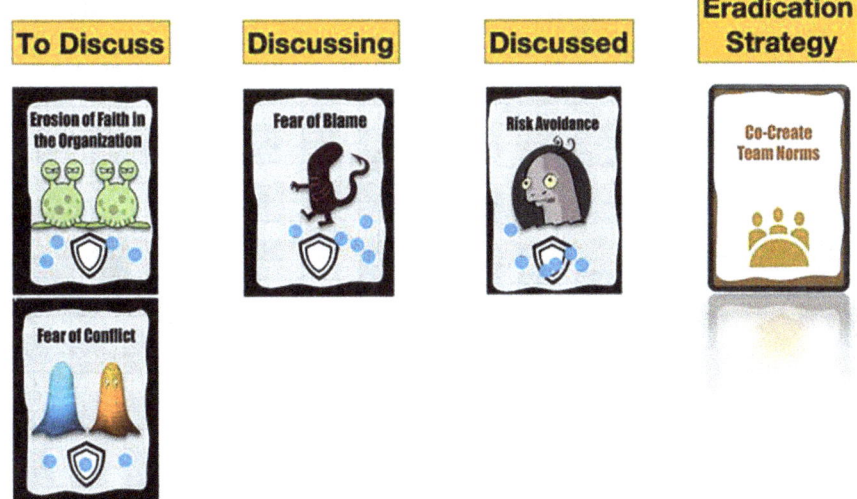

Figure 15-18. Experimenting with Lean Coffee dynamic at AgileCamp, NYC, September 2018

The feedback from these experiments confirmed that the game was ready for an upgrade from the current paper prototype version to a more professional look and feel. After reviewing several card printing options, I selected The Gamecrafter platform and published the first version of the *Fear in the Workplace* game on October 15, 2018.

Agile + DevOps East Conference, Orlando, Florida, November 2018

Right around the same time, I was invited to run my *Introduction to DevOps* as a half-day tutorial at the Agile + DevOps East 2018 conference by TechWell (Figure 15-19).

CHAPTER 15   PLAY HISTORY AND MODIFICATIONS: IT'S ALL ABOUT THE FEEDBACK!

Figure 15-19. *Agile + DevOps 2018 participants playing the Fear in the Workplace game*

I used this opportunity to supplement the *LEGO and Chocolate* simulation with the *Fear in the Workplace* game, specifically in the context of teaching the group about the Third Way of DevOps. In addition to the *Fear* cards, the game had new *ClassifyMe* cards with direct quotes and scenarios of what people say or do when they work in organizations with fear-ridden or bureaucratic cultures. The two games complemented each other in offering complete coverage of the Three Ways of DevOps learning. However, from the facilitation perspective, the games were evoking two different energies in the room. I felt a need to bring up the energy in the room after the deep reflections and conversations enabled by the *Fear in the Workplace*. This is how I started incorporating the 25/10 Crowdsourcing,[14] Tiny Monsters,[15] and other Liberating Structures into my workshops. You can read more about facilitating them in the appendix.

Train-the-Trainer Workshops

As the workshop became popular, I started receiving inquiries from various clients about bringing DevOps coaching games into their organizations as well as training their internal trainers to scale these DevOps training offerings. By September 2018, I officially started my own business with the first large contract for bringing these workshops and the train-the-trainer sessions to a client's eleven global technology hubs.

This inspired me to iterate once again on the design of the role cards[16] for the *LEGO and Chocolate* game, to create the DevOps Simulation Starter Kit (see Figure 15-20) with all the components required to run the game with a group of 21 participants. I later started offering these workshops as public training as well.

---

[14] https://www.liberatingstructures.com/12-2510-crowd-sourcing/
[15] https://fullcirc.com/2018/01/25/drawing-monsters-thanks-to-lynda-barry/
[16] https://www.thegamecrafter.com/games/devops-culture-role-cards

CHAPTER 15   PLAY HISTORY AND MODIFICATIONS: IT'S ALL ABOUT THE FEEDBACK!

Figure 15-20. *DevOps Simulation Starter Kit and the new Role Cards created for Train-the-Trainer workshops, 2018*

2019–2020: More Workshops, Design Iterations, and Global Pandemic

I continued running these workshops at various conferences, incorporating feedback and making minor modifications to the games:

- January 2019 – Continuous Delivery Meetup, New York, NY, US

- April 2019 – Deliver Agile 2019, Nashville, TN, US

CHAPTER 15   PLAY HISTORY AND MODIFICATIONS: IT'S ALL ABOUT THE FEEDBACK!

- May 2019 – Global Scrum Gathering, Austin, TX, US[17]
- June 2019 – Agile + DevOps West 2019, Las Vegas, NV, US

AgileCamp2019, New York, October 2019

By the time the AgileCamp conference came back to NYC in 2019, I redesigned and published the first professionally printed version of the *Safety in the Workplace* game on the Gamecrafter (Figure 15-21). Fun fact: there were several participants in my workshop who also attended its earlier version in 2018, who have played with the original paper prototype version of the game, and whose feedback inspired the final version of the cards, and the workshop[18] they were attending now.

Figure 15-21. *Safety in the Workplace, released in time for the AgileCamp2019 conference*

---

[17] https://www.slideshare.net/danapylayeva/team-up-to-eradicate-fear
[18] https://www.slideshare.net/danapylayeva/journey-without-fear

CHAPTER 15   PLAY HISTORY AND MODIFICATIONS: IT'S ALL ABOUT THE FEEDBACK!

OOP2020, Munich, Germany, February 2020

While there were no significant modifications made in preparation for this conference, it is worth mentioning as it became the very last pre-Covid in-person conference (Figure 15-22).

Figure 15-22. *OOP2020 participants, Munich, Germany*

Agile India 2020 and the Failed Attempt at Online Conversion

This is the conference I was invited to speak at in March of 2020. As you already know, right around the time when the whole world went into lockdown. As the conference organizers decided to postpone the conference to October and make it virtual, I was then faced with the need (and opportunity) to create an online version of the *LEGO and Chocolate* workshop.

CHAPTER 15   PLAY HISTORY AND MODIFICATIONS: IT'S ALL ABOUT THE FEEDBACK!

While I did manage to create a Mural board and translate the game components into their online equivalents (Figure 15-23), the balance between fun and learning was completely lost in translation. The online version required an advanced level of Mural skills and couldn't recreate the ease of cross-table and cross-room collaboration.

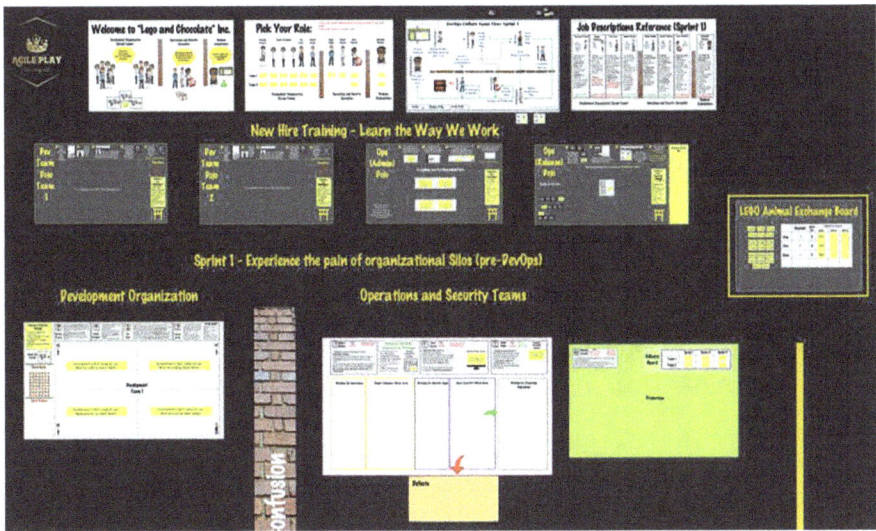

Figure 15-23.   A failed attempt at an online version of the LEGO and Chocolate workshop

After a few other attempts, I made a conscious choice to NOT convert the *LEGO and Chocolate* game to an online experience.

2021: *Fear in the Workplace* and *Safety in the Workplace*, Online Edition

I first considered converting these games into an online experience while building a curriculum for an internal leadership training. Since the main point of these games was to enable conversations, the move from an in-person experience of holding and shuffling physical cards to an online

CHAPTER 15   PLAY HISTORY AND MODIFICATIONS: IT'S ALL ABOUT THE FEEDBACK!

experience of moving the virtual cards in Mural did not create a drastic loss of user experience. After a few experiments, I released a publicly available version with an upgraded card design, a reduced number of Fear cards, and simplified versions of the Safety cards. Instead of the three original categories (Individual, Team, and Leadership), the new Safety cards were now subdivided into five categories (Knowledge, Transparency, Autonomy, Blameless, and Team) (see Figure 15-24).

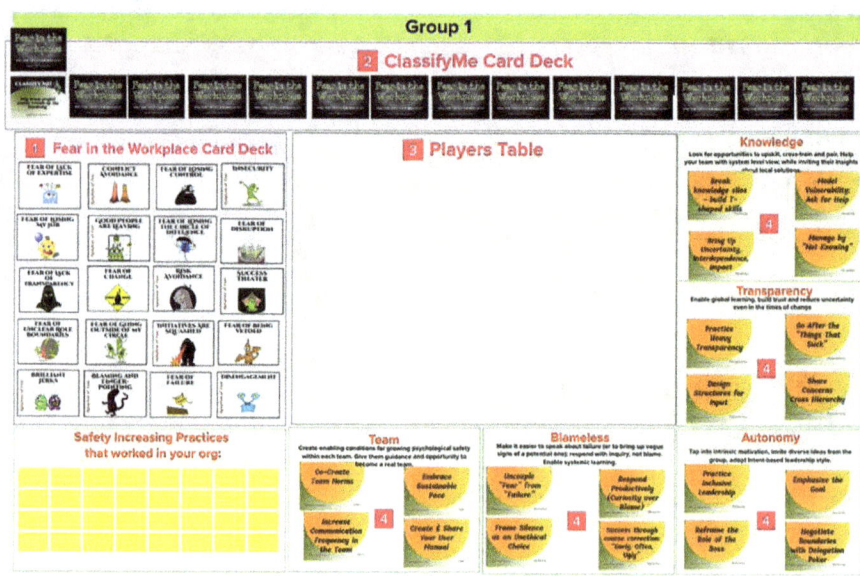

Figure 15-24. *The online version of the Fear in the Workplace and the Safety in the Workplace games*

2022: DevOps Coaching Games Are Back!

I am delighted to report that the *LEGO and Chocolate* game is back! I've been running it again with my clients, as well as offering the half-day tutorial version at the Agile + DevOps East conferences by TechWell.

CHAPTER 15 PLAY HISTORY AND MODIFICATIONS: IT'S ALL ABOUT THE FEEDBACK!

Several of the trainers who trained with me before the pandemic are reaching for their DevOps Simulation Starter Kit again and successfully bringing this simulation to their organizations. Now it's your turn!

In the final chapter of this book, I will share with you several field stories from other coaches and trainers who've experimented with the *LEGO and Chocolate* simulation, the *Fear in the Workplace* game, or both. I had a great time interviewing them for this chapter and appreciate their contribution to this book.

Will there be a new game version at some point? While the game has a good balance now, the feedback from participants can always trigger new ideas. How can you as a future facilitator help the game evolve? Run the game and share your story!

CHAPTER 16

Kickstarting Transformations with Games: Field Stories

This final chapter is a collection of field stories from several coaches and trainers who've been using my coaching games in their practice. I chose to interview these six experts for a very specific reason. Through these years, as I was iterating on the games, they were also running them in their parts of the world, adjusting them to their local contexts. Thanks to social media, we kept an eye on each other's progress, cheering the experiments and occasionally sharing notes.

My hope is that after reading about their unique situations and experiences with these games, you too will be inspired to bring these coaching games to organizations to kickstart their transformational journeys. Even more so, I hope that you too will start experimenting with evolving these games on your own, using the feedback from your groups and tailoring these coaching games to your context.

CHAPTER 16   KICKSTARTING TRANSFORMATIONS WITH GAMES: FIELD STORIES

Karl Métivier, Canada

About Karl Métivier:

Karl is an Agile, Lean & DevOps Coach and Value Stream Enthusiast from Quebec, Canada, who created the French translations of the *LEGO and Chocolate* and *Fear in the Workplace* games. Karl facilitated these games with 15+ groups while working as a consultant at a private telecommunication company. A frequent speaker at Agile Tour conferences, he also ran these games at several French-speaking public meetups and conferences.

LinkedIn: https://www.linkedin.com/in/karlmetivier/

Our collaboration with Karl started with a LinkedIn message I received in May of 2017:

> *"Dana, I am a technical agile coach working in Canada. We are looking to use your DevOps game and we are wondering if we can translate your training materials in French?"*

I was looking at the message and couldn't believe my eyes. An Agile coach was offering to translate my DevOps game material to French, the language I've always been fascinated with and tried to learn so many times?! Fast forward a few months, and I was looking at the masterful translation that Karl created together with his colleague Mariana Vielmas. Similar to the approach I'd taken earlier with my Russian translation, they'd chosen to localize the names of the game characters. I was smiling at Robert Release's new identity as Luc Livraison, Benjamin Business's turning into Alan Affaires, and so on. Karl and Mariana also translated the training deck,[1] and following this translation facilitated the *DevOps with LEGO and Chocolate* simulation for more than 15 internal groups across several organizations. They also delivered it as a workshop at French-speaking conferences, where they facilitated the simulation with groups of up to 60 people.

When I published my *Fear in the Workplace* game, Karl, Mariana, and their colleague Hachem Gaas offered to collaborate on the game's translation again. You can find the results of their work as a *Peur au Travail*[2] coaching game on the Gamecrafter site. As I was interviewing Karl for this chapter, I learned that he had also experimented with running the *Fear in the Workplace* game in various contexts: as an independent game for leaders, development teams, and mixed groups from various parts of an organization. I've summarized the highlights from our interview into the following five tips, sprinkling in several soundbites from Karl.

1. Ensure Buy-in and Continuity

When bringing these games as an external consultant it is critical to get the initial management buy-in. As Karl noted, management is often buzzword-driven and asks for a training because:

> *"We have to be DevOps!*
>
> *- Okay, but what is DevOps for you?*
>
> *- Well, people work faster, or we have tooling.*
>
> *- Well, it's not that . . ."*

---

[1] https://www.slideshare.net/excellenceAgile/atelier-de-simulation-devops
[2] https://www.thegamecrafter.com/games/peur-au-travail

This initial confusion can be used as an opportunity to bring in a different type of DevOps/DevSecOps training. The one that will guide the teams through experiential learning of flow, of the pull notion, and help them move beyond the buzzwords. To increase the "stickiness" of learning from this training, nudge people into taking on roles that are different from their real-life roles:

> "Ah, you're a manager? Why don't you do the dev role? You are a developer, go try the Ops role."

Finally, remember to include internal coaches in your workshop. As an external trainer, you often don't get to see the long-term impact of the workshops you facilitate. Bringing in other coaches can enable long-lasting results from your training as the coaches can experience and see what other participants experience through this simulation. Most important, they can hear the reflections, participate in the debriefing, help connect the learning with the organizational context, and later refer to the learning from this shared experience.

2. Watch Out for Habitual Behaviors

A funny thing that happens in this simulation: people bring in their current way of acting and thinking. As a facilitator, pay close attention to those participants who bring in behavior that can be at odds with the generative culture of DevSecOps. As Karl noted:

> "Some roles (the business owner or the product owner) are crucial in the game. If the wrong person is in that role, it can divert the flow of the game. Just like a wrong person in the product owner or product manager role can also derail the functionality of the team in real life."

What are some of the most typical examples? "Command and control" management style of the Scrum Master or the Product Owner, operating within the boundaries of one's role even after being cross-trained, and expecting a "detailed requirement" for each animal, which can be blindly followed without a need to ever talk to the business.

3. Draw Attention to Business Needs

People often don't pay close attention to the Animal Exchange Board or the current needs of the business. Karl shared a story of a business owner who invented an animal in one of the workshops. He asked for a "wuss." To his surprise, the team didn't even blink when taking a card with "2 Wuss" to build. It took them close to 10 minutes to come back to him and ask, "What is a wuss?" The important insight that the team derived in the debriefing was:

> "If something is not clear, you have to clarify it before putting it forth into development."

To help your teams feel the importance of paying close attention to the needs of the business, add something unusual to the Animal Exchange Board. A funny animal, or a dragon with a price of 100—I want one! Observe what happens. Most people will start building a dragon based on the way they think about a dragon, but what is a dragon to the Business Owner?

4. Ask: "How Can We improve?"

After playing the games, take time to debrief the experience and help the team uncover potential improvement opportunities in their work. Some of the questions to ask are:

> "We have played the game, now what can we improve?
>
> Do we modify our team design?

Are we okay?

How do we collaborate?

How can we balance resources and flow?"

5. First Master the Games, Then Modify Them

If you are considering bringing these games to your group, take the time to prepare. Do a practice run with a small group. Do it several times to master them. Perhaps you will tweak these games after a few times to adjust them to your contexts. With both games, Karl has been making modifications. With the *LEGO and Chocolate* simulation, Karl introduced visible signs for team names, improved the clarity of instructions, and brought it into the French-speaking Agile/DevSecOps community.

With *Fear in the Workplace* (or *Peur au Travail* for French speakers) he tailored the set of Fear Monster cards and the game dynamic to the specific audience. With a group of DevOps leaders, he used a subset of the cards and invited leaders to talk about their department by asking: "Do you see these kinds of fears in your teams?"

With development teams, he alternated between two different ways of playing the game. In the first one, the team was asked to select their top three fears for discussion. In another one, they used the ClassifyMe cards with various scenarios, selecting the ones that they found most relevant to their situation. The second version seemed to be harder for the teams to put in context. Where it became more applicable is with the teams that occasionally had trouble working together. In this case, the game could drive some insightful conversations. Another variation was to bring this game when working with a group of people from different departments. When the group uncovered similar fears, even though they were not working in the same team, this could point to a larger issue at an organizational level.

One of the most unusual modifications that Karl shared was his experience of combining it with the Marshmallow Challenge:[3]

> *"We did a marshmallow challenge and talked about 'Are you safe to fail?'*
>
> *You can fail the design of your marshmallow challenge and start from the beginning: a new strategy, a new architecture. Some people stay with the current design, and they fail at the end. So, we wanted to talk about failing. We ran the Marshmallow Challenge, and after that we talked a little bit about the fears, then played Fear in the Workplace."*

Karl noted how in all these modifications the game enables candid conversations about the difficult topic of emotions and feelings. The funny monster cards create a safe space for people to open up, explore together, and find ways to address the current issues in the inner workings of the team.

Dr. Peter Fassbinder, Germany

About Dr. Peter Fassbinder:

Peter has over fifteen years of hands-on experience in Lean/Agile and more than six years in implementing Continuous Delivery and DevOps in industrial enterprises. He was one of the first trainers to create a virtual adaptation of the *LEGO and Chocolate* simulation.

LinkedIn: https://www.linkedin.com/in/peter-fassbinder-3a8209194/

---

[3] https://www.ted.com/talks/tom_wujec_build_a_tower_build_a_team

CHAPTER 16   KICKSTARTING TRANSFORMATIONS WITH GAMES: FIELD STORIES

Peter reached out to me with questions about the *LEGO and Chocolate* simulation in February 2020, just before the global pandemic made all in-person trainings out of reach. He attended one of my first virtual DevOps Culture Certified Trainer classes and began experimenting with taking this simulation into the virtual space. One year later, he shared the results of his experiments on LinkedIn. Since then, he has been able to facilitate his virtual adaptation of this simulation with over 20 groups ranging from 12 to 20 people. I was thrilled when he agreed to sit down with me for an interview and share his field story.

Virtual Adaptation with a Focus on Flow

As you know, after a few of my own attempts with Mural and Zoom in 2020, I decided not to pursue creating a virtual version of the *LEGO and Chocolate* simulation. I wasn't willing to let go of any elements, dynamics, or characters of the original game. Peter's approach was different. Instead of trying to keep as much of the original game as possible, he decided to focus the game on one key learning—the benefits of the smooth, uninterrupted flow of Continuous Delivery.

Major Simplifications

Acknowledging the difficulties of running a complex simulation in a virtual space, the shortened attention span of the participants, and the required learning curve for the new online collaboration tools, Peter cut down the game to its bare minimum.

First, he removed the roles of Benjamin Business, Patricia Product, Samuel Scrum, and Harry Hacker, and dropped the game dynamics associated with these roles. Next, he replaced the task of building the LEGO animals on a physical table with the task of coloring simple geometric shapes on a virtual collaboration board. Finally, he eliminated the cross-training (T-shaped skills building) activity, which in person required simultaneous conversations between multiple, random, self-organized pairs of participants.

Tools and Setup

Peter used Conceptboard[4] (a German collaboration tool for digital teams, comparable to Mural) to set up three different boards—one per round of the simulation game. Each board had pre-defined virtual tables with the names of the training participants pre-assigned. On each table, there was a built-in link to a pre-created team-specific Microsoft Teams meeting.

When people joined the training, they could immediately find their respective tables and their roles. When they needed to communicate with someone from another team (Sara Security, Robert Release, or Adam Admin), all they needed to do was click on the link on the other group's table. Just like in real life, a Microsoft Teams window would pop up, inviting them to join another call. As Peter recalled:

> *"Talking to someone from administration, in round one, really required the people not just shout over to the next table. They actually had to leave their meeting. They had to go to another meeting, and this reflected the reality even more. From this aspect, I think we even had a better simulation than the original one."*

Key Observations

As we continued discussing the simulation, Peter pointed out several important observations derived from facilitating it with 20+ virtual groups.

---

[4] https://conceptboard.com/

This Simulation Works Well as an Eye-opener

The simulation works well when introduced at the beginning of a digital transformation. It works as an eye-opener because people typically don't associate these types of transformations with a need to change their processes, their current ways of working, and their current team design.

Peter typically includes this simulation at the very beginning of his DevOps awareness trainings. After guiding the participants through the experience and allowing them to generate the "Aha!" moments, he follows up with an extensive debriefing session. Here are a few sample questions from these discussions:

- What are the application scenarios of what you just learned?
- How does it apply to your organization?
- What is the impact on your organization?
- What are the required changes in processes, organizational setups, etc., that you need to do?

"Shift-left" on Security Benefits the Team

Through this simulation, people quickly understand the benefit of shifting security testing to the beginning of the process. "Shift-left" on security is the very first improvement that they identify during the debriefing, with minimal prompting from the facilitator. In addition, they are typically quick to acknowledge the positive impact of becoming cross-functional on the team's' ability to address bottlenecks.

The "One-Piece Flow" Requires a Mindset Shift

The ability to influence a shift in mindset is the biggest benefit of this simulation. In larger companies, people have been running large releases and projects for their entire careers. Often, they don't even think about the possibility of doing it differently.

The simulation shows them that there is another way. Large releases are not mandatory; we can challenge that!

New Processes and a Competency Build-up Are Necessary for Avoiding Chaos

This final key learning will resonate strongly with anyone involved in organizational transformation of any kind; Cloud, DevSecOps, Digital transformation—they all require time for the new processes to take hold and for people to develop competencies in new areas. When this learning emerges through the simulation, it helps raise awareness and bring focus to this often-neglected topic.

As Peter observed, during the final debriefing people consistently noticed that with the move to a one-piece flow, their processes became a bit chaotic, and they experienced several quality issues in the simulation. This is where he usually jumps in to help solidify learning:

> "Yes, of course. We cannot just simply say 'everybody does everything and one-piece flow and when it's ready, we throw it into production.' We need a lot of tools and mechanisms, like a high degree of test automation to ensure the quality in every step or real-time status transparency. We cannot simply all deploy into production; we need a competence build-up on t-shaped profiles."

Taking this to a broader context, DevSecOps transformations require re-thinking of the upstream and the downstream processes as well. Can the customer handle so many frequent deployments? What about

CHAPTER 16   KICKSTARTING TRANSFORMATIONS WITH GAMES: FIELD STORIES

businesspeople, salespeople, support, and installations? As we introduce the technology and change processes to enable frequent releases, a lot of other functions will be affected by this and need to be brought into the information loop.

Wayne Hetherington, Canada

About Wayne Hetherington:

Wayne is an Enterprise Coach from Toronto, Canada, who is helping people find better ways to work. Wayne has been using the *Fear in the Workplace* card game with teams and leaders to facilitate difficult conversations at work.

LinkedIn: `https://www.linkedin.com/in/wayne-hetherington/`

Here are some observations about his experience that he shared with me in our private email exchange.

What role do the Fear in the Workplace (and other coaching games) play in what you do?

> "The Fear cards are an interesting way to get into the difficult conversations at work. People often feel uncomfortable talking about issues, and playing a game like this can make it easier for everyone to speak their mind. As a coach, I am always looking for ways to help people improve their work environment, and the game/cards helps me do that."

CHAPTER 16 KICKSTARTING TRANSFORMATIONS WITH GAMES: FIELD STORIES

What have you noted when you followed up with the participants after these games?

> "I have noted that people are discussing what they learned in the game weeks afterward. I even sometimes overhear them using the terms/phrases off the cards in their discussions with each other."

What is a typical scenario when you would bring this game to an organization?

> "I have used the 'Fear' cards in two scenarios:
>
> 1) In a team setting, typically during a retrospective, where the team gets to examine some of the things that might be holding them back. **This setting tends to be more personal,** and team members get to discuss their feelings and experiences first-hand.
>
> 2) In a leadership setting, where leaders use the cards to discuss what they see happening with their people. This **third person discussion** tends to be **less personal and safer** to have."

What patterns have you noticed when facilitating the game with various groups?

> "I have noticed that either people are well aware of the problems that are causing the fear, or that they have completely missed the issues altogether. One conversation will lead to a diagnosis and hopefully corrective action, the other leads to discovery and awareness."

In what setting have you seen the game resonating?

"The game seems to resonate more with leaders who are responsible for creating positive working environments. Although teams can identify with the fears, I have found that they often feel helpless to make any changes so the game becomes a validation of what they already know."

Is there anything else you'd like to share about the game?

"The 'Fear' cards are powerful! They can uncover some deep emotions and may even surface conflict. Be careful! It is a good idea to set some boundaries before starting the game. Are there any issues that you will not discuss? How will we know when to stop?"

What has been your experience running the Fear in the Workplace game?

"It has been challenging to run an effective 'Fear' discussion since I often feel unqualified to guide the conversation and keep it positive. Good teams can have this discussion relatively easily but bad teams (who probably need to discuss the issue more) can be hard to facilitate positively."

Have you seen any new fears emerging in these conversations?

"Fear of losing my job seems to come up often (similar to fear of layoffs) as does fear of speaking up or reporting problems—which may result in job loss."

CHAPTER 16 KICKSTARTING TRANSFORMATIONS WITH GAMES: FIELD STORIES

Norma Hernandez Garcia, José Luis Ortiz González, and Jorge Gándara, Grupo Salinas, Mexico

About Norma Hernandez Garcia:

Norma is an Agile Coach and Trainer who introduced the DevOps with LEGO, Chocolate, and Scrum Game in Grupo Salinas.

LinkedIn: https://www.linkedin.com/in/norma-hernandez-garcia/

About José Luis Ortiz González:

José Luis is an Agile Coach and Trainer who designed a virtual adaptation of this simulation in 2021 in Grupo Salinas.

LinkedIn: https://www.linkedin.com/in/jlortizg-7966a3202/

About Jorge Gándara:

Jorge is an Agile Coach and Trainer from Grupo Salinas who helped make our interview possible as an English/Spanish translator.

LinkedIn: https://www.linkedin.com/in/jorge-gandara-255654179/

Together, these coaches facilitated the *LEGO and Chocolate* simulation over 60 times (in person and virtual) with a total of 10 trainers for various internal groups in technology, business, and even human resources at Grupo Salinas.

CHAPTER 16   KICKSTARTING TRANSFORMATIONS WITH GAMES: FIELD STORIES

I've been getting occasional glimpses into Norma's work ever since she tagged me in one of her first LinkedIn posts about my *LEGO and Chocolate* game. Starting with a small pilot group, then gaining momentum and bringing it to a larger audience (both in person and virtual), she and her colleagues have really embraced the simulation and made it a part of their DevSecOps training curriculum at Grupo Salinas. When I reached out to Norma with an interview invitation, I couldn't even imagine how much fun we would have on that Zoom call! (Figure 16-1.)

Figure 16-1. Interview with DevSecOps trainers from Grupo Salinas

Norma and I were joined by two of her colleagues—José Luis Ortiz González and Jorge Gándara—and the interview couldn't have been timelier. The group was getting ready to run the simulation at their internal conference, in person, for the first time since the pandemic. In a lovely mix of English and Spanish, we chatted about their experience facilitating the game in Grupo Salinas, shared ideas and observations about the game, discussed their virtual adaptation of it, as well as discussed our encounters with skeptics. Here are a few highlights from this interview.

CHAPTER 16   KICKSTARTING TRANSFORMATIONS WITH GAMES: FIELD STORIES

Virtual Adaptation

After José Luis completed the virtual adaptation of this game in the ConceptBoard collaboration tool, the trainers fully integrated it into their Business Agility training curriculum to support the Introduction to DevSecOps material. This virtual training was offered to participants from Mexico and Latin America.

Unlike the adaptation described in a prior interview, this one retained most of the roles, the rules, and the dynamics of the original game. Even in the virtual space, participants were building animals as they were learning about DevSecOps. While the formal role of Harry Hacker was gone, the trainers had taken it upon themselves to introduce "unplanned emergency issues," drawing a little bug, putting it on a team's virtual board, and causing a little bit of panic: "Oh, there is a bug!"

Dealing with Skeptics

Occasionally, the trainers from Grupo Salinas would run into a small number of skeptics. Typically, these are participants from a very technical background, who complain that they are being treated like children with this simulation: "Why are we playing? We should use a more serious approach!"

When Norma and José Luis noticed this feedback after the training, they modified their approach. In the next training session, after introducing the group to DevSecOps culture with the simulation, they invited a director of DevSecOps to share his experience and offer some real-life examples of DevSecOps implementation in parts of the organization.

I was excited to hear about this great augmentation, which undoubtedly enhanced the experience of the participants. One other thing to keep in mind: this game is a model. It is a simulation of a process with all the bottlenecks and dysfunctions. When we take the process outside of the real world, we make it easier to experiment with changing it. Talking about bottlenecks becomes less personal. It is easier to experiment with a new way of doing work when it doesn't affect people's jobs, or doesn't hurt anyone's feelings. While it is all done in the game, the people still learn from this experience when we create space for a powerful debriefing, helping them to connect it back to real-life recommendations.

Trainer's Attitude Plays an Important Role

Finally, José Luis made a point about the game that really resonated with me: The trainer's attitude plays a major role in the success (or failure) of this simulation:

> *"If the trainer is bored, and gives instructions in a monotonous way, participants will not learn well. Attitude plays a big role! As we are enjoying running this game, participants are enjoying it too. They learn, and they have a great experience."*

I couldn't agree more! Every time I have an opportunity to facilitate the *LEGO and Chocolate* simulation, I am bringing in my own playfulness and curiosity. What will emerge this time? Will the participants fall into the same traps designed in the game flow? How will this group be different from any other groups I ran this simulation with? What will they share as their "Aha!" moments? How will they inspire me to modify the game further?

It's a Wrap!

As I am wrapping up this book, I want to thank you, the future facilitator of my coaching games. It takes a special kind of trainer to walk into a serious workplace and bring a gamified workshop. I hope that this book will serve you well: guiding you through preparation and facilitation, arming you with answers to tough questions, and giving you enough insights into DevSecOps and Safety culture to introduce your clients and your teams to these fascinating topics.

I have full confidence in you and your ability to create a safe space for the participants to go deep in their debriefing, uncover connections with their day-to-day challenges, and instill energy to instigate organizational change.

Don't be a stranger! I'd love to hear about your experiences running these games. Share your "Aha!" moments, ask questions, share feedback on the game's Facebook page: http://bit.ly/chocolegogameconnect, or connect with me on LinkedIn: https://www.linkedin.com/in/danapylayeva/.

Be awesome, my friend, and bring joy and playfulness to the teams and the workplaces you encounter on your trainer's journey!

APPENDIX

Design Assets, Posters, and More...

In the first part of this appendix, you will find the latest version of all the materials I use to facilitate these games: photos of the in-room posters you may want to create, images of the workshop handouts, the role cards, and a packing checklist. The second part of the appendix offers you facilitation instructions for the six Liberating Structures referenced in this book. I also provided some guidance on how to run these Liberating Structures if you have a fully remote group (on Zoom or MS Teams). The electronic version of the book's appendix provides facilitator slides, workshop handouts, packing checklist, and print-ready versions of the *LEGO and Chocolate* role cards, the *Fear in Workplace* cards, and the *Safety in the Workplace* cards. You can access it by clicking on the "Download Source Code" on the book's information page on Apress.

Part 1: Design Assets and In-room Posters for Running the *LEGO and Chocolate* Game

I've included here my own version of the in-room posters as a reference. You may choose to draw them fresh every single time or laminate them and reuse them in your next workshops.

APPENDIX   DESIGN ASSETS, POSTERS, AND MORE...

I recommend printing and laminating the workshop handouts. As far as the role cards, if you have time to wait for shipping, order them from the Gamecrafter. I've been very pleased with the quality of the material and the longevity of the role cards produced by this print-on-demand shop for game makers. Alternatively, use the electronic version of the appendix to download, print, and cut the role cards.

Role Cards

Scrum Team (Danny Developer, Tim Tester, Patricia Product, and Samuel Scrum)

APPENDIX   DESIGN ASSETS, POSTERS, AND MORE...

DANNY DEVELOPER

- I work in a Scrum Team.
- I **build and test software** (a small package with a LEGO animal and a chocolate candy).
- I always remember to paste a small **label with a number** on each LEGO animal as I build it.
- I instil quality by adhering to a Definition of Done.

Copyright © 2017 - 2024 Dana Pylayeva All rights reserved

DEPENDENCIES

Adam Admin: to build and patch the environments, to authorize deployments

Tim Tester: to perform a variety of tests as per team's Definition of Done

Robert Release: to build a deployment package and deploy it into production

Sara Security: to educate about security issues, safeguard products and environments

Patricia Product: to clarify, prioritize PBIs, facilitate feedback collection

MY GOAL: CREATE A USABLE PRODUCT INCREMENT EACH SPRINT.

TIM TESTER

- I work in a Scrum Team.
- I run **acceptance test** on each small development package (Definition of Done: LEGO animal, a candy, a number label and the package is closed).
- I run **integration tests** (deployment package has a PBI card, small packages, team name, and a Sprint number).

DEPENDENCIES

Danny Developer: to build software (a small package with LEGO and chocolate) as per Definition of Done

Patricia Product: to clarify, prioritize PBIs and get feedback from the business

Adam Admin: to build and patch the environments, to authorize deployments

Robert Release: to build a deployment package and deploy it to production

MY GOAL: ENSURE PRODUCT QUALITY

APPENDIX   DESIGN ASSETS, POSTERS, AND MORE...

PATRICIA PRODUCT

- I help the Scrum Team pick their next Product Backlog Item (PBI) for the implementation.
- I **clarify** the needs with the business (a type of LEGO animal to build).
- I get **feedback** and share it with my team.

Copyright © 2017 - 2024 Dana Pylayeva All rights reserved

DEPENDENCIES

Scrum Team: to build and test products fast (small packages with LEGO and chocolate)

Ops Team: to package and deploy products built by Dev Team, to handle emergencies

Samuel Scrum: to enable team effectiveness, facilitate empirical product planning, remove impediments

Benjamin Business: to place orders, set prices, accept or reject products, give feedback and pay

MY GOAL: MAXIMIZING THE VALUE OF THE PRODUCT RESULTING FROM THE WORK OF THE SCRUM TEAM

SAMUEL SCRUM

- I work in a Scrum Team.
- I ensure Scrum events take place, are positive, productive, and **kept within the timebox**.
- I **coach** the team in self-management, cross-functionality, & creating **high-value** usable Increments every Sprint.
- I am a true leader, I serve the team & the larger organization.

Copyright © 2017 - 2024 Dana Pylayeva All rights reserved

DEPENDENCIES

Scrum Team: to build and test products (small packages with LEGO and chocolate)

Patricia Product: to clarify, prioritize PBIs and get feedback from the business

Ops Team: to package and deploy products built by Dev Team, to handle emergencies

MY GOAL: SCRUM TEAM'S EFFECTIVENESS

APPENDIX   DESIGN ASSETS, POSTERS, AND MORE...

Operations Team (Adam Admin, Robert Release)

ROBERT RELEASE

- I work in an Operations team.
- I assemble the PBI work card and small LEGO/Chocolate packages into a large **deployment package**.
- I write a Sprint number and the team name on that package.
- I am the only one who can **deploy into production**.

DEPENDENCIES

Scrum Team: to build and test products (small packages with LEGO and chocolate)

Adam Admin: to build and patch the environments, to authorize deployments

Sara Security: to educate about security issues, safeguard products and environments

MY GOAL: **STABLE PRODUCTION ENVIRONMENT**

APPENDIX   DESIGN ASSETS, POSTERS, AND MORE...

ADAM ADMIN

- I work in an Operations team.
- I **build environments** for each developer/tester (using my masking tape).
- I install **security patches** after hacker's attacks and **monitor production** environment.
- I am the only one who can **authorise the deployment.**

Copyright © 2017 - 2024 Dana Pylayeva All rights reserved

DEPENDENCIES

Scrum Team: *to build and test products (small packages with LEGO and chocolate)*

Robert Release: *to build a deployment package and deploy it into production*

Sara Security: *to educate about security issues, safeguard products and environments*

MY GOAL: **STABLE PRODUCTION ENVIRONMENT**

Security Team (Sara Security)

SARA SECURITY

- I work in a Security Team.
- I am always up to date on the latest security **vulnerabilities** (I have 3 new numbers in my security catalog every Sprint).
- When I run a **security scan**, I look for these numbers on each LEGO animal label. I will fail the entire deployment package, if even one animal fails

Copyright © 2017 - 2024 Dana Pylayeva All rights reserved

DEPENDENCIES

Scrum Team: to build, test and remove security bugs from products (small packages with LEGO and chocolate)

Adam Admin: to build and patch the environments, to authorize deployments

Robert Release: to build deployment packages and bring them for my security scans

MY GOAL: SECURE PRODUCTION ENVIRONMENT

APPENDIX   DESIGN ASSETS, POSTERS, AND MORE...

Business Team (Benjamin Business)

BENJAMIN BUSINESS

- I work with external stakeholders and know the **price and demand** on products at the current LEGO animal market.
- I **place orders** with a Product Owner, accept or reject them, **provide feedback** and pay, if I like what I get!

DEPENDENCIES

Patricia Product: to maximize the value of the product resulting from the work of the Scrum Team

Scrum Team: to build and test products (small packages with LEGO and chocolate)

Ops Team: to package and deploy products built by Dev Team, to handle emergencies

MY GOAL: **RESPOND QUICKLY TO CHANGES IN THE MARKET DEMAND**

Hacker (Harry Hacker)

HARRY HACKER

- I am an intruder.
- I seek to breach defences and **exploit weaknesses**.
- I take advantage of the **Heart bleed bug** (draw a heart on a masking tape) and **tamper with environments**.

DEPENDENCIES

Sara Security: to stop the development and request environment patching when security breach occurs

Adam Admin: to install security patches (a new layer of tape) after a hacker attack

Scrum Team: to be stopped from development until all security patches are applied

MY GOAL: EXPLOIT SECURITY VULNERABILITY

Copyright © 2017 - 2024 Dana Pylayeva All rights reserved

APPENDIX DESIGN ASSETS, POSTERS, AND MORE...

Mod Cards

Adam Admin, Sara Security: Sprint 1

ADAM ADMIN

- We are in a **Code Freeze**.
- NO DEPLOYMENTS in Sprint One.

You can share this information with Robert Release and only when he asks for your permission to deploy to production.

MOD CARD

KEEP CALM CHRISTMAS IS COMING

DURING SECOND PART OF SPRINT ONE ONLY

APPENDIX   DESIGN ASSETS, POSTERS, AND MORE...

SARA SECURITY

MOD CARD

1. At the start of each Sprint, write down 3 random numbers between _____ and _____. These numbers will be your **known security issues** for this Sprint for team_____.
2. Check the **deployment packages**. If any of them contain an animal with a label that's matching your number, send the **entire package back** to the Scrum team for a fix.

Sprint 1 ____   ____   ____
Sprint 2 ____   ____   ____
Sprint 3 ____   ____   ____

THREATS AND SECURITY BUGS CATALOG

APPENDIX   DESIGN ASSETS, POSTERS, AND MORE...

Sara Security, Benjamin Business: Sprint 2

SARA SECURITY

MOD CARD

- Check all the environment for potential security issues. Do you see any marks on the tape?
- If you recognise hearts (Heartbleed Bug) or ghosts (Ghost vulnerability), stop the Scrum Team!
- Environment has been compromised and must be patched!

DURING SPRINT TWO ONLY

APPENDIX   DESIGN ASSETS, POSTERS, AND MORE...

BENJAMIN BUSINESS

- These teams are being **too slow**.
- Our competitors just released a bunch of cats, dogs and snakes! The price on them has dropped significantly.
- Update the board, **drop prices**.
- Start asking for **new animals** and offer to pay a lot more for them.

MOD CARD

STARTS IN SPRINT TWO

APPENDIX   DESIGN ASSETS, POSTERS, AND MORE...

Patricia Product: Sprint 3

APPENDIX DESIGN ASSETS, POSTERS, AND MORE...

Workshop Handouts

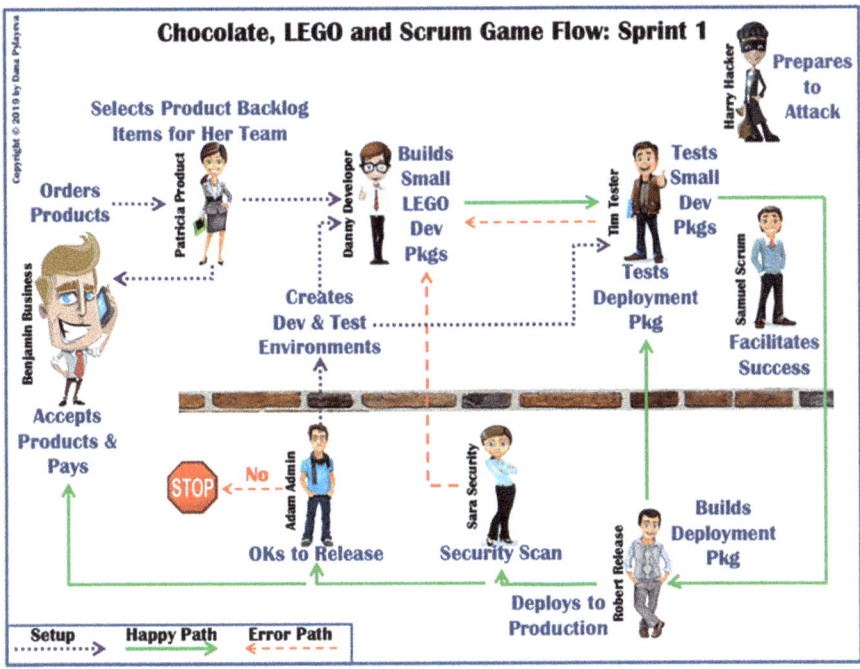

APPENDIX DESIGN ASSETS, POSTERS, AND MORE...

Small Dev. Package

Definition of Done

1. Each small package contains one LEGO animal (as requested in a Product Backlog Item - PBI) and a chocolate candy.
2. Each LEGO animal has a small label with a number affixed to it.
3. The package is closed, the contents don't fall out if turned upside-down.

Deployment Package

Definition of Done

1. Contains a PBI work card.
2. Contains a number of small packages with a LEGO animal and a chocolate candy in each.
3. Has a label with Team Name and Sprint Number on it.
4. The package is closed.
5. Type of animals and their quantity same as in PBI work card.

APPENDIX   DESIGN ASSETS, POSTERS, AND MORE...

Packing Checklist (21-person group)

		Sprint 1 Supplies	Sprint 2 Supplies	Sprint 3 Supplies
Scrum Team: 7 people (Supplies are listed for one team. Don't forget to pack for 2!)				
		LEGO Classic or similar building bricks		
		1/2 pound of small chocolate candies		
		One package (20 ct) of 9 1/2" x 4" clear party bags		
		~ 50 small rubber bands		
		One page of small number labels		
		Game flow sheet		
		Role Card - Danny Developer - 4		
		Role Card -Tim Tester - 1		
		Role Card -Patricia Product - 1		
		Role Card -Samuel Scrum - 1		
Ops Team + Security - 4		**Game flow sheet**		
	Adam Admin	One rolls of 1" masking tape.		
	Robert Release	14 gallon-size resealable bags		
	Robert Release	20 all-purpose 1" X 3" rectangular labels		
	Sara Security	2 "Known security issues" catalog cards		

APPENDIX   DESIGN ASSETS, POSTERS, AND MORE...

		Role Card -Adam Admin - 1		
		Role Card -Sara Security - 2		
		Role Card -Robert Release - 1		
	Business Team - 2	Game flow sheet		
		3" x 5" Index cards of any color (about 20 per each team)		
		Role Card -Benjamin Business - 2		
		2 Sharpies + 1 marker		
		Play money		
	Harry Hacker - optional 1			
		Role Card -Harry Hacker - 1		
		One red marker		
	Facilitator set			
		1 x Mod card - Adam Admin		
			2 x Mod Card - Benjamin Business	
			2 x Mod Card- Sara Security	
			Small stickers in 3 different colors (Red - dev, Orange - Ops, Green - security)	
			One roll of 1" painter's green masking tape	
				5"x11" transparent green party bags (about 30 per development team)
				2 x Mod Card - Patricia product

APPENDIX DESIGN ASSETS, POSTERS, AND MORE...

In-room Posters

LEGO Animal Exchange poster with PBI cards

Delivery Board Poster for 4 Scrum Teams and 3 Sprints

APPENDIX DESIGN ASSETS, POSTERS, AND MORE...

Key Takeaways Poster

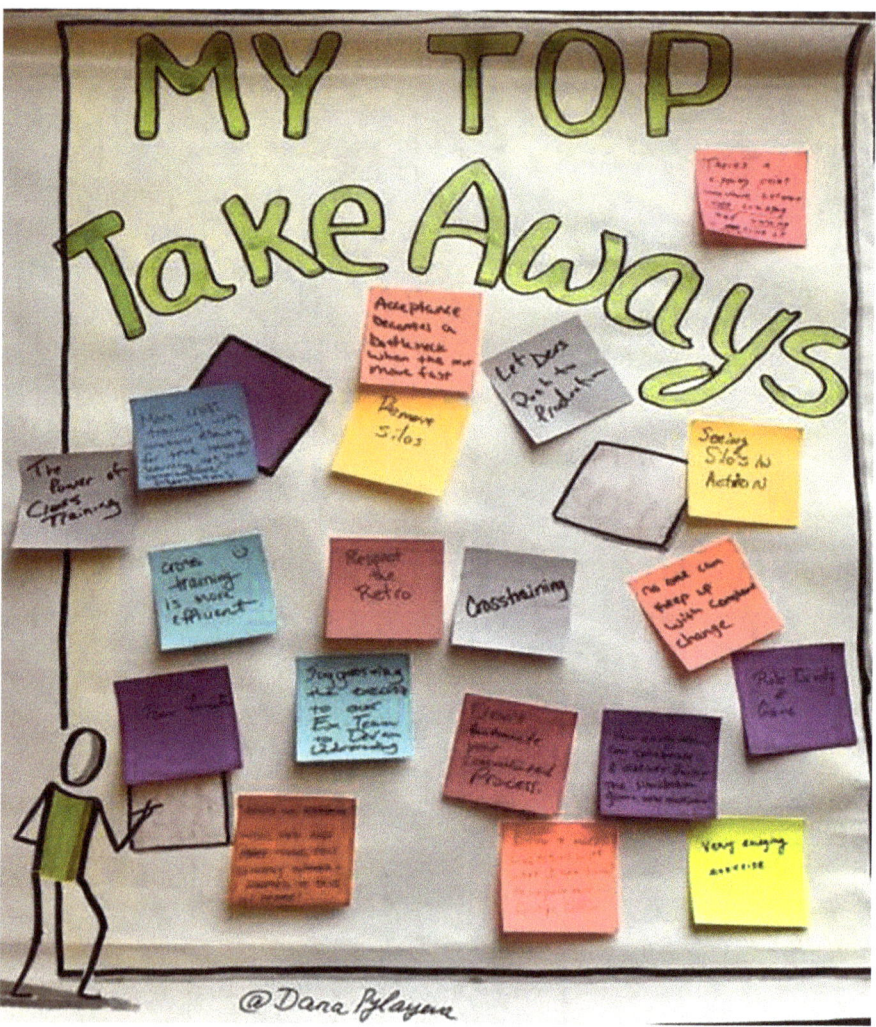

Cross-training (FEEL) Poster

APPENDIX   DESIGN ASSETS, POSTERS, AND MORE...

Known Good Environment Configuration Poster

Part 2: The Liberating Structures Referenced in This Book

In this part of the appendix, you will find my variation of the Liberating Structures (LS), applied to debriefing and idea crowdsourcing with the participants of my coaching games and simulation. When I discovered this library of 33 facilitation techniques, collected, simplified, and distilled to their essence by Keith McCandless and Henry Lipmanowicz, it immediately resonated with me. Liberating Structures enable the collaboration of a group in a special and unique way. They create space and interaction patterns for engagement, co-creation, and inclusion in a group of any size.

APPENDIX DESIGN ASSETS, POSTERS, AND MORE...

All LS have the same elements (structural "DNA" or microstructures). This allows for a reduced learning curve for new facilitators, letting them start integrating these powerful methods into their work right away. Every LS has a purpose, a structured invitation, a specific arrangement of space, a thoughtful group configuration, a specific sequence of steps with timing, and a mode of participation (how is it distributed). Whether you are trying to learn about LS from the community-supported Liberating Structures website[1] or from the app[2] developed by a team at Holisticon, you can always count on finding these elements in the description of individual LS.

The intent of this part of the appendix is to take you through the application of these structures in the context of the coaching games described in this book. I will be providing the references to their standard definitions for you to check out and to experiment with in other contexts.

1-2-4-All

Source: `https://www.liberatingstructures.com/1-1-2-4-all/`

Purpose: Engage everyone simultaneously in reconstructing the experience, reflecting on it, and harvesting learning.

Invitation: What is the biggest "Aha!" moment you had so far in this simulation?

Space: Unlimited number of groups, formed with people from other tables, enough space for people to walk around the room.

---

[1] `https://www.liberatingstructures.com/`
[2] `https://apps.apple.com/us/app/liberating-structures/id1206361128`

Group configuration: First solo, then pairs, then quads, then entire group.

Participation Distributed: Everyone has an opportunity to contribute and has an opportunity to share their ideas with at least three people. A spokesperson from each quad shares with the large group.

Sequence of Steps:

- 1 min (solo) – Invite people to reflect on their experience and write down the biggest "Aha!" moments that came up for them.

- 3 min (in pairs) – Ask people to form a pair with someone from a different table and share with each other the insights they wrote in step 1.

- 5 min (in quads) – Next, instruct them to keep the same partner, and merge with another pair to review all "Aha!"s. Select one that is worth sharing with a larger group, and pick a spokesperson to represent this quad.

- 6 min (entire group) – Quads take turns to share 1-2 insights from each group. As the spokespeople offer their insights to the group, acknowledge the feelings, changes in perspectives, and shifts in the group's mental models that emerge during debriefs. Collect all the written insights in one visible place. I like using "Key Takeaways" poster for that.

APPENDIX   DESIGN ASSETS, POSTERS, AND MORE...

If You Need to Run It Virtually:

- 1 – Invite participants to join an online collaboration tool and add their individual reflections there.
- 2 – Use breakout rooms (Zoom or MS Teams) to create pairs. Open the rooms for the duration of the timebox for step 2. Bring everyone back into the main room.
- 4 – Combine breakout rooms to keep pairs together, as they join the groups of 4. Open the rooms for the duration of the timebox*.
- All – Bring everyone back into the main room for final share-outs from each group.
- **Mural Template** – If you are a Mural user, you can create your board from this template: `https://tinyurl.com/template-124all`

*It is also possible in Zoom to combine pairs while the breakout rooms are still open. In the setup, let people know that you will start moving them from 2 to 4 at the end of the first timebox. This option will feel less disruptive to the flow of this structure. Unfortunately, it is not available in MS Teams.

What? So What? Now What?

Source: `https://www.liberatingstructures.com/9-what-so-what-now-what-w/`

Purpose: Together, look back on the shared experience, engage in sensemaking, and identify potential improvements in the next round of simulation

Invitation: What? So What? Now What?

Space: Groups are formed with people at their current tables, allowing for a deep dive into the experiences of each functional group in the simulation.

Group Configuration: First solo, then in small groups, then entire group. Same configuration for all 3 questions.

Participation Distributed: Everyone has an opportunity to contribute, and has an opportunity to share their ideas in a small group. Anyone can share with the large group in the final round of the discussion.

Sequence of Steps:

- *What?* Reflect and discuss with others: *What happened in the first sprint? What have they noticed? What observations stood out from their perspective?* (no judgment, simply stating the facts, just like a video camera would record it). Invite people to:

  1 min – write down individual reflections

  2 min – discuss at their tables

  5 min – share the most salient insights with the entire group. (start share-outs from development teams, then the business team, followed by the operations and security teams)

- *So What?* Let's make sense of the facts. Why is that important? What hypotheses can we make about our way of working in Sprint 1? Invite people to:

1 min – write down individual reflections

2 min – discuss at their tables

3 min – share the most salient insights with the entire group

- ***Now What?*** What can be done differently in Sprint 2? *Based on what we explored, what changes make sense now?* While you will not be applying all of them in Sprint 2, it will be useful to connect to their ideas when you start introducing modifications for Sprint 2. Invite people to:

1 min – write down individual reflections

2 min – discuss at their tables

5 min – share the most salient insights with the entire group

If you need to run it virtually:

Repeat the following steps for each of the three questions in this LS (What? So What? Now What?):

- Invite participants to join an online collaboration tool and add their individual reflections to the designated board.
- Use breakout rooms (Zoom or MS Teams) to create small groups. Open the rooms for the duration of the timebox.
- Bring everyone back into the main room to hear the insights from each group (continue the same steps to explore the next question).

APPENDIX   DESIGN ASSETS, POSTERS, AND MORE...

- **Mural Template:** If you are a Mural user, you can create your board from this template: https://tinyurl.com/template-w3

User Experience Fishbowl

Source: https://www.liberatingstructures.com/18-users-experience-fishbowl/

Purpose: Share individual insights from the shared experience with the entire group.

Invitation: What have we learned from this simulation and how might we bring these ideas to life to influence change?

Space: Five chairs, arranged into a semi-circle in front of the group

Group Configuration: Up to five people in the fishbowl, unlimited number of people in the audience

Participation Distributed: Everyone has an opportunity to join the fishbowl and speak when there is an empty chair available. When all the chairs are taken, someone has to leave the fishbowl. Anyone not in the fishbowl (including the facilitator) is a listener.

Sequence of Steps:

- 2 min – Explain the rules of the fishbowl.
- 1 min (solo) – Invite people to reflect on their experience and write down a few thoughts.

APPENDIX DESIGN ASSETS, POSTERS, AND MORE...

- 15–30 min – Fishbowl is open, invite people to join the fishbowl when there is a chair available and they have something to share or add to the conversation. Once in a fishbowl, engage in an open conversation. Follow the rules of the fishbowl, keeping one chair always open as an invitation to join. When a new participant joins (and takes the last available chair), one of the existing fishbowl participants will have to leave the fishbowl. The conversation goes on until it ends on its own.

If you need to run it virtually:

Instead of using chairs in the physical space to create a container for the conversations (the Fishbowl), you will be using a video on/off feature in Zoom to differentiate between people in the fishbowl and the observers (see Figure A-1). Once the conversations in the Fishbowl conclude, you can create multiple breakout rooms with 3–4 people and open them for 5 minutes for the final round of debriefing.

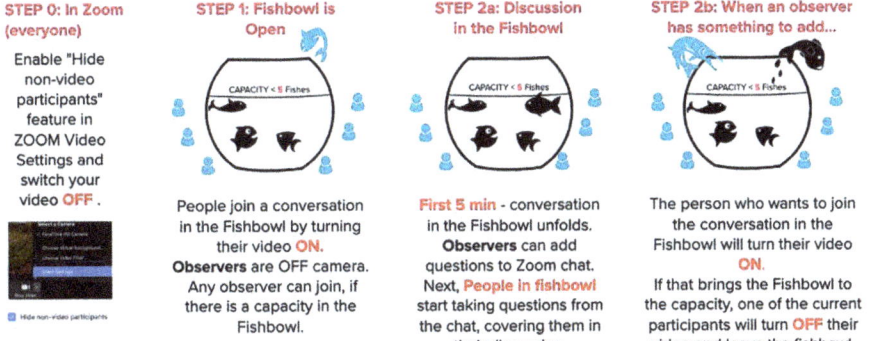

Figure A-1. How to run User Experience Fishbowl LS in virtual space

APPENDIX   DESIGN ASSETS, POSTERS, AND MORE...

25 – 10 Crowdsourcing

Source: https://www.liberatingstructures.com/12-2510-crowd-sourcing/

Purpose: Engaging everyone in generating big ideas, and quickly selecting the best 10 of them via a randomized group voting

Invitation: If you were 10 times bolder, what big ideas would you experiment with in your organization?

Space: A larger space for people to stand in a circle, and then move around in random order.

Group Configuration: First write on an index card (solo), then pass around the cards in the group, then individually rate the current card.

Participation Distributed: Everyone has the opportunity to contribute their idea, rate at least five other ideas from the group, and represent the idea of the group if it receives the top 10 rating.

Sequence of Steps:

- 2 min – Explain to the participant that they are going to engage in an idea crowdsourcing and you will guide them through 5 rounds of it, resulting in 10 best ideas.

- 1 min – Invite them to write their best idea on an index card in response to the invitation.

- 10 min – Signal to start passing the cards to each other without reading. After about a minute, signal to stop, read the card in their hands, and rate it on a scale from 1 (not feeling it) to 5 (the most powerful idea!). Signal to continue passing the cards without reading. After about a minute, signal to stop, read, and rate the cards. Continue for 3 more rounds (5 rounds total). At the end of the last round, ask them to tally the ratings on the card in their hands and circle the total rating.

- 10 min – Discover the top 10 crowdsourced ideas as a group. Ask a person who is holding an idea with a 25 rating to step forward. Continue calling forward the participants with ideas rates as 24, 23, 22 . . . until you have 10 ideas at the front of the room.

  Ask people to read the ideas that are written on their top-rated cards out loud. Optionally, you can have the group explore these top-rated ideas further and identify a small next step to advance them forward.

If you need to run it virtually:

- Invite participants to join your favorite online collaboration tool and create one sticky per person with an idea, responding to the invitation.

- Instruct them to pass the stickies around until you ask them to stop.

- Ask them to provide their ratings on the sticky they hold at this time by using the "Add Comment" feature on that sticky. Continue with the rest of the in-person dynamic.

- After completing all 5 rounds, ask participants to tally the ratings on their card and arrange the top 10 in one column (no special board is required).

APPENDIX   DESIGN ASSETS, POSTERS, AND MORE...

TRIZ

Source: https://www.liberatingstructures.com/6-making-space-with-triz/

Purpose: Stop counterproductive actions, dysfunctions, or toxic ways of working to make space for DevSecOps culture.

Invitation: How can we reliably design a perfect way to **fail a DevSecOps transformation**? List all actions, behaviors, and organizational design choices we can use to ensure it **fails in the most spectacular way**!

Space: Unlimited number of small groups seated at tables or in circles of chairs near flipcharts.

Group Configuration: 4–7 people from the same group, or a mix of people from different functional groups.

Participation Distributed: Everyone has an opportunity to contribute and everyone is involved in the work of the group.

Sequence of Steps:

Step 1: How can we reliably design a perfect way to fail a DevSecOps transformation?

- 2 min (solo) - Think and write your ideas on sticky notes.
- 5 min (group of 2-3) - Share with your group and add more. Be evil!
- 5 min (all) - Share a few of your most evil ideas. Enjoy a good laugh!

Step 2. Look at your collection again. Which ones are you already doing today?

- 5 min (group of 2–3) – Review your original list (or collection of sticky notes) and mark the ones that resemble your current practices or actions.

Step 3. Which ones will you STOP doing?

- 1 min (solo) – Select one item from the previous step that you are willing to commit to STOP doing.
- 5 min (group of 2–3) – What will be the most impactful for us to STOP doing as a group?
- 5 min (all) – Share your commitments and observations with the large group.

If you need to run it virtually:

- Invite participants to join an online collaboration tool and add their individual reflections to the designated boards.
- Use breakout rooms (Zoom or MS Teams) to create small groups. Open the rooms for the duration of the timebox in Step 1.
- Bring everyone back into the main room to hear the insights from each group (continue using breakout rooms and collaboration tools for Steps 2 and 3).
- **Mural Template:** If you are a Mural user, you can create your board from this template: `http://tinyurl.com/TRIZBoardTemplate`

APPENDIX DESIGN ASSETS, POSTERS, AND MORE...

Tiny Monsters (a.k.a. Tiny Demons)

Technically, not a Liberating Structure (yet), this activity is used often by Liberating Structures practitioners as it is perfect for a playful exploration of (and way to deal with) fears and worries that we all may experience at the time of change. I learned this from Nancy White, experienced LS Maestro, when I volunteered to shadow her at a workshop for the NY Department of Parks and Recreation in February of 2019.

Source: https://fullcirc.com/2018/01/25/drawing-monsters-thanks-to-lynda-barry/ **and** https://agilefacil.wordpress.com/2023/11/26/tiny-demons/

Purpose: Bring fears out in the open with playfulness, build empathy, and identify shared concerns in the group.

Invitation: Make a list of things that worry you the most about the upcoming DevSecOps transformation initiative.

Space: Unlimited number of people, space to walk around, one blank sheet of paper per person.

Group Configuration: First solo, then impromptu pairs

Participation Distributed: Everyone has an opportunity to explore their worries, share their biggest fears, and get advice from at least three people in the larger group.

Sequence of Steps:

Part 1 (solo):

- 2 min – Invite everyone to think and write down on a blank sheet of paper all the concerns, worries, or fears they have about the upcoming transformation.
- 1 min – Ask them to flip the page to the other side, divide it into 4 quadrants, and draw 4 shapes (one in each quadrant): a circle, a square, a spiky shape, and a random squiggle.
- 5 min – Ask the participants to turn these shapes into tiny monsters by adding fur, teeth, beaks, claws, and other scary features.
- 1 min – Map each of the top four fears to one of the four monsters.

Part 2 - Monster walk (in pairs):

- 10 min – Invite participants to find a random partner in the room and introduce their monsters to their partner. Take turns learning about the monsters and offering advice on how to deal with these monsters. Switch partners several times to tire out your monsters.

If you need to run it virtually:

- Use physical paper and markers to draw the monsters even in the virtual space. Follow the same steps for Part 1.

- Create multiple breakout rooms with 2–3 people in each. Instruct the participants to keep their video turned ON. Send them to their breakout rooms for a monster walk and ask them to hold their drawings close to the camera, while introducing their monsters to their partners. Reconfigure breakout rooms several times to allow for multiple pairings and conversations to occur.
- Optionally, ask for volunteers to share their learnings in the main room after the final round of the Monster Walk is completed.

Index

A

Agile, 4, 30, 54, 187, 190, 191, 239, 286, 291
Agile + DevOps East 2018 conference, Orlando (November 2018), 301, 302
Agile2015 (August 2015), 291–293
Agile Alliance Technical Conference (AATC2017), 297
AgileCamp2018 Conference, New York (September 2018), 300, 301
AgileCamp2019, New York (October 2019), 305
Agile community, 1, 5, 279
Agile Days 2015, Moscow, 286–288
Agile games, 117, 239
Agile Games conference, 297, 298
Agile India 2020, 306, 307
Agile Retrospective, 242
Amplifying feedback loops, 41, 49, 55
Amplify Signal (Helpful Cassandras), 214, 215
"Amygdala Hijack", 183, 209
Anti-gossip policies, 235

B

Blaming and finger-pointing, 185
Bloom's Taxonomy, 242, 243
Brilliant Jerks, 184
Bureaucratic cultures, 15, 30, 178, 181, 188, 302

C

Change management models, 8
Check-in protocol, 228
ClassifyMe cards, 194, 195, 199, 302, 316
Coaches and trainers
    Fassbinder, P., 317–322 (*see also* Fassbinder, P.)
    Gándara, J., 325–328 (*see also* Gándara, J.)
    Garcia, N.H., 324–328 (*see also* Garcia, N.H.)
    González, J.L.O., 325–328 (*see also* González, J.L.O.)
    Hetherington, W., 322–324
    Métivier, K., 312–317 (*see also* Métivier, K.)

INDEX

Coaching games, 8–10, 15, 19, 261, 308, 309, *See also* Fear in the Workplace; Safety in the Workplace
"Code freeze", 24, 67, 78, 145, 168
Collaborative game, 195, 196
Community of practice (CoP), 1, 6
Competitive game, 194–195
Containerization, 39, 46, 50, 82, 155, 159, 266
Continuous delivery (CD), 44, 45, 80–83, 159, 174, 290, 318
Continuous integration (CI), 44, 45, 49
Core Protocols, 212, 228, 231, 233
Cross-training
   benefits, 256, 257
   concerns, 257, 258
Cultural change, 6–9, 182

D, E

DASA DevOps Competence Model, 187
Database administrator (DBA), 9, 23, 219
Debriefing
   activities, 251, 252
   aspects, 240, 241
   connections, 251
   DevSecOps training workshop, 244, 245
   feedback loop, 241
   LEGO and Chocolate simulation, 240
   Liberating Structures, 244
   models, 242, 243
   1-2-4-All structure, 247
   open-ended questions, 251
   Operations team, 241
   participant experiences, 241
   User Experience Fishbowl structure, 248, 250
   What? So What? Now What? structure, 246
Debriefing for Meaningful Learning (DML) model, 242
DevOps, 36
   audience, 4
   coaching games, 9, 10
   communities, 5
   cultural changes, 6–9
      2013, 28
      2014, 29, 30
      2018, 31
      2019, 32
   definition, 137
   enterprises, 138
   facilitation instructions, 2
   facilitators, 4, 5
   Fear in the Workplace, 1, 4, 14, 15
   functional manager, 3
   functional silos, 22–24
   goals, typical product development organization, 5

INDEX

LEGO and Chocolate game, 3, 13, 27
low-trust culture, 22–24
organizational cultures, typology, 29
organizations, 5, 27
The Phoenix Project, 1
psychological safety, 32–34
redesigning, 296
safety culture, 1
Safety in the Workplace, 1, 4, 14, 15
technical/non-technical participants, 3
Three Ways, 40
transformation initiatives, 2
tried-and-true workshop, 2
unicorns, 138
The #DevOps hashtag, 26
DevSecOps, 34–37
    impact, business, 259, 260
    psychological safety, 202
    security role, 258, 259
    transformations, 186–188, 214, 267, 273
DevSecOps training, 115
    accelerate metrics, 136
    Adam Admin, 151, 153
    audience, 142
    bottlenecks slide, 147, 148
    break, 155
    CI/CD pipeline, 156, 157
    continuous value delivery, 160
    cross-training activity, 151
    cyclical value delivery, 143
    debriefing
        organizational changes, 153, 154
        organizational dynamics, 145
        User Experience Fishbowl, 161–163
    evolution, 136, 137
    game flow, 139
    Harry Hacker, 151
    instructor introduction, 133
    intervention, 144, 152, 161
    LEGO and Chocolate simulation, 244
    misalignment goals
        culture, 135, 136
        delivery timeline, 135, 136
        development teams, 133, 134
        information security team, 133, 134
        operations teams, 133, 134
        traditional organization, 134, 135
    patching, 152
    players handouts, 139, 140
    process improvements/modifications, 149, 150, 158–160
    Sara Security, 143
    Second Way of DevOps, 155, 156
    Three Way of DevOps, 146, 147
    timeboxes, 143, 150, 151

INDEX

DevSecOps training (*cont.*)
    timer/operations table, 144
    turn and talk slide, 132, 133
    vulnerability discovery to exploit, 157, 158
Disengagement, 177, 184

F

Facilitation script
    Adam Admin, 171, 172
    Aha! Moments, 176
    continuous value delivery, 175
    debriefing
        Benjamin Business, 168
        delivery board, 168
        1-2-4-All activity, 172, 173, 176
        Scrum teams, 167
        security issues, 168
    DevSecOps, 169, 170
    game introduction, 164–166
    intervention, 167, 171, 175
    patching, 171
    poster/whiteboard, timebox, 169
    process improvements/modifications, 168, 174, 175
    Samuel Scrum's role, 166
    Sara security, 166
    timeboxes, 166
    timer/operations table, 167

Facilitators, 4–5, 72, 92, 93, 112–114, 263, 355
Fassbinder, P.
    LEGO and Chocolate simulation, 318
    observations
        eye-opener, 320
        new processes/competency build up, 321, 322
        one-piece flow, 321
        Shift-left, security, 320
    virtual adaptation
        simplifications, 318
        tools/setup, 319
Fawn response of Conflict Avoidance, 184
Fear cards, 188, 190, 195, 207, 300, 308, 323, 324
Fear Eradicated game, 297, 298
Fear in organizations
    impact, 183–186
    symptoms, 183–186
Fear in the Workplace game, 4, 8, 10, 262
    Agile + DevOps East 2018 conference, Orlando (November 2018), 301, 302
    AgileCamp2018 conference, New York (Septemper 2018), 300, 301
    ClassifyMe cards, 194
    as coaching tool, 179
    collaborative game, 195, 196
    competitive game, 195

INDEX

DevSecOps, 181, 182
fear and fear symptoms cards, 194
fear-focused retrospective, 299, 300
fear FS, dysfunctions in organizational cultures, 184
fear-inducing organizational changes
  DevSecOps transformation, 186–188
  mergers and acquisitions, 188, 189
fear in organizations
  impact, 183–186
  symptoms, 183–186
fearless conversations, 179
LEGO and Chocolate workshop, 180
Mural template, 272
online edition, 308
organizational culture collide, 181, 182
remote-friendly version, 271
reorgs and layoffs, 189–192
risk-discourages cultures, organizations, 183
role cards, 16
short activity, extra-large group, 196, 197
team-level fears, 193
Third Way of DevOps, 197, 198
Fearless culture, 261–262

Fear of Failure, 187, 216, 274
Fear of Lack of Expertise, 187, 274
Fear of Stagnating, 193
Fear/Symptoms cards, 196
Feedback loop, 40, 41, 50, 82, 100, 163, 181, 250
Fight response, 184
Fire Slimy Weasels, 235–236
Flight response, 184
Freeze response, 184

G

Gándara, J.
  attitude, 328
  skeptics, 327
  virtual adaptation, 326
Garcia, N.H.
  attitude, 328
  colleagues, 326
  Grupo Salinas, 326
  LinkedIn posts, 325
  skeptics, 327
  virtual adaptation, 326
Generative cultures, 15, 30, 182, 198, 206, 218
Global scrum gathering, Berlin (September 2014), 282, 283
Global scrum gathering New Orleans (May 2014), 280, 281
Global Scrum Gathering, Prague (November 2015), 293, 294

373

INDEX

González, J.L.O.
   attitude, 328
   skeptics, 327
   virtual adaptation, 326
Gossip and rumors, 185
Grupo Salinas, 324–327

H

Hidden posters, 18, 101, 102
Host Failure Parties (Fail–Learn–Move on), 217–218

I, J, K

Infrastructure as Code (IaC), 39, 41, 47–49, 152, 171
In-room posters, 15, 18, 331–332, 351–354
Interval timer, 116, 123, 132, 143
Introduce and Use Core Protocols, 231
IT Operations team
   Adam admin, 66–68
   dynamic, 66
   Robert release, 68, 69
   roles, 65
   supplies, 89, 90

L

Leaders, 27, 65, 82, 205, 225, 235, 313, 323
Leadership, 212, 215, 216, 218–221, 224–226, 234–236

Lean Coffee style, 206–208, 300
Learned Helplessness, 193
LEGO and Chocolate simulation, 13, 14, 27, 115
   abstraction, 267
   Adam admin, 141
   aim, 57, 58
   Animal Exchange board/product backlog, 59
   assembly instructions, 265
   avatars, 58
   batches size, 267
   Benjamin Business, 73, 74, 76, 77, 141
   Business team, 59
      Benjamin Business, 73, 74
      supplies, 91
   challenges, 269, 270
   component links, 94
   cross-training, 266
   cultural aspect, 267
   Danny Developer, 141
   end-to-end development, 268
   facilitation script (*see* Facilitation script)
   facilitator, 72, 92, 93
   First Way of DevOps
      CD, 44, 45
      containerization, 46
      IaC, 47, 49
      microservices, 46
   flow/modifications, 76, 77
      Adam admin, 77, 80, 81
      Benjamin Business, 79, 80

continuous delivery of value, 82, 83
Danny Developer, 76
group, 78
Harry hacker, 80
instructions, 78, 79
Patricia Product, 76
Robert release, 77
Sara security, 80
Scrum team, 81
Tim Tester, 77
T-shape building steps, 78, 79
Harry hacker, 75, 92
interaction patterns/process bottlenecks, 97
IT Operations team (*see* IT Operations team)
mod cards, 86, 87, 293
online conversion, 306
Patricia Product, 141
The Phoenix Project, 40–42
player roles, 58
public workshops (*see* Public workshops (v 1.0); Public workshops (v 1.2)
remote team, 270
Robert release, 141
role cards, 16, 85, 86, 138, 279, 280
role of security, 41
room configurations (*see* Room configurations)
room posters (*see* Room posters)
Sara security, 142
Scrum guide, 266
Scrum team (*see* Scrum team)
Second Way of DevOps, 49–50
Security team, 59
Sara security, 70, 72
supplies, 90, 91
segregation of duty, 267
separate roles, 266
session plan, 125–127, 129
"shield right" approach, 52
"shift-left" approach, 52
summary, 57, 58
table setup, 97
team changes, 266
technical reviewer, 268
"The Three Ways of DevOps"
feedback loop, 41
supplemental material, 41
systems thinking, 40, 42, 43
Tim Tester, 141
workshop, 180
Liberating Structures (LS), 6, 14, 15, 120, 200, 215, 303, 354–355

M, N

Métivier, K.
attention, business needs, 315
and colleagues, 312, 313
Fear in the Workplace, 313
French translations, 312
game improvement, 315, 316

Métivier, K. (*cont.*)
  games buy-in/continuity, 313, 314
  habitual behaviors, 314, 315
  LEGO and Chocolate simulation, 313
  LinkedIn message, 312
  master, games, 316, 317
Microservices, 39, 41, 46, 50, 155, 156
Mod cards, 17, 61, 85–87, 149, 168, 292, 342–346
Mole cards
  Adam Admin, 342–344
  Patricia Product, 346
  Sara Security, 344–346
Multiple coaching styles, 180

O

1-2-4-All structure
  group configuration, 356
  invitation, 355
  participation distributed, 356
  purpose, 355
  sequence of steps, 356
  source, 355
  space, 355
  virtual space, 357
OOP2020, Munich (February 2020), 306
Open Space Technology (OST), 225, 226
Organizational cultures
  bureaucratic, 30
  generative, 30
  pathological/fear-ridden, 29
  typology, 30
Over-functioning, 185

P, Q

Participants, 2, 58, 100, 130, 190, 240, 280, 314, 319, 320, 327, 328
Pathological/fear-ridden cultures, 29, 177
The Phoenix Project, 1, 9, 40–42, 147, 278
Play4Agile Rückersbach, Germany (February 2015), 284
Practice heavy transparency, 216
Practice Inclusive Leadership, 224
Product backlog items (PBIs), 60, 61, 76, 99, 141
Psychological safety, 32–34, 37, 193, 198, 211, 215, 222, 234
Public workshops (v 1.0)
  global scrum gathering, Berlin (September 2014), 282, 283
  global scrum gathering, New Orleans (May 2014), 280, 281
  Play4Agile Rückersbach, Germany (February 2015), 284
  Toronto Agile and Software, Canada (November 2014), 283, 284

Public workshops (v 2.0)
    Agile2015 (August 2015), 291, 293
    Agile Days 2015, Moscow, 286–288
    conferences, 295
    Global Scrum Gathering, Prague (November 2015), 293, 294
    Rakuten Technology Conference, Tokyo (November 2015), 294
    XP2015 (May 2015), 288–290

R

Radical transparency culture, 216
Rakuten Marketing, 277, 278
Rakuten Technology Conference, Tokyo (November 2015), 294
Reorg, 189–192
Risk avoidance, 185
Rochester Institute of Technology (RIT), 242
Role cards, 16, 17
    business team, 340
    Harry Hacker, 341
    operations team, 337–339
    scrum team, 332–337
Room configurations
    extra large group setup, 111, 112
    large group setup
        28-42 players, 109
        38-42 players, 111
        38-56 players, 110
    medium group setup
        15-25 players, 106, 107
        18-28 players, 108
    optimal configuration, 105
    scaling, 112, 113
    small group setup, 106
Room posters
    hidden posters
        cross-training "FEEL" poster, 102, 103
        known good configuration, 103, 104
    visible posters
        delivery board, 99, 100
        learning/debriefing, 100, 101
        LEGO animal exchange board, 98, 99
Room setup, 14, 95, 105–111, 130

S

Safety enhancers collection
    autonomy
        abandon "trust-destroying" practices, 225
        design structures, input, 226, 227
        discover & amplify voices, open space, 225, 226
        experiment with dynamic reteaming, 224

INDEX

Safety enhancers collection (*cont.*)
  practice inclusive leadership, 224
  success through course correction, 223
 certainty
  adopt an experimental (*vs.* operational) mindset, 221
  Bring Up Uncertainty, 216, 217
  change terminology, reframe error, 219, 220
  frame silence, unethical choice, 218
  Host Failure Parties (Fail–Learn–Move on), 217
  Interdependence, Impact, 216, 217
  practice heavy transparency, 216
  reframe the role of the boss, 220, 221
  uncouple fear from failure, 218
 fairness
  anti-gossip rule, 235, 236
  co-create team norms, 233, 234
  description, 232
  embrace sustainable pace, 232, 233
  goal, 237
  measure team's health & safety, 234, 235
  Negotiate Boundaries with Delegation Poker, 234
  respond productively (curiosity over blame), 236
  things that suck, 235
 individual safety enhancer, 211, 213, 216
 relatedness
  communication frequency, team, 230
  feelings, 228
  Introduce and Use Core Protocols, 231
  run frequent retrospectives, 230, 231
  take team outside, 229
  user manual, create and share, 229, 230
 SCARF® model, 208, 209
 status, 211
  ambiguous threats, 213, 214
  amplify signal (Helpful Cassandras), 214, 215
  feedback, 211
  help, 212
  "Not Knowing", 212, 213
  questions, 210
  share concerns cross-hierarchy, 214
Safety in the Workplace game, 4, 205
 cards, 16
 categories, safety enhancers, 205

diagnostic tool, 206
Lean Coffee style, 206–208
mini catalog, practices, 206
Mural template, 272
online edition, 308
remote-friendly version, 271
safety enhancers collection (*see* Safety enhancers collection)
Sara Security
  known vulnerabilities and security threats catalog, 53
  role, 52
SCARF® model, 208, 209
Scrum, 5, 54, 116, 125, 266
Scrum team, 59
  Danny Developer, 61, 62
  Patricia Product, 60, 61
  roles, 59
  Samuel Scrum, 64, 65
  supplies, 87, 88
  Tim tester, 63, 64
Security, 34, 35, 108, 134, 149, 258–259
Service-oriented architecture (SOA), 46
Session plan, 117
  connection activity, 117
  DevSecOps training, 117
    break, 122
    buffer time, 125
    concrete practice, 119
    continuous value delivery, 123
    debriefing, 120, 122, 124
    instructor introduction, 118
    participants, 118
    process improvements/modifications, 121, 123
    setup, 119
    simulation flow, 119
    steps, 121
    topic introduction, 118, 120, 122
    user experience, 124
  learners' engagement/content retention, 117
  LEGO and Chocolate simulation, 125
    debriefing, 126, 128, 129
    game introduction, 126
    instructions, 129
    process improvements/modifications, 127, 128
    steps, 127
    timeboxes, 126
"Shield right" approach, 52
"Shift-left" approach, 41, 42, 52, 149, 156, 258, 320
Shortening the game, 130
"Simple math of DevOps", 24, 25
Static code analysis tools, 49, 51, 157
Success theater, 183, 185, 186, 218
Systems thinking, 39, 40, 42, 43

INDEX

T

Team, 214, 217, 223, 229, 230, 232, 320
Team Handouts, 17, 93
Team-level fears, 193
Team-level safety enhancer, 228
Team working agreements, 230, 233
Teardown timebox, 130
Technical reviewer, 268
The Back of the Room (TBR) workshop, 296, 297
"The Three Ways of DevOps"
    feedback loop, 41
    generative culture, 182
    supplemental material, 41
    systems thinking, 40, 42, 43
Tiny monsters, 273, 274
    group configuration, 366
    invitation, 366
    participation distributed, 366
    purpose, 366
    sequence of steps, 367
    source, 366
    space, 366
    virtual space, 367, 368
Toronto Agile and Software, Canada (November 2014), 283, 284
Train-the-Trainer Workshops, 14, 303, 304
TRIZ structure, 272, 273
    group configuration, 364
    invitation, 364
    participation distributed, 364
    purpose, 364
    sequence of steps, 364, 365
    source, 364
    space, 364
    virtual space, 365
Trunk-based development, 45, 47
"T-shaped" skills, 8, 40, 58, 80, 121, 169, 186, 247, 256
25-10 Crowdsourcing structure
    group configuration, 362
    invitation, 362
    participation distributed, 362
    purpose, 362
    sequence of steps, 362, 363
    source, 362
    space, 362
    virtual space, 363

U

User Experience Fishbowl structure
    group configuration, 360
    invitation, 360
    participation distributed, 360
    purpose, 360
    sequence of steps, 360, 361
    source, 360
    space, 360
    virtual space, 361

V

Visible posters, 18, 98

W

What? So What? Now What? structure
    group configuration, 358
    invitation, 358
    participation distributed, 358
    purpose, 357
    sequences of steps, 358
    source, 357
    space, 358
    virtual space, 359
Workshop handouts, 347–349
    in-room posters, 351–354
    packing checklist, 349–351

X, Y, Z

XP2015 (May 2015), 288–290

GPSR Compliance
The European Union's (EU) General Product Safety Regulation (GPSR) is a set of rules that requires consumer products to be safe and our obligations to ensure this.

If you have any concerns about our products, you can contact us on

ProductSafety@springernature.com

In case Publisher is established outside the EU, the EU authorized representative is:

Springer Nature Customer Service Center GmbH
Europaplatz 3
69115 Heidelberg, Germany